D1591181

Space, Time, and Culture
among the Iraqw
of Tanzania

This is a volume in

STUDIES IN ANTHROPOLOGY

Under the consulting editorship of
E. A. Hammel, University of California, Berkeley

A complete list of titles appears at the end of this volume.

Space, Time, and Culture among the Iraqw of Tanzania

ROBERT J. THORNTON
Department of Anthropology
University of Cape Town
South Africa

ACADEMIC PRESS
A Subsidiary of Harcourt Brace Jovanovich, Publishers
New York   London   Toronto   Sydney   San Francisco

ACADEMIC PRESS, INC.
111 Fifth Avenue, New York, New York 10003

United Kingdom Edition published by
ACADEMIC PRESS, INC. (LONDON) LTD.
24/28 Oval Road, London NW1 7DX

Library of Congress Cataloging in Publication Data

Thornton, Robert J
    Space, time, and culture among the Iraqw of Tanzania.

    (Studies in anthropology)
    Bibliography: p.
    Includes index.
    1. Wambulu (African tribe) 2. Anthropo—geography—
Tanzania. 3. Folk—lore, Wambulu. 4. Space and time.
I. Title.
DT443.T47   967.8'26004963   79—6793
ISBN 0—12—690580—0

PRINTED IN THE UNITED STATES OF AMERICA

80 81 82 83   9 8 7 6 5 4 3 2 1

Contents

Chapter 1

The Iraqw and the Problem of Space

Chapter 2

The Cultural Organization of Domestic and Political Space

Chapter 3

The Aya: *Territory as Image*

Chapter 4

The Masay *Ritual: Realization of Spatial Categories*

Chapter 5

The Definition and Evaluation of Groups

Chapter 6

Social Order and Social Control

Chapter 7

Talking about the Past: Time in the Iraqw World View

Chapter 8

History

Chapter 9

Territorial Expansion

Chapter 10

Conclusions   249

List of Illustrations

List of Texts

Preface

Recently there has been a resurgence of interest in the conceptual and practical problems of space in the social and psychological sciences in general. The problem is, in fact, a perennial one since space and spatial order pervade every aspect of our lives and thought. It is also a very knotty problem, both philosophically and practically. I have addressed these problems in this study of the Iraqw, an agricultural people living along the Rift Valley Escarpment in North-Central Tanzania, because a concern with spatial order is central to their political process, ritual, oral literature, and history. But the particularities of the Iraqw use and conceptualization of space are simply aspects of more general psychological and sociological issues. I have found, therefore, that my attempt to understand Iraqw culture and society has provided both the means and the challenge to attempt to formulate statements about the role of spatial order in politics, ritual, settlement patterns, definition of groups, ethnic interaction, oral literature, and ethnohistory that may be more generally useful to other anthropologists and to scholars in other fields.

It is a fundamental premise of this book that space and time are cultural constructs. This is not to deny that elementary perception and cognition of space and time may be biologically programmed, but only to say that the specific realization in concepts and action is historically and culturally conditioned and contextually relative. For a study such as this to be possible at all, however, we must assume that at some level, categories of time and space are shared by all human beings. I do not address myself to this epistemological problem, but assume its truth. There are, nevertheless, differences in perspective, context, and application between the Iraqw and my notions of space and time, and it is these which I attempt to elucidate. There are, then, two sides to the problem: (*a*) How space is perceived and ordered in the cultural and cognitive processes of the subject; and (*b*) how we, as observers and analysts, are to treat space in our theoretical formulations. Since solutions to one side of the problem inform inquiry into the other, I treat both alternately throughout the work.

In the field of anthropology, since Lewis Henry Morgan pointed out the central importance of kinship, and distinguished societies organized in terms of kinship (*societas*) from those organized in terms of territory and space (*civitas*), the study of the former "primitive" type has diverged from the study of the latter "modern" type in method, theory, and disciplinary organization. Study of the nature of kinship found it to be a cultural logic of human relationships and a calculus of mutual rights and obligations. Study of space and spatial organization, however, proceeded as if it were simply a practical or material logic of property or sovereign domain. Here I argue that the nature of spatial organization in human society is to be found in another cultural logic of relationships and images. I give this argument fuller statement in the first chapter of the book and seek to demonstrate the usefulness of this view in the chapters that follow. Since this is a new perspective, I try in a short historical discussion to show why it has not been exploited before now and how it can make our understanding more complete.

The theoretical view developed here has implications for psychologists, linguists, geographers, and sociologists whose research interests include the cross-cultural study of cognition, especially "cognitive mapping," "environmental psychology," spatial perception and cognition, context analysis, and settlement pattern. Since I also try to place the study in temporal perspective and to show how the Iraqw notions of space have led to and shaped a process of territorial expansion, historians of frontier interactions, of demographic change, or of African societies in general may find the book interesting as well.

In addition to its theoretical contribution, I hope this study will begin to fill a rather large gap in the ethnographic description of East Africa. Iraqw society has been little studied. There are a few monographs on some of the other peoples in the immediate area of the Iraqw, such as the Sonjo (Gray, 1963), the Wanyaturu (Schneider, 1970), the Barabaig (Klima, 1970), and the Gogo (Rigby, 1969), but there are no studies of comparable length on the Tatoga (other than the Barabaig), Iramba, Iambi, Hadza, Gorowa, Alagwa, Mbugwe, Sandawe, or Tanzanian Masai, all of whom participate in the history of the Iraqw and interact intensively with them. This study of the Iraqw cannot hope to be complete with so much of the picture missing. This is especially so since the sociological and linguistic complexity is greater here than in almost any other place on the

African continent. One feature to emerge clearly, but with which I could not deal because of limitations of scope and time, was that no single ethnic unit in North-Central Tanzania could be considered as an isolated whole. The Iraqw political system simply would not operate without the Masai warrior–herdsman, the Tatoga ritual expert, or the Colonial or Independent government's courts and coercive power. Population is continually exchanged among most of these groups, and virtually all males and many females are multilingual. The agricultural, pastoral, and hunting economies of the peoples of the region are interdependent. Indeed, it seems to me that it is not a question of *societies* interacting within a regional system, but of a *regional social system* in which groups interact. For this reason, I do not attempt to describe the Iraqw society or culture as a "systematic whole." To do so would be misleading. Instead, I try to show wherever possible that the small part of Iraqw society and culture that I do describe is part of a larger system, the boundaries of which I would not, at this moment, attempt to delimit.

The book is organized in 10 chapters. The first chapter sets the theoretical frame about the rest. The second and third chapters present the layout and cultural logic of domestic and political space, and the fourth describes the ritual practice whereby the Iraqw mark and resanctify their land. Chapters 5 and 6 are concerned with the definition and evaluation of groups both within the Iraqw domain (defined by their characteristic ritual and speech) and within the region generally. A discussion of the means and practice of social control and politics leads into three chapters that deal in different ways with time and history. The final chapter provides a summary of evidence and of the argument, advanced throughout, that space is a cultural construct.

The research was conducted over a 15-month period. For the first 6 months or so, I spoke Swahili, which many Iraqw know except, unfortunately, the old men or most women over the age of 30. Thereafter, more research was conducted in Iraqw. All Iraqw texts were recorded on a tape recorder and transcribed first in Iraqw, then translated into Swahili with the help of research assistants and, when possible, the performer of the text himself. Finally, I prepared an English translation working from both the Iraqw and Swahili transcripts. Although this method was time consuming, it produced accurate and reliable texts of interviews and most of the examples of Iraqw narrative genres that I collected. This study is based mainly on these texts. Other methods and materials included population surveys, maps, photography, observations, and a general acquaintance with the Iraqw way of life, acquired while I was working in the gardens, walking, hunting, and working with my Iraqw friends and companions.

Acknowledgments

It is with regret that I acknowledge that the fieldworker can never repay the tremendous debt of kindness to the people with whom he has lived and worked. I can only express my thanks in the most general terms. The people of Kwermusl have added a great deal to my life and to my understanding of others' lives. I miss them. I shall not forget Father Augustino and Father Silvini, whose courtesy, trust, and friendship were always to be relied upon. I cannot adequately express my deep gratitude to Dionis and Paskal and their families, but I like to think that they do understand how great their contribution is to this book and receive some compensation from that knowledge. I owe Mzee Tua Masay a great deal for his encouragement, his pointing me in the right direction, and for his wisdom and honesty.

I also wish to thank the University of Dar es Salaam, particularly M. H. Kaniki of the History Department and I. Kimambo, the Dean for academic affairs. Dr. Kimambo managed to get me the necessary permission to do research in Tanzania; Dr. Kaniki was my liaison with the university while I was in Mbulu district.

The research for this book was conducted with the assistance of a Fulbright–Hays Doctoral Dissertation Research Grant, held from December, 1974 to December, 1975. I also received invaluable assistance and support from the British Institute in Eastern Africa. As a research student associated with the Institute, I was given the use of one of their Land Rovers and the driver from the Institute, Ali Ramadhani, for my first 2-month period in Mbulu district, Tanzania. Without this assistance, my fieldwork would have been delayed and hampered immeasurably. Indeed, without it I probably could not have conducted the study that I had planned. My warmest thanks go to the director of the British Institute, Neville Chittick; to members of his staff, David Phillipson and Patrick Pender-Cudlipp; and to the executive secretary, John Mascarenhas.

In addition to the assistance that I received from the British Institute and the Fulbright–Hays Grant, I received a small grant from the Committee on African Studies of the University of Chicago for equipment that was valuable in the field.

For reading various drafts of the dissertation, I am grateful to the members of my committee: Ralph Nicholas, Marshall Sahlins, George Stocking, Ralph Austen, and John Comaroff. As much as I appreciate the assistance that I have received from colleagues and mentors, governments and universities, I could not have achieved the level of understanding that I hope I have without the moral and material support of my family. My parents, Givens and Barbara Thornton, have devoted their lives to teaching; they taught me how to learn. My brother Jonathan and my sister Wendy have encouraged me and helped support me during the writing. My wife Lucy must share with me the credit for what I have accomplished. She has provided the time and stability that has allowed me to undertake this research and to carry it through to completion.

Orthographic Note

A few bible texts, available in Mbulu District, have been published in Iraqw by Catholic and Lutheran missions. The orthography used by one mission differs from that of the other in a number of respects. Since most of the people in the area of my intensive research were exposed to the Catholic system, if they could read, I chose to use it, though it is less precise. For example, both the unvoiced glottal stop and the unvoiced pharyngeal stop are indicated by an apostrophe. Where the pharyngeal stop is followed by a pharyngealized vowel sound this is indicated by a circonflex diacritic mark. Thus, *a'i*, 'journey' is pronounced with a simple glottal stop, while *fa'â*, 'food', is pronounced with a pharyngeal stop followed by a pharyngealized vowel. This system has proved adequate for my needs, although it does not yield an accurate phonological transcription. Indeed, such a transcription would be very difficult since there is a great deal of variation among speakers of the language, depending on whether the Speaker also speaks a Bantu language (e.g. Swahili), a Nilotic language (e.g. Masai or Tatoga), or a language containing clicks (e.g. Hadza). Thus, the uvular plosive, *q*, becomes a *gh* for many speakers of Swahili, but remains strongly articulated for a speaker of Tatoga or Hadza.

Vowel sounds, too, are variable. "Average sounds" are represented here by *a, e, i, o, u* which have values corresponding to their values in Swahili or Italian. Long vowels are represented by doubling, thus: *aa, ee, ii, oo, uu.*

The consonants *b, d, f, g, k, l, m, n, p, s, t, w,* and *y* represent the same sounds they do in English.

The characters *tl* and *ts* are strongly plosive, and *q* represents a uvular plosive as it would in transcriptions of Arabic. It is often pronounced with lip rounding and is then represented with a *w* as *qw,* as in *Iraqw.* The *x* represents a uvular fricative articulated in the same position as the plosive *q.*

The *sl* represents a lateral fricative.

The single *h* represents the same sound that it does in English, but the double *hh* is a forcefully produced pharyngeal unvoiced aspirate.

Tone may be significant in Iraqw, but much more research needs to be done on this feature of the language. I have not attempted to represent it consistently here.

Introduction

On March 3, 1975, I crossed from Kenya into Tanzania for the first time. I was riding in a Land Rover provided by the British Institute in Eastern Africa and was driven by the institute's capable driver, Ali Ramadhani, under whose tutelage I began to learn properly the national language of Tanzania, Swahili. I had lived in Uganda for several years before traveling to Tanzania to do research and had thought I knew some Swahili. When I entered Tanzania for the first time, however, I must admit that I did not appreciate how beautiful and expressive the language could be, nor did I realize how little of it I really knew. Ali and I arrived in the town of Mbulu, the district seat of the District of Mbulu, after spending a day in Arusha, the regional capital. Mbulu is a tiny town at the crossing of two dirt roads. It was immediately apparent that sufficient provisions would not be available in Mbulu. In fact, many food items, paper, research supplies of all sorts, and an occasional, usually badly needed, conversation in English were at least 240 km away in Arusha, or nearly 500 km away in Nairobi. There was no lodging in Mbulu, so I settled myself, with the help of Ali Ramadhani and the permission of the District Officer, Bwana Mambo, on the parade grounds behind the offices of the District Administration in a tent provided by the British Institute. I stayed there for nearly a month and a half, finalizing arrangements with the government for permission to conduct research in the district, reassuring everybody of my intentions, and learning Swahili as fast as I could. Although communicating was frustrating at the time, I am now grateful to the government officials who insisted on speaking to me in Swahili in all our dealings, even when they knew English perfectly well. At the same time, I began to get a feel for the district, and began to try to contact some of the Iraqw people who live all around the town of Mbulu, but who do not, by and large, live in it. From my position in the town it soon became obvious that I would not be able to research the Iraqw if I remained there.

Very few government personnel, shopowners, and town residents are Iraqw. The Iraqw continue to be suspicious of life in the towns. As I sat under the awning of my tent or walked about the town learning what I could of the district, I saw Iraqw men in their long cloaks with their staves carried over their shoulders walk through the town, but I could not strike up a conversation with any of them.

On an afternoon in the fifth week of my stay in Mbulu, I had just brewed a large pot of tea with sugar and dried-milk powder stirred into it and resumed my study of Swahili grammar when I noticed that I was being carefully observed by an old man dressed in a heavy green cloak of *merikani* (denin, originally imported from New England, hence the name). He had a rolled umbrella carried over his shoulder in place of the familiar meter-long fighting stick that all Iraqw men carry. On his head he wore a green cap of the type usually worn by devout T.A.N.U. party members, and on his feet he wore a good pair of Bata shoes, rare in the district, and even more uncommon among the Iraqw. He stood at a distance, watching me drink my tea.

This was unusual because, quite unlike the experience of many other cultural anthropologists who have been observed more closely and more constantly than they have been able to observe, the Iraqw had so far been completely indifferent to me and my inquiry. I invited the old man over to my tent for tea, and poured him two or three large cupfuls before he began to speak to me. He asked me what I was doing in Mbulu since he had seen me there for several weeks and wondered if I planned to stay. I told him that I was a student from America and that I had come to Tanzania to learn about the language and ways of a Tanzanian people. I told him that I wanted to live with the Iraqw and learn their language. He asked what I wanted to know about the Iraqw. I said that I was especially interested in ritual and politics. He looked at me and told me that he could tell me right then, everything I wanted to know! Completely taken aback, I did not even know the right questions to ask, and I told him so. He sat and drank a fourth cup of tea. When he finished, he continued to interview me with great astuteness. Finally he paused and told me, "If you want to stay here, you must plant a garden and work. There is not enough food in this district for people who don't work." I said I would be happy to work but that I needed a place where I could live with other Iraqw people to learn how to plant, how to speak Iraqw, how to talk with people, how to live. He said I should first of all forget about Swahili and learn Iraqw because Iraqw was a difficult language for outsiders to learn. He said that he expected me to know Iraqw thoroughly by our next meeting. "We can talk now in Swahili," he said, "but you will not learn anything about the Iraqw by using this language." Then he pointed east to a line of hills that could be seen over the treetops of the government reforestation center. He asked me if I could see the road winding up the side of the hill farthest to the south, beside the dark line of the forest. I said that I could. "Take the road, go over that mountain, down the other side, up the next mountain you find, and over that one. You will then be in the *aya Kwermusl*. You should stay there. I will be back to see you in a few months." He finished his tea, set the mug on my table, and left.

The next day I packed my tent and supplies into the Land Rover, and Ali and I drove to the mountains the old man had indicated, not by the same path, but by another road that seemed to lead in the same direction. We ended up in the *aya* (territory) called *Kainam*. I was introduced to an Iraqw Catholic priest, Father Augustino, who lived in that area, and to the government clerk. They gave me permission to pitch my tent on the old colonial parade ground. I did not realize it then, but I recognize now that my being situated in *places* associated with the colonial government was not accidental. In fact, this characteristic *placing* of both things and people in their appropriate places is one of the central themes of this ethnographic study.

As it turned out, however, I did not stay in *Kainam* very long. After returning the Land Rover in Nairobi, I returned to Mbulu by bus, a 3-day trip from Nairobi. Once in Mbulu, I began the 13-mile climb up and down the mountains to what I had since learned was called *Irqwar Da'aw* in Iraqw, the land most Iraqw consider to be their "homeland," their cultural center. I returned to my tent after a 2-week absence. Nothing had been touched. I had left all of my equipment and supplies in place in the tent. It was all there. In fact, Father Augustino had sent someone down each day to check it and to sweep it. After a few weeks in *Kainam,* I met a family in the neighboring *aya* of *Kwermusl* whom I liked very much. I asked them if I could live with them. They agreed, and I began a relationship with the family of Dionis De'engw of *Kwermusl* that has been tremendously satisfying on all counts. Dionis and his brother-in-law, Paskal, became my closest friends and advisors during my stay in Iraqw land. After 6 months in *Kwermusl,* my fiancee came to join me; we were married in *Kwermusl* and were treated as family. Dionis and Paskal helped me build the house in which Lucy and I lived for the duration of our fieldwork.

The old man who had sent me to *Kwermusl* in the first place did eventually check up on me as he had said he would. He helped me understand Iraqw history more than any other person. He did, however, tell me that I was not learning Iraqw fast enough and that I would have to do better before his next visit. He continued to check my progress throughout my stay. His name was Mzee Tua Masay. He was an Iraqw ritual expert who had pioneered the area of *Maghan* in the dry western part of the district for Iraqw settlement. He was the only Iraqw ritual expert who managed to be a member of the national T.A.N.U. party as well. He was widely respected. He always carried an umbrella, but I never saw him use it.

Chapter 1

The Iraqw and the
Problem of Space

Principles of Spatial Order

This book is about the Iraqw, or Wambulu, people of the Arusha
region in North-Central Tanzania. It is not simply description, however, for
I am seeking to develop a clear approach to the nature and potentialities of
space in social organization. The thesis of this study is that under certain
historical conditions, an ideology of spatial relations may serve to organize
sociopolitical action and cultural forms in a technologically simple and
egalitarian society. Considerable attention has already been given by
anthropologists to the way in which ideologies of descent and kinship,
patrimonial authority or chiefly hierarchy, fulfill the organizational function in other African societies such as the Nuer, Tallensi, Baganda, or
Swazi. For the Iraqw, however, categories and relations of space, not kin
or chiefship, underlie all social organization above that of the domestic
group. It is the principles of a spatial order—not principles of hierarchy, "shared substance," or economy—that integrate independent single-
family homesteads, the smallest productive and reproductive units, into
larger social and political units. These principles, which are given expression in ritual and oral performances, create social space and provide the parameters for political action. This amounts to a cosmology
that defines political means and ends by placing both Iraqw people and
others who surround them in a valued social universe. The cultural
categories of space that emerge in this study of the Iraqw provide the
framework for the organization and evaluation of social action. They
therefore create polarities and tensions that generate social processes and
that lead to historical changes. As a result, I have not been content to

1

elucidate a timeless structure of spatial concepts. I have endeavored to show that these ideas have themselves emerged from a particular historical process in a particular social and natural environment, and have in turn given rise to historical events.

The Iraqw and Their Environment

The Iraqw people live in the Mbulu and Hanang districts of Arusha region in the north-central part of Tanzania. There are about 150,000 Iraqw people distributed over much of northern Tanzania, but concentrated primarily in the district of Mbulu on the Mbulu Plateau, stretching southward for about 160 km (100 miles) from Ngorongoro Crater National Park in the north. The western escarpment of the Great Rift Valley of East Africa runs along the eastern edge of this plateau separating the Iraqw from their neighbors on that side, the Masai and the Mbugwe. The Masai are also permitted to graze in the Ngorongoro Park lands to the north, so they border the Iraqw on that side, too. The plateau slopes off to the west, gradually merging with the Serengeti Plain. The plateau lands inhabited by the Iraqw, however, are separated from the Serengeti by several low ranges of mountains and by a long shallow salt lake, Eyasi, which runs along the low western edge of the plateau from north to south. On this side the Iraqw are bordered by and live amongst several different ethnic groups including the Tatoga (speaking a language belonging to the Kalenjin branch of the Nilotic family of languages) and the hunting and gathering Hatsa (who speak a Click language without traceable links to any other African language). To the south, southeast, and southwest, the Mbulu Plateau merges with drybush savanna inhabited by various groups of agricultural peoples who speak Bantu languages (Iramba, Ihanzu, Irangi, Turu, and Gogo). To the southeast, the Iraqw are bordered by several small clusters of people speaking languages that are closely related to their own (Gorowa and Alagwa).

The plateau on which most of the Iraqw live is composed of eroded crystalline rocks (schists, granites, and gneisses) of the ancient continental massif. The plateau surface is highly dissected. Constant erosion has prevented the buildup of soil. Soils in most of the district are immature and composed primarily of the decomposition products of the underlying rocks. Except for the northern portion of the district, which has volcanic soils, the earth is not fertile. Vegetation, under constraints of high altitude (1524–2133 m [5000–7000 feet]), low fertility, and high-grazing pressure, is confined to very short grasses, tough woody forbs (*Cordia, hybiscus* spp., *solanum* spp., *labiatae* spp., and the like), and occasional fire- and drought-resistant trees (*euphorbia candelabra, erithrina abysinica, combretum*, among others).

The research for this study, however, was conducted in a relatively small area of this plateau. This area, called Irqwar Da'aw ('Iraqw land of the East') in Iraqw, "Mama-Isara" or "Kainam" in other literature, is located right on the east edge of the plateau overlooking the escarpment that drops nearly 610 m (2000 feet) to the Masai Steppe below. Irqwar Da'aw is cut off from the rest of the plateau by a low but steep line of hills on the west and by a dense virgin forest on the north and south. The forest is populated by elephants, leopards, hyenas (on the margins), and occasional buffalo; it is, in short, a formidable barrier. It has appeared to a number of observers that this isolated mountain area has tended to preserve remnants of earlier populations with their languages (Bagshawe, 1925; Fosbrooke. 1954; Tucker & Bryan, 1956; Tucker, 1967; Sutton, 1966). The ebb and flow of Bantu and Nilotic migrations, the Arab slave and ivory trade, and even European incursions and administrations have left the area largely untouched (Roberts, 1969:58; Gwassa, 1969). Other geographical features contribute to its isolation. The area is a self-contained drainage basin, with rivers flowing neither into nor out of it toward the Indian Ocean, Lake Victoria, or Lake Tanganyika. The two salt lakes, Eyasi and Manyara, trap the runoff from the hills that lie between them. Although the plateau on which the Iraqw live is relatively well watered, it is surrounded by large, flat, dry areas that are unsuitable for agriculture. This geographical isolation has no doubt contributed to the social and political isolation of the area. There is no doubt that it has also been an area of refuge that has received people from all of the surrounding areas at various times in the past, and this constant movement has been an important factor in the attenuation of kinship as an effective means of social organization on any scale above the household.

There are no very reliable population estimates for the early part of this century for the Arusha region, but Winter and Molyneaux (1963) have presented clear evidence that the population of the Mbulu district, of the Iraqw in particular, has expanded rapidly. Large family size in the Irqwar Da'aw area (average of 5 living children, ranging up to 12 children), and decrease in epidemic diseases (there were several plague epidemics in the 1920s and 1930s) indicate that the growth is not an artefact of better statistical methods. It is clear that population growth has permitted a rapid expansion recently, but it has not been a cause of expansion. Rapid population growth only began after territorial expansion began to be successful. Before that, the practice of infanticide, serious diseases, and warfare seem to have kept the population low and stable. The mere physical constraint of population "pressure" does not, in any case, explain the particular form that territorial expansion will take in any historical instance. The implications of these geographical and demographic facts for Iraqw history and social structure are dealt with from different viewpoints in the chapters that follow.

Language

The area in which the Iraqw live is distinctive in other ways as well. In this small area bounded by Lakes Eyasi and Manyara on the west and east, by Ngorongoro Crater on the north and by the dry Gogo Plain on the south, live small groups of peoples who speak languages belonging to four (by present classifications) major language families: Bantu, Khoisan, Nilotic, and Cushitic. There is, however, considerable doubt about the classification of a number of these languages.

The Iraqw are one of a group of apparently related peoples who speak a group of languages which have, as yet, remained unclassified, or are tentatively classified as "Southern Cushitic" (Greenberg, 1966; Ehret, 1974). The Goroa (also Gorowa or Wafiome) are closely related to the Iraqw and their languages are mutually intelligible. The Alagwa (also Alawa or Wasi) and the Burunge, situated to the south and west of the Iraqw, differ enough in their speech that communication with the Iraqw or the Goroa is difficult, but their languages are formally quite similar and clearly genetically related (Whiteley, 1958). The languages of all of these peoples, living in close proximity—the Iraqw, Goroa, Alagwa, and Burunge—are separate but closely related. I did not work with any of these peoples other than the Iraqw of Irqwar Da'aw, and since there is little other historical or ethnographic information about the others, it is not possible to suggest what the historical or sociological relationships among these groups are at present.

But the languages of these peoples remain an anomaly in current schemes of linguistic classification. It was suggested by H. H. Johnston and F. J. Bagshawe in 1925 that the languages were "Hamitic," but in those times this is what officials of the colonial administration called any East African people who did not speak a Bantu language and who kept cattle. They were unable to find any evidence to support their surmise, despite their informal comparisons with Semitic and Ethiopian languages (Bagshawe, 1925). J. Greenberg (1966) classified the language as "Southern Cushitic," an isolated branch of his large "Afro-Asiatic" family of languages. This classification is based on very slim evidence. Greenberg lists only six examples of possible cognates from "Iraqwan" languages (i.e., examples selected from all four of the Iraqw-related languages) in a comparative word list of 78 items, and some of these seem to me to be doubtful. Furthermore, the suggested cognates are selected from a wide range of languages classified by Greenberg as "Afro-Asiatic." His classification of Iraqw must be seen as extremely tentative.

Those more familiar with the Iraqw language reject this classification. Whiteley (1958) failed to find any connection with the Cushitic languages of Ethiopia, although he acknowledges that there are some features that "seem to invite comparison with Hamitic and Semitic languages," but evidence, he contends, is inconclusive. Tucker and Bryan (1956, 1966) concur with Whiteley. Although a number of other ethnologists, historians, and linguists have insisted on classifying these languages with the Cushitic languages of Ethiopia (e.g., Murdock, 1959; Ehret, 1971, 1974; Oliver, 1963, among others), I think that we must conclude that there is no strong evidence to support this classification. These languages, like the Basque language in Europe, are linguistic and historical isolates, anomalies in any classification system.

A Sketch of Iraqw Society

Politics among the Iraqw is characterised by a commitment to equality and consensus. Throughout this study I attempt to show the way in which these values are expressed and the effects they have on daily life, social structure, and history. Characteristically, they are expressed in spatial metaphors, rather than in metaphors of kinship. The ire of ancestors, so important as sanctions in many African societies, is largely irrelevant.

The Iraqw have maintained throughout this century a consistent and independent political system despite the imposition of chiefs and subchiefs during the Colonial period. Since independence, a new system of the T.A.N.U. Party (now renamed *Chama Cha Mapinduzi,* 'Revolutionary Party') and government officials has been instituted, but even so, the indigenous political order has persisted. This order is founded on public meetings, called *kwasleema,* that are held regularly in specified places. All male, adult heads of households attend. All decisions affecting the public order are made in this forum. Hierarchies of government officers appointed by the colonial government, or since independence, are inimical to this system. The ritual state of the land is dependent on the spirit of consensus that the meeting fosters, and on this, in turn, depends the spiritual state of people and animals and the success or failure of agriculture. Clearly more than "just politics" is involved, so despite the provision of alternate political systems and government courts for the settlement of disputes, the Iraqw *kwasleema* persists. Indeed many Iraqw, especially those of Irqwar Da'aw, express suspicion and hostility toward all governmental institutions. This is partly because government officials speak Swahili and have always been insensitive or hostile to Iraqw concerns. Practices that have resulted from the Iraqw concept of pollution, exile, or infanticide, for example, have been regarded as barbaric by colonial and independent government officials alike. Even the semisubterranean house-type of dwelling, favored by some Iraqw, especially earlier in this century, has sparked the animosity of outsiders (see Bagshawe, 1925:72 and Fosbrooke, 1954:51). Nevertheless, resistance by many Iraqw to external systems of authority arises primarily from its contradiction of Iraqw values of egalitarianism, consensus, and the segmentation and territorial expansion that these values have produced.

There are no markets among the Iraqw, and until recently cash crops for external sale have not been important except in the wheat-producing region around the town of Karatu in the northern part of the district. Wheat farming was begun during World War II by the British administration and did not exist on a large scale before that time. Cattle, sheep, and goats are sold at government-administered auctions that circulate around the district. In the higher parts of the district, such as Irqwar Da'aw, pyrethrum is grown and sold to the government. None of these resources bring much income. They are insignificant in the subsistence economy of the vast majority of Iraqw. Any surpluses that are produced are exchanged among neighbors for specialized services such as thatching and potting, or for assistance in carrying building materials or grindstones from forests, swamps, or rock-outcroppings where they are found. Extra maize and millet are grown expressly for the purpose of brewing beer which is sold to neighbors and visitors. Since neighbors can usually cite an instance when they helped the beer-brewer at some time in the past, and can therefore make a claim for free beer, the sale of beer can scarcely be called economic. Nevertheless, beer parties are important for many other reasons that will be discussed in later chapters.

The household is the unit of production and consumption. Both men and women participate in agricultural tasks, and when men are not available for herding, girls sometimes herd the cattle and goats. Most households grow a wide range of food crops including maize and sweet potatoes (the principle starchy staples), beans, pumpkins, wheat, finger millet, sorghum, and bullrush millet (roughly cited in decreasing order of importance). I have also seen small quantities of cocoyam (*colocasia*), cow peas, green peas, onion, cabbage, Irish potatoes, and bananas raised by some Iraqw of Irqwar Da'aw.

Marriage is monogamous and neolocal. Most sons move out of their parents house and set up their own house and begin to cultivate their own fields well before they marry. It is a serious pollution for a daughter to give birth to a child within her parents' house. If it occurred, the daughter would be exiled and the parents who permitted it would be ostracized from the community. Consequently, sons and daughters move to places that are considerably distant. Land distribution is managed by the consensus of the meeting (*kwasleema*). Rights to land are never permanent, but are viewed as temporary usufruct privileges. When the user of a piece of land dies it does not go automatically to his kin or descendants. Its reallocation is decided upon by the meeting. With one exception (the *Kahamusmo*), there are no heritable titles or political roles; descent and inheritance are of little importance. The houses of parents are left to fall down when they die. It would be bad luck to reinhabit them, and in any case most off-spring are independent by the time parents' deaths are likely to occur. If there is property to inherit, generally items of Western material culture such as books or metal pots, they go to the youngest child who is likely to remain closest to the parents in their old age. If there is an inheritance rule, one might say it is ultimogenitor-by-default.

The religious conceptions of the Iraqw are, like many other aspects of their culture, unusual in East Africa. There are two spirits or supernatural beings, opposed as good and bad, supplicable and capricious. *Lo'a* is associated with the sky, the "above," the sun, and with rain; *netlangw* are associated with the earth, the "below," with stream beds, springs, and damp. *Lo'a* and *netlangw* are supplicated in prayers, but it is *lo'a* who is held to be the most responsive, while the *netlangw* are capricious. Both may work good or evil, but on balance, *lo'a* is the more positive and "good" of the two. *Lo'a*, the word that refers to the 'spirit of the sky' is grammatically feminine, and *netlangw,* the 'spirit of the below,' is grammatically plural. In the Iraqw concept, however, they are both immanent and nonmaterial. It is of great significance that they are associated with directions (above–below) and with nature (the sun, bright and hot versus the spring, dark and cool). The nature of these spirits and their effect on human life is critical to the Iraqw practice of politics and their conception of the cosmos that gives life its meaning. The Iraqw believe that man has a spiritual essence or soul as well. A person's soul, *fuqurangw,* persists after death, and becomes an ancestral spirit or *gii.* The ancestors' *gii* are not commemorated or regularly propitiated, and there are no organized ancestor cults or cults of other spirits. The spirits of the dead persist in the area in which they died. People do not remember where their grandparents lie buried, however, for there is no reason for them to retain this knowledge. Along with a lack of spiritual cults, one must also note that witchcraft is very rare. The Iraqw know that such beliefs exist among their neighbors, especially among those who speak Bantu languages, and many Iraqw can give accurate accounts of what this entails in terms of accusations, confessions, and divination. The Iraqw concepts of pollution and ritual state of the land have many of the same functions that witchcraft beliefs have in other societies, but the manifestation of these beliefs in daily life are radically different. Features or groups of features can be compared with other societies, but the particular constellation that makes Iraqw society what it is is unique. In general, however, the emphasis on space among the Iraqw is surely nothing more than *emphasis.* The organizational forms that they have realized in a given historical instance exist as potentials in all human societies. But the role of space has been little studied in anthropology. To this end, it is necessary to develop a number of concepts with which to analyze the Iraqw case. It is my hope that these analytical concepts will prove useful in other ethnographic contexts.

The Study of Space in Anthropology: Some Concepts

In the latter half of the nineteenth century, Sir Henry Sumner Maine and Lewis Henry Morgan distinguished sharply between kinship and territory as two incontrovertible and mutually inconsistent modes of social organization. Maine asserted in his *Ancient Law* (1861) that kinship was the "sole possible ground of community in political functions" in "early" or "ancient" society. In this well-known passage, he continued, "nor is there any of those subversions so startling and so complete as the change which is accomplished when some other principle—such as that, for instance, of *local contiguity*—establishes itself for the first time as the basis of common political action [1861:137]." His distinction had great force in the development of anthropology and is quoted with approval by contemporary anthropologists who continue to operate with this orientation (Colson, 1968:190; Balandier, 1972:9,26; Fortes, 1969:126). In the United States, Lewis Henry Morgan, like Maine, a lawyer, undertook his monumental study of *Systems of Consanguinity and Affinity* in 1859 and published his results in 1871. The theoretical capstone of his career, *Ancient Society* appeared 6 years later in 1877 and was based in large part upon his earlier work. Like Maine, he distinguished between primitive society that was based on ties of kinship (or consanguinity and affinity) and modern, civil society which was based on relations of property and territory. Indeed, he wrote

All forms of government are reducible to two general plans. . . . In their bases the two are fundamentally distinct. The first, in order of time, is founded upon persons, and upon relations purely personal, and may be distinguished as a society (societas). . . . The second is founded upon territory and upon property, and may be distinguished as a state (civitas). The township or ward, circumscribed by metes and bounds, with the property it contains, is the basis or unit of the latter and political society is the result. Political society is organized upon territorial areas, and deals with property as well as with persons through territorial relations. . . . In ancient society this territorial plan was unknown. When it came in it fixed the boundary line between ancient and modern society [1877:13–14].

This position was argued brilliantly by the two jurists who brought the best evidence available to them at the time to bear in support of their argument. Their combined force had the effect of moving the discipline almost entirely toward the study of kinship alone (Radcliffe-Browne, 1965:49–51; Fortes, 1969:27ff). Maine and Morgan argued for the evolutionary and logical priority of kinship as the "earliest tie" and "the basis of society". In the natural evolution of human society, Maine contended, territory gradually came to substitute itself for kinship as the primary political bond, but this was "slow and not accomplished without very violent struggles" (Maine, 1875:75). In addition to its temporal priority, kinship was also logically prior, since in "ancient society" the territorial plan was not only nonexistent, it was also inconceivable. Morgan believed that in dealing with contemporary primitive societies he was "dealing substantially with the ancient condition of our own remote ancestors." He compared the logic he perceived in the social organization of the American Indians with the ancient writings of Greeks and Romans to show that what was logically prior was historically prior and vice versa. Maine followed a substantially similar line.

When Radcliffe-Browne argued against such speculative history, he still gave kinship logical priority in the constitution of primitive societies. Given his orientation and goals, Radcliffe-Browne's choice of focus was logically entailed in his formulation of the problem. Kinship presented itself very clearly in manifest word and deed among the peoples they studied. Their primary concern, of course, was sociological. They studied the practical ends and means of social relations as they were observed in behavior and reported behavior. Territory and space, however, contrary to what Maine and Morgan believed, are fundamentally cultural and conceptual phenomena.

Writing with respect to the Iraqw, Edward Winter remarked that Evans-Pritchard's work, *The Nuer* (1940), "showed in detail that one is faced not with determining whether or not the system of a particular society is based upon a kinship or territorial basis, but rather with the problem of showing how kinship principles are utilized to structure territorial groupings [Winter 1966:173–174]." In Evans-Pritchard's work, the relationship between kinship and territory was entirely in agreement with at least part of Maine and Morgan's posited relationship. Kinship was logically prior to practical activity. The question of evolutionary priority was never laid to rest, however; it was merely ignored since it was held to be unanswerable. The idea of the logical priority of kinship, seen as a practical calculus of rights and obligations over persons and things that was expressed and played out in terms that denoted degrees of consanguinity (shared "blood" or "substance") and affinity (a jural bond), became even more convincing after *The Nuer* and similar works showed the analytic power of this view.

     According to this approach, territory was usually defined as a "locus of use" for a group constituted on the basis of kinship, or it was the "limit of sovereignty" for such a group. These two ideas about the nature of territory are common to Western jurisprudence since Roman times at least, and were brought into the body of theoretical concepts of anthropology by Maine. The current subdisciplines of anthropology, such as ecology, ethnology, and sociobiology, that operate with ideas of territory have made no theoretical advances on this definition (e.g., see Dyson-Hudson and Smith, 1978). These definitions of territory are not really definitions of the spatial category they appear to be; rather, they are concerned with political phenomena that involve *prior concepts of spatial categories* for their realization. In Maine's words, for example, this notion of territory was constituted by "the idea that a number of persons should exercise political rights in common simply because they happened to live in the same topographical limits." Morgan's notion of the unit of territorial organization, the township, "circumscribed by metes and bounds, with the property it contains," is similarly political. The error that they made, and which continues to be made, is to confuse territory, the *conceptual category*, with territory, *the object of a political bond*. Maine's confusion resulted from the fact that he attributed to "topographic limit" an independent meaning in and of itself. Even in fully political nation states of modern times, it is not topography alone but convention and culture (conceptual system or ideology) that determine spatial limits. Boundaries are given meaning through a large number of practical acts (surveying) and processes of legitimation (registration). They exist through and only because of the attribution of meaning through such processes.

     Morgan's confusion, similarly, resulted from the fact that he did not conceive of "metes and bounds" as wholly separate from "the property they contain." Boundaries do not entail relations of property or ownership. Boundaries are literally *imaginary:* they consist of the images of continuity and closure applied to a continuous material reality. Boundaries are communicated in "practical" acts (e.g., the scientific survey, or the Australian Aboriginal "walkabout," or *masay* ceremony described later). Once constituted they may be related to human individuals or groups in many ways. A relationship or ownership is only one sort of relationship among many. Why, then, did Morgan and Maine think the idea of territory was so revolutionary? Because they believed that it entailed property relations and these, demonstrably, did not exist among many primitive communities.

They may have been correct that marriage—a jurally constituted bond between two people—was evolutionarily prior to property—a jurally constituted bond between a person and a thing or even between two things, for example, "Crown Lands"—but they were wrong in associating territory with only one of these relationships. It must now be made clear that a *concept of differentiated space* must underlie both territorial and affinal relationships. Briefly, the principle of exogamy is implicit in the practice of marriage, and it entails a division of *we* and *they* which, given the nature of spatial reality, entails the spatial differentiation *here* and *there.* A notion of boundary is as implicit in the act of marriage as it is in the politicization of territory. Both marriage and ownership, however, must be kept analytically distinct from the image of a spatial category or area that constitutes territory, as I define the term here.

The notion of the sovereign territory as the basis of political association in modern civil society is the product of a particular tradition in Western jurisprudence and political thought. Maine was aware of this. In a chapter of *Ancient Society* entitled "Modern History of Law of Nature," Maine discussed the development of the concept that there is such a thing as natural law, distinct from civil law. One of the "greatest functions" of the idea of a Law of Nature, according to Maine, was the development of International Law. He presented several postulates which form the foundation of international law. The first is "expressed in the position that there is a determinable Law of Nature"; second, that natural law is binding on all states since they are natural entities. The latter postulate derives from the prior distinctions between civil and natural order: Civil order was held to have an "author," natural order had no author except God. States, therefore, were deemed natural because no one person was their author. But at the same time the international law of dominion was, in Maine's words, "pure Roman property law," that is, civil law. In order to apply the civil concept of dominion to the "natural" state, Maine tells us that dominion was resolved "into the double proposition that sovereignty is territorial, that is, that it is always associated with the proprietorship of a limited portion of the earth's surface, and that sovereigns *inter se* are deemed not paramount but absolute owners of the state's territory" (Maine, 1875:105). In other words in the development of international law in the European context, sovereigns were held to be related to each other like members of a group of Roman proprietors.

Maine's discussion of international law was intended to document the development of a few concepts, but in the frame of his larger project, he also meant it to show that the territorial basis for political community was historically late to appear and logically dependent on several prior conditions. Returning to consider his argument a century later, however, it can be taken to show that the supposed indissoluble link between territory and sovereignty was the product of a *particular* historical development and is not logically entailed. This means that the same linkage of space and sovereignty may or may not arise as the result of other historical sequences. But this, rather than solving a problem, presents us with another problem, namely, the investigation of the historical conditions that produce particular relationships between a community and the way in which it chooses to define the space it occupies.

Maine's example also shows that the definition of territory always implies a larger system. In European jurisprudence an international "law of dominion," or "territorial sovereignty," was not necessary until there were other sovereigns and other territories. Thus, the spatial boundary never defines the limit of the sociocultural system since the idea of an inside implies that an outside must also exist. A boundary necessarily creates a polarity of value, one pole of which must be associated with the outside just as the other pole is associated with the inside. To define the political community as a territorial community, for example as Max Weber has done (1978:901) is always, in one sense at least, an error.

It ignores the implied outside that is the opposite term of the polarity (we–they) which creates the community and gives it meaning in the first place. In international law it is this larger system that is at issue. Territories become significant where they represent a differentiation of space within a larger community of interests. All of this enables us to see, again, why it is that space was not taken up as readily as kinship in the ethnographic monograph. So long as the notion of "tribe" remained legitimate, the boundary of the tribal territory was taken to be the boundary of the social system. Space only becomes a critical problem at the level of the cosmological concept or image in a larger world view that includes both poles of the valued dichotomies "we–they" and "inside–outside." A research program that concerns itself with social behavior alone, takes the cultural creation of space for granted. Deriving its concepts from traditional jurisprudence in England and America, British structural-functional monographs were subject to some of the same confusions and presuppositions that were inherent in that tradition. At least from the time of Radcliffe-Brown, the social anthropological monograph did not address the social-cultural system as a whole. The study of space was consequently neglected.

Although influential, Maine's and Morgan's principle distinction did not go unchallenged. Robert Lowie described his *Primitive Society* (1921) as a "persistent critique of Morgan [1947, *Preface*]." While Lowie agreed that the distinction between kinship and territorial organization was valid, he objected to the logical and the evolutionary priority given kinship. Lowie argued that the relationship between the two bases of organization was not one of logical exclusion (either–or) or evolutionary sequence (before–after), but was instead a relation of systematic interaction. Lowie was quite clear that although some societies "conform admirably to the theory that kinship is the one factor in all governmental relations," the territorial organization was never absent and constituted a possibility at all levels of political and technological complexity (1921: 377; 1927:59).

> What matters is that even in very humble cultural levels local contiguity is one of the factors determining social solidarity independently of blood-relationship. Now I have designated as associations those social units not based on kinship, and the territorial group may veritably be conceived as a specialized form of association [Lowie, 1921:380].

Relying on the very wide command of ethnographic knowledge for which Lowie was noted, he demonstrated these statements with examples and lucid argument. But more important than his insistence on the systematic interaction of the two modes of organization, was Lowie's contention that the two modes were *independent,* and that they varied in emphasis according to different historical conditions (1927:51–54). Lowie believed that the "germ of territoriality" was universally present in human society. For him, the existence of valued social space was not at issue, but only its relationship to other bases of social organization such as age and sex. Although he offered no theory to account for the cultural constitution of space, his discussion of the relationship between territory and kinship represented an important advance.

The elements of a cultural theory of space came from Europe. Emile Durkheim and his associates in the *Année Sociologique* began to elaborate a theory of social differentiation. The differentiation of space into areas of different values (sacred or profane, for example) was for him an integral aspect of social differentiation. He wrote

> Space is not the vague and indeterminate medium which Kant imagined; if purely and absolutely homogeneous, it would be of no use, and could not be grasped by the mind. Spatial representations consist essentially in a primary coordination of the data of sensuous experience. But this co-ordination would be impossible if the parts of space were qualitatively equivalent and if they were really interchangeable. To dispose things spatially there must be a possibility of placing them differently, of putting some at the right, others at the left, those above, those below, at the north of or at the south of, east or west, etc., etc., just as to dispose of states of consciousness temporarily there must be a possibility of localizing them at determinable dates. This is to say that space could not be what it is if it were not, like time, divided and differentiated [Durkheim, 1915:23].

Durkheim's socially differentiated space was a far cry from the notion of a sovereign territory, discussed above. For a political community to exist in a territory, Durkheim saw that it was not sufficient that they have a relationship to that territory, for example, sovereignty. What was crucial was that space be differentiated and valued so that it represented the differentiation and evaluation of social groups. Georg Simmel expressed a similar position: He pointed out that "spatial relations not only are determining conditions of relationships among men, but also are symbolic of those relationships [Levine, 1971:143]."

It is beyond cavil that spatial dispositions represent or are symbolic of social relationships, but I do not agree that spatial relationships, spatial images, or spatial concepts are simply representations of social relations and, therefore, are wholly determined by them. Before space can represent anything at all, there must be imposed upon it a structure of differentiation, or *topology,* which allows other relationships to be expressed in its terms. This topologization is logically prior to representation, and is a conceptual and cultural function.

Durkheim and Simmel made the first moves in the direction of a theory of meaningful space, but for them spatial differentiation was fully accounted for by social structures that it merely represented. In a different vein, Arnold Van Gennep, in *Rites de Passage,* used spatial structure to account for a broad range of other social phenomena. When he used the term *passage* in this important and influential essay on the "rites of passage," he had in fact invented a rich metaphor. In the first substantive chapter, "The Territorial Passage," Van Gennep established his premise.

Territorial passage can provide the framework for the discussion of
rites of passage which follows. . . . The frontier, an imaginary line
connecting milestones or stakes, is visible—in exaggerated fashion—
only on maps. But not so long ago, the passage from one country to
another, from one province to another, within each country and still
earlier from one manorial domain to another was accompanied by
various formalities. These were largely political, legal, and economic,
but some were of a magico-religious nature. . . . It is this magico-
religious aspect of crossing frontiers that interests us. . . . It is this
situation which I have designated a transition, and one of the purposes
of this book is to demonstrate that this symbolic and spatial area of
transition may be found in more or less pronounced form in all the
ceremonies which accompany the passage from one social and magico-
religious position to another [1960:15–18].

By "magico-religious," Van Gennep meant both the practical or
ritual (magical) aspect of territorial passage and the theoretical or conceptual (religious) aspect of this. It was, in fact, in the interest of contrib-
uting to the understanding of the sacred that he advanced the territorial
passage as a conceptual model. The concern with the sacred, however,
obscures for us today as it did for him the fact that the "largely political, legal, and economic formalities" involved in the frontier crossing
were as much a part of culture as the category of the sacred. The sovereign territory is, after all, a cognitive image of space with which a
group has established a political, rather than a religious, relationship.
The frontier is an *imaginary* line in the etymological sense of this word:
It is an image. It has no other reality apart from the "customs" or "formalities" that serve to mark it as either political space (e.g., the territory
of the sovereign nation) or as religious space (the precinct of the temple
or altar). The political, legal, and economic formalities together with
the magico-religious formalities need not be distinguished as Van Gennep
thought. They are all means of designating a particular sort of relationship to what is fundamentally a cognitive image of space.

Van Gennep's metaphor, as metaphor, has had a powerful influence
on many anthropologists since *Rites de Passage* was originally published
in 1908 (see Gluckman, 1962; Turner, 1969:14, 166; Stoeltje, 1978).
In this essay, he argued, for example, that being married was *like* crossing
a boundary. His metaphor was immediately seen to be a very apt one,
not only for marriage but for a whole range of social transitions of status,
state, condition, category, or disposition, which were in numerous ways
like spatial transitions. By seeing for the first time the relations of likeness
that appeared between social distinctions and spatial boundaries, or between changes of social status and movements in space, Van Gennep was

able to demonstrate an essential unity among a group of social beliefs and practices that had until then appeared disparate and unrelated. It is odd that, although the metaphor that Van Gennep suggested has been widely accepted and applied, little consideration has been given to the initial perception on which it is based, that of spatial neighborhood, boundary, and transition. These are, in the terms which I have adopted, topological relations of space, and it is these relations *as* relations that have so wide an applicability.

It is partly because the metaphor it established was so successful that the *Rites de Passage* essay did not stimulate a study of space in and for itself. Max Black (1962:38–41) discusses some of the implications of metaphor in a way that allows us to see why this was so. One kind of metaphor, he explains, consists of putting new meaning into old words in a way that "plugs the gaps" in the vocabulary. Van Gennep's extension of the meaning of the word *passage* is an example of this. Such a metaphor serves to organize thought about something. But there are, in fact, two "somethings" in a metaphor, namely, a principle subject—for example, marriage or initiation in our case—and the subsidiary subject—crossing a territorial frontier. The two meanings interact in such a way that the "system of associated commonplaces" of frontier crossing organizes our thought about the great variety of customs and beliefs attendant upon getting married or being initiated into a new status. The metaphor, says Black, acts like a filter: It emphasizes some traits and pushes others into the background. Such metaphors allow us to think more clearly. Indeed, they may shift attention entirely away from the subsidiary subject—in Van Gennep's case, the nature of spatial categories and passages—upon which the analytic edifice is built.

With respect to space itself, Van Gennep's achievement was to show that territory was a cultural phenomenon. He recognized that boundaries were not "natural," but collectively conceived and ritually established.

This recognition provides the basis upon which an adequate cultural theory of territory may be built.

The Ritual Creation of Space: A Definition

Natural, physical, or "ecological" space is only of secondary concern in this study. Only insofar as the natural order is given meaning and value (including economic as well as ritual value) does it become relevant to the study of society and culture. The Iraqw say they "make" or "create" their land (*aten ayaren aga tlehh*) and it is this cultural "creation" of space that is of interest. The cultural creation of space entails at least three definable symbolic processes.

First, selected landforms—natural or physical patterns of space— are *appropriated* into a specifically cultural frame by attributing to these things, or features of them, certain specified values. I call this process appropriation because, from the Iraqw point of view, natural features, land, resources, and so on, are taken out of the wild (*slaa'*) and brought into the familiar world of meaningful objects and relations. In another sense of the term, that which is selected is "appropriate" to the context or frame into which it has been drawn by virtue of features that influenced its selection in the first place. As we shall see in Chapter 2, the slope of a hill, the "ridge" which is a prominent feature of this dissected-plateau landscape, the door of the house, and so on, are given values, or meaning, within a system of values that relates these features to each other in systematic ways. Thus, naming something that has not been named, or assigning to something a significance that it has not had before constitutes an *appropriation* of that thing, place, or capacity into the cultural system. In the Iraqw case, giving a new place a new name, or defining and evaluating a "frontier" or a place of exile (*sehha*) is first of all a cultural appropriation of space.

Second, the ritual creation of space involves the specialization and differentiation of multiplex spatial meanings and the selective valuation of space thus defined. In other words, a cultural logic develops that serves to order values and meanings attached to the patterns of space that emerge. The development of a cultural logic is an historical process.

For example, the cultural logic concerning the relations of space, particularly the delineation of boundaries and areas and the preservation of continuity between them (or the negation of continuity, as in the case of "cursing the land" or exile) reveals itself as a set of topological concepts. These concepts provide the fundamental metaphor in the Iraqw conceptual ordering of the past, just as the tree has served as the fundamental metaphor for the European's conceptualization of "branching" lines of the family genealogy ("the family tree") or of evolution of man itself. Furthermore, these topological concepts (not simply topographical since they are used to apply to both time and space) are applied in ordering certain ritual performances (the *masay* ritual, for example—see Chapter 4), and have motivated and shaped important social movements in Iraqw society.

I develop this idea of "topology" in order to "translate" a set of concepts that are central to Iraqw culture. I do not use *topology* in the strictly mathematical sense, but in the way that Piaget (1970:23 and following) has used the term to refer to a type of logical structure that relies on ideas of continuity, boundary, neighborhood, openness, and closedness as some of its fundamental elements or assumptions. The mathematical science of topology has given these ideas strict mathematical content. While my use of *topology* does not preclude a more rigorous treatment, the aim in this discussion is to *establishing an ethnological content,* and to suggest that there are a set of related spatial concepts that are appropriate to the discussion because they approximate the cultural order that the Iraqw themselves see and use. Topological space is distinguished from the idea of a Euclidean space that a set of axes introduces. Axes permit a different evaluation and use of space that is called *projective space* to distinguish it from elementary topological space and from metric space. The ideas of a measured, metric space are not relevant to this discussion. This study investigates the way topological and projective space are given value (good–bad, pure–polluted, dangerous–benevolent, powerful–innocuous, etc.) such that it may provide the underlying structure in observed behavioral and cultural products of many varieties.

Thus, the idea of boundary and of closure is, in the Iraqw cultural order, a specialized notion derived from an abstract cultural system and applied in the definition of residential groups, in the practice of sacrifice, in the legitimation of authority, and so on. The spatial order, when differentiated and selectively valued within a system of values, provides the overall framework for organizing and articulating small kin groups of many ethnic backgrounds into a larger, functioning social group with a distinct identity and orientation to its environment.

Third, the ritual objectification of spatial concepts may generate a series of motivated variants, all of which are derived from a set or "kernel" of spatial principles. Throughout the book I attempt to show how a small set of basic postulates about the order of space are manifested in politics, the conduct of ritual, the "conditions of appropriateness" for certain types of discourse, the exercise of social sanctions and the definition of social transgressions, the organization of discourse about the past, as well as in the historical process itself. In each instance I also try to show how these principles are selectively applied according to the variations of context and historical conditions.

The cultural study of space must be both structural and historical. In fact, we must deal with two different scales or levels of phenomena: the structure of social process over time and the structure of logical process in the mind of the subject who perceives and orders the events. By analyzing both levels in terms of the symbolic processes and logic I have mentioned, we are more easily able to relate these levels one to the other in order to achieve a better understanding of the whole. The research is necessarily interdisciplinary between history and ethnology. Piaget (1973) would find this connection congenial since he feels that the nature of the relationship between the various disciplines of the social sciences

> remains an open question so long as the central problem of sociology, that of society considered as a whole and the relations between the sub-systems and the whole system, is still not solved. . . . It is very likely that new light will be thrown on the problem of the hierarchy of scales of phenomena and the related studies by future progress of two essentially synthetic disciplines and their repercussions on the question of infrastructure and superstructures. These are ethnology, the multidimensional character of which is manifest, and history, regarded not as the mere reconstruction of events, but as interdisciplinary research dealing with the diachronic aspects of each of the fields studied by the various human sciences.

One result of the ritual creation of space—but not the only result—is the definition of territory. According to the view taken here, the creation of the territory is essentially no different from the creation of the "house space," or the isolation and sacralization of a "ritual space" or sacred precinct. The distinction that has been previously drawn between territory and other defined spaces—which treats territory as political and the subject or limit of sovereignty and domination—is rejected. Territory is political because it is shared, public, and because it defines limit or locus of use of resources. It is not shared, public, and used because it is "political." What is essential in the definition of territory is that it is an image or icon, a symbolic representation. Such representation may take the form of a graphic map (as it does in the modern West), or it may be presented kinesthetically in ritual as it is among the Iraqw. It may also be imaged (and imagined) in myth as is the land of the Aboriginal Australians in "dreamtime."

We may define territory, then, in the following terms: *Territory is the symbolic differentiation of space (topologization) and the appropriation of this topologized space into a structure of meaning by attributing shared and public values to places, directions, and boundaries such that it may be graphically, cognitively, or ritually represented as a coherent and enduring image.*

The initial differentiation of this space may be accomplished by means of boundaries or by defining a locus about a point, or by using a combination of these means. As Van Gennep pointed out, it is the convention of marking and respecting a boundary that is real and observable, not the boundary itself, for that is imaginary. Particular economic, political, religious, or legal relationships that individuals or groups may have with an area so defined, such as sovereignty, dominion, ownership, usufruct, tenure, leasehold, defense, rental, and so on, are secondary, and of an entirely different nature.

This definition of *territory* goes well beyond other definitions such as the ecological "locus of use" or the political "limits of domination and sovereignty" definitions that have usually guided the approach to the phenomenon. The definition employed here constitutes a theoretical orientation and a program for research. This book is an attempt to work out some of its theoretical implications through an examination of the cultural system and social action of the Iraqw.

Ritual and Politics

Ritual and political action among the Iraqw cannot be easily distinguished. It seemed to one observer (Winter, 1955) that the only discussions among the elders were "confined to the discussion of ritual which the elders carry out for the country as a whole." My own experience confirms this. It would appear, in the light of much recent theory (Douglas, 1966; Dumont, 1970; Turner, 1974) that such ritual, involved as it is with concepts of pollution, category, and territory, are complex metaphors of political interaction. Mary Douglas (1966:3) believes that "some pollutions are used as analogies for expressing a view of the social order," and claims that "pollution beliefs can be used in a dialogue of claims and counter claims to status." Among the Iraqw, many social processes, which appear more obviously "political" or "economic" in other societies, are given expression and form as part of ritual.

In other words, the personal relationship with which we are concerned here are multiplex rather than simplex (Swartz, 1968:1 after Gluckman, 1955). They are multiplex because they are defined according to multiple criteria (age, sex, neighborhood, kinship, etc.), and they function in various contexts and in multiple capacities (ritual, political, economic, etc.). Political relationships constituted in the process of seeking political goals are not differentiated from those that are constituted for the activity of achieving a "blessing" for the land, or for promoting an economic exchange. This is especially true of relationships arising from spatial contiguity (neighborhood) or from mutual enclosure within a boundary (in this case, the boundary of the *aya*). The spatial definition of relationship (i.e., "we are related because we are neighbors or because we are enclosed by the same boundary") is itself neutral: It must be invested with value before it can serve as the basis for organizing activity or mobilizing resources. It is the ritual process that invests the spatial schema with cultural meaning, "energizing" it, as it were, so that it becomes both a part of the cultural "structure of meaning" and a means to political and other social ends. The *masay* ritual, by posing the spatial dichotomy of a "good" inside to a "dangerous" outside realizes just this cultural valuation of spatial order in practice.

But to what end? To consider the goals for which people strive and compete is to study politics. *Politics,* as it has been defined by Marc Swartz in *Local Level Politics* (1968:1), "refers to the events which are involved in the determination and implementation of public goals and/or the differential distribution and use of power within the group or groups concerned with the goals being considered." I proceed with this definition of politics because it emphasizes the event—the process—over the structure. One immediately recognizes, in confronting Iraqw society, that it is in a state of flux. It is not political structures or statuses, for example, that are legitimized in the Iraqw political process, but rather it is the verbal *means* to achieve power that is legitimized. The exercise of power depends on the performative competence in "legitimizing genres" of oral literature and ritual by those who would wish to exercise power. In practice, however, the exercise of political power is much less an issue than the political rhetoric used to forge consensus among the participants of the public meeting.

Iraqw society is a society of equals. There are no leaders who hold political office. With the exception of the speaker (*kahamusmo*) who represents the community to outsiders and who leads the meeting, no one person holds a title or regularly performs political functions. Indeed, the most powerful persons, the ritual experts (*qwaslare*), are not integrated into the political community at all. In the Iraqw concept they are external to the normal political process, tied as it is to the ritual condition of the land. Their powers are sought in extraordinary circumstances. They are outside of the boundaries of the political community, but not outside of the political system. Within the community the exercise of power depends on the creative and integrative competence with which the elements of oral literature and ritual practice are put together into new ritual forms. Political change among the Iraqw is much like the political change through competitive innovation that Franz Boas drew attention to in 1897 in his discussion of the "Secret Societies of the Kwakiutl" (see Chapter 8).

More recently, Ralph Nicholas (1968:296 after Bailey, 1960 and Swartz *et al.,* 1966) noted that the "understanding of new forms of political cooperation and conflict—or new forms of social relationship generally—is facilitated by an analytic focus on social process rather than on social structure." He distinguishes between the event itself (the political process) and the environment that "both sustains the political system, in that it provides the actors and provisions them while they are engaged in political activity, and at the same time places some restraint upon political activity [1968:300]." Nicholas makes the useful distinction between the rules and resources which comprise the political environment. In general, *resources* include both the material and the human. Among the Iraqw, who lack an elaborated material culture or a monetarized economy, land is the primary material resource. It is also the primary object of ritual and of economic activity. These multiple relationships to land reflect exactly the same lack of differentiation that produces the multiplex relations among people that we have already mentioned.

The role and definition of rules, however, is slightly more complex. Nicholas discusses five categories of *rules* that he considers to be part of the political environment. They are *moral principles* (statements about what one should or ought to do), *jural rules, technical facts, pragmatic rules,* and *regularities.* The first four types, briefly stated, are conscious rules that can be formulated by at least some of the actors, while "regularities" are the features of the observer's model, the observed patterns that exist and endure but that cannot be explicitly formulated by the actors. For this study of Iraqw politics we are concerned primarily with "moral principles." What we think of as "jural rules" play very little part in the conduct of Iraqw political life. Nicholas cites "the basic idea of the caste system, of the propriety of hierarchical social relations," as an example of moral principle. His example recalls the salience of neighborhood and other topological principles in Iraqw social relations. Moreover, it makes clearer the differences between the Iraqw and the South Asian practice of a highly ritualized politics, while indicating the functional analogy between the topological and the hierarchical mode of social discrimination of groups in competition for resources.

In the course of this study I try to reveal the intermingling of politics and ritual in the constitution of multiplex relations between men and the land, and between men and other men. I attempt to show that inasmuch as the expansion of relative control over resources (here, the land) is a central objective of political activity (Nicholas, 1968:302), ritual plays the critical organizational function. By the same token, the ritual practice also sets up the categories and dichotomies that both constrain and sustain the political process.

For example, this valued spatial ideology provides a means for social control by making possible certain sanctions. Wrongdoing is punished by exile, or by seclusion in one's house and exclusion from all social contact. A notion of space that defines a boundary that distinguishes a good inside from a dangerous and inherently punishing outside underlies the effectiveness of exile as a social sanction. Other ethnic groups are classified, named, and evaluated according to their position in space relative to the Iraqw lands, (not, for example, in terms of a model of descent, as the sons of Noah defined the races for the ancient Hebrew, or the sons of Ruhanga defined them from the Banyoro of Uganda). Changes of status within internal Iraqw hierarches (for example, the *marmo* ritual among women—see Chapter 8) were celebrated, marked, and talked about in terms of categories of space. The ideology of space is functionally analogous to other types of structural ideologies, such as the lineage model.

Among the Iraqw, authority is legitimated by its relationship to the meetings (*kwasleema*) in which political decisions are made, and by its relationship to certain genres of oral performance. Both the meeting and the performance of these genres of oral literature are constrained by the underlying ideology of space. History does not have the same legitimating function that it does in societies organized according to a lineage ideology or according to a succession of chiefs. The Iraqw narrative presents events that happened in the past as examples of effective ritual and oral performance. The Iraqw narrative is not a charter for contemporary authority. Instead it legitimates the performance of ritual on which authority, in turn, depends. This fact gives "history" quite a different character, and this must be examined if we are to use their account of the past to write an objective, critical history of social processes.

Politics and History

Part of this work is an ethnohistory; that is, a history of a non-Western, nonliterate people based on the informed interpretation of "oral tradition" and other ethnological, geographical, and linguistic information. This, however, is only half of the project. I make a radical distinction between "history," our own rationalized interpretation of texts that relate to the past, and what John Plumb has called "the past." Plumb is talking about the cultural representation of the past that is a part of the culture of the people and must be considered as such if we are to preserve, in describing it, its structural characteristics that relate it to the rest of the cultural "text."

Therefore, I separate my discussion of "history" in Chapter 8 from my discussion of "the past" in Chapter 7, called "Talking About the Past." This is a distinction drawn by Plumb (1970) in *Death of the Past:*

> I have tried to draw a sharp distinction between the past and history. Man from the earliest days of recorded time has used the past in a

variety of ways: to explain the origins and purpose of human life, to sanctify institutions of government, to give validity to class structure, to provide moral example, to vivify his cultural and educational process, to interpret the future, to invest both the individual human life or a nation's with a sense of destiny. . . . But the past, used in the way it was, is never history, although parts of it may be historical. History, like science, is an intellectual process. . . . History is not the past.

The past is always created ideology with a purpose, designed to control individuals or to motivate societies [Pp. 11–17].

My purpose in distinguishing history from the Iraqw concept of the past is different from that of Plumb's, who is concerned with the function of the past in any given society. Here, I investigate the structure of the idea of the past among the Iraqw, examining it as one cultural text among others so that its nature, as part of a larger cultural whole, may be elucidated.

This approach to the text of oral traditions is a complement to much of contemporary African historiography, the guiding principles for which have been set out by Jan Vansina (1961). In Vansina's view, the oral text is analogous to, and only superficially different from, the written documents with which the Western historian is accustomed to working. He issues the caveat, however, that since history is "no more than the calculation of probabilities," we can never have a complete understanding of the past because "the past is something outside our experience, something that is other [p. 185]." Clearly, Vansina's use of the term *the past* differs from Plumb's in precisely the same way that the two halves of this inquiry differ. The ethnological examination of *the past* (Plumb's term, i.e., the particular cultural concept) that *is* an accessible part of culture, enriches history by enabling us to reinsert culture into the historical account. This historical account of *the past* (Vansina's term i.e., the description of events and processes of preceding times that have had, as their result, contemporary society and culture) is complicated by the very nature of oral tradition. Nevertheless, according to Vansina:

What the historian can do is to arrive at some approximation to the ultimate historical truth. He does this by using calculations of probability, by interpreting the facts, and by evaluating them in an attempt to recreate for himself the circumstances which existed at certain given moments of the past. And here the historian using oral traditions finds himself on exactly the same level as the historian using any other kind of historical source material. No doubt he will arrive at a lower degree of probability than would otherwise be attained, but that does not rule out the fact that what he is doing is valid, and that it is history [p. 186].

In Chapters 8 and 9 of this book, then, oral texts are used in conjunction with other materials to write history. I take two approaches to the same cultural material: one produces history, the other a description of a cultural logic.

Ultimately, this study is concerned with meaningful action in the observable world; that is, with politics and with history. My first step is to describe a "structure of meaning," a system of ideas about the order of space that partially constitutes Iraqw culture. I then will attempt to show how this cultural order is instantiated, for example, in the pattern of residence, in different forms of literature, in the exercise of political sanctions, in the definitions of ethnic/ecological boundaries, and in the acquisition of territory in an expansion movement. The spatial patterns that are observed in culture and in social action are not arbitrary patterns: They are conditioned by historical antecedents and motivated by political and social contingencies.

It is one of the aims of this work to demonstrate that the particular way the Iraqw talk about and organize space is the result of a history that has left them feeling vulnerable, as they say, "caught in the middle." In direct consequence of this, they have adopted a particular strategy of organization of space. It will at once be recognized that this is a different form of organization that distinguishes Iraqw social structure from that of many other African societies that are organized by kinship (consanguinity, lineality, affinity, filiation, etc.). There are, however, perfectly comprehensible reasons—rational within their own frame, and conditioned by historical events—for organizing society in terms of spatial categories.

The Anthropological Problems

In the foregoing sections of this chapter I outlined a theory of cultural space that has grown out of my experience with the Iraqw. I have suggested ways in which these elementary spatial relations articulate with politics and help to generate a particular social process, the account of which is history.

My 15 months of residence with the Iraqw, together with my use of numerous other resources, has enabled me to sketch the outlines of Iraqw history. Since I do not deal with history until later chapters, a brief overview of its main movements is essential for the understanding of the rest of the discussion.

The Iraqw have moved in this century from a remote mountain fastness into a much larger area at the expense of the Masai and other pastoralist, agricultural, and hunting peoples (Winter and Molyneaux, 1963). Their expansion has been relatively rapid. Most of the Iraqw living in the newly settled areas were either themselves born in Irqwar Da'aw, their mountain "homeland," or their fathers were. This territorial expansion confronted them with a diversity of experience. Along their frontiers they have met with no less than eight distinct ethnic groups speaking languages representative of at least three major language families of continental Africa practicing economies as various as mixed cattle-goat-sheep pastoralism; grain-legume-cucurbit sedentary agriculture; hunting, gathering, and honey collecting, and inhabiting environments ranging from salt flats to montane evergreen forests (Murdock, 1959). Both prior to and during the expansion of the Iraqw, they have absorbed small groups and even individuals from all of the groups that today surround them. Diversity of language, economy, and culture exists both within and outside of Iraqw society.

In view of this diversity, a central problem, both for the anthropologist and for the peoples involved, is to locate the frontier—the boundary along which competitive interactions among various groups is likely to occur.

It is important to note that frontiers do not develop in all cases of interethnic interactions. Sometimes one group is quietly absorbed by another. In the century or more prior to 1870, small groups of diverse origins were absorbed into the Iraqw society. But where the frontier does exist, it is a clear-cut area where intraethnic rules of reciprocity in exchange of all types seem no longer to apply, and where hostilities frequently erupt. Among the Iraqw these boundaries that create the frontier are defined ritually in a ceremony called *masay*.

The *masay* ceremony creates a sacred precinct. The delineation of a sacred precinct is a common feature of African public rituals. This has been amply discussed by Victor Turner (1967a) for the Ndembu, Monica Wilson (1951) for the Nyakyusa, C. Hallpike (1972) for the Konso of Ethiopia, and Peter Rigby (1968) for the Gogo of Tanzania, to list a few ethnographic examples. This feature of ritual and other forms of social life was clear to Durkheim (1915:23) and Van Gennep (1960) even earlier.

But what is unusual about the Iraqw case is that this sacred precinct is drawn to include all of the territory to which a particular part of the Iraqw people lay claim. This ritual reaffirms rights to the land. It also creates a strong polarity between the pure and blessed settled area and the impure cursed outside; that is, the frontier. In fact three categories are created: the homeland (*aya*), the frontier (*sehha*), and the dangerous wilderness (*slaa'*), which may be inhabited by people of other ethnic groups (*homo*).

Emigration, then, becomes a movement from the pure to the impure. Movement out of the homeland area began as persons accused of witchcraft or other misconduct were exiled—either by the elders meeting in council or by popular disapprobation—into the frontier by the formula *sehha keer*, "get thee to the frontier." When exiled persons in the frontier had settled and prospered enough to declare, by means of the *masay* ritual, an *aya* of their own, they were reincorporated into the larger society by the elders who formally lifted their curse in a ceremony that was the precise inverse of the original cursing. On the other hand immigrants, by virtue of their exogenous origins in the impure wilderness (*homo*), were believed to have special powers. In the last century the paramount ritual office was successively accorded to representatives of three "foreign" ethnic groups. During the Colonial period, appointed chiefs, who in the course of their official duties had traveled widely, were accorded special respect and spoken of as "men who walked in the wilderness."

In the case of exile and reincorporation, the frontier moved by a process of transcendent redefinition in which the impure frontier was declared pure and incorporated into the mother society, thereby creating a new frontier beyond the first. Historically this process was eventually superseded by a movement led by a class of "priests" (*kahamuse*, literally 'speakers') who moved with groups of supporters directly into the frontier area, performed the *masay* ritual, and immediately declared the new area pure and a part of the mother society. In many cases the men who led these movements were able to transform their political status from that of ritual functionary to outright chiefship in the newly settled lands. This process continues today.

When I went into the field in 1975 several articles were available that indicated both the importance of space and the centrality of ritual in social and political action. Wada (1975) and Yoneyama (1970), two Japanese ethnologists who had worked in a different part of Mbulu District with the Iraqw, indicated the outline of territorial organization but did not account for it in historical, structural, or functional terms. Edward Winter, who had conducted research in Mbulu District in the early 1950s, was the first to understand that spatial categories, not kinship categories, provided the principles of organization for the Iraqw. In an article, "Territorial Groupings and Religion among the Iraqw," Winter (1966) pointed out that:

The structural principle utilized within Iraqw territorial groupings is *spatial contiguity* itself. Although Anthropologists working in Africa have not isolated this as a principle in the way they have isolated the lineage principle, there seems to be no intrinsic reason why it should not be utilized. However, when it is used, certain peculiar problems are raised for the analyst which are not raised when a lineage principle is employed. Granted that the people within a territorial group are held together by ties of neighborliness, there is still the problem of why such a group exists in the form that it does [p. 168].

Although Winter's statement of the central problem that Iraqw social organization presented to anthropology was clear, he neither pursued it further nor did he attempt to present much evidence in the attempt to solve it. He did indicate that the means for defining the territory were ritual, but he gave no description of what these rituals might have been. My research some 25 years later showed that very little had changed. My findings supported Winter's earlier perception and enabled me to shed light on this central problem of space as an organizational principle.

There was of course other ethnographic evidence from peoples near the Iraqw that indicated that research focused on space, spatial concepts, and rituals of spatial demarcatior would be particularly rewarding. Among the Gogo, a Bantu-speaking people living to the south of the Iraqw, Peter Rigby noted the importance of the "ritual area" (called *yisi* in Kigogo) in many aspects of Gogo social life. In a discussion of purification rituals, Rigby (1968) commented that:

Whatever events necessitate them, the purification rites in particular circumstances, the "control" and manipulation of the ritual state (*mbeha*) of an area of space, and the prevention of the destructive forces of a bad ritual state (*libeho*), are the central issues in Gogo thought.

Indeed, the Gogo and the Iraqw are not alone in their strong concern for "ritual state of areas of space." This concern is characteristic of a broad area of northern, western and central Tanzania. This area has been called the Ntemi area, after the most commonly encountered name for a particular kind of ritual expert, or *ntemi*, that distinguishes their political mode from that of other Tanzanian and other African peoples. While the Iraqw do not use the term *ntemi*, and while their political organization does not revolve around such people, certain features of their political ideology are consonant with that of other peoples in the Ntemi area. Indeed it is this sharing of underlying political and ritual forms and concepts that leads non-Iraqw neighbors to attribute efficacy to the Iraqw rituals that serve to mark their boundaries. For the Iraqw, as for other peoples in this area, politics and ritual are very closely linked. The nature of this linkage was not clear when I went into the field. It constitutes another of the central problems with which this study deals.

There are three ethnographic problems that confront us at the outset: (*a*) What is the reason for the Iraqw focus on space?; (*b*) Why are "politics" and "ritual" apparently inextricably interlinked?; and (*c*) Why, or how, did the Iraqw, who lacked any institutions of central authority and who characteristically used no force in their social interactions, manage to expand rapidly and inexorably into a much larger region at the expense of hostile and militarily able pastoralists such as the Masai?

I try to show that their central, organizing ideology is constituted on the basis of an elementary topology—a systematic set of ideas about spatial categories and relationships. I have tried to demonstrate that in this egalitarian society, social order is primarily ritual order, and that ritual order is a practically motivated activity (that is, one that is carried out for practical ends) in which the terms and gestures composing it are valued and revalued according to historically determined social needs. These needs, furthermore, are political needs, having to do with the legitimation of authority and right over land use. Ritual, therefore, is politics for the Iraqw.

Finally, I try to show that the Iraqw practice of exile produced a gradual migration into surrounding "cursed" frontier lands by exiled youths. These young people were frequently followed by others into the frontier. As the Iraqw-speaking population increased in these areas, these places were frequently legitimated and reincluded in normal Iraqw society by means of the performance of a boundary-defining, land-purifying ritual called *masay*. Subsequently, under the British colonial aegis, certain ritually expert individuals used this ritual deliberately to carve out new territories which, since they were agriculturally productive, could be taxed by the colonial authority, and were therefore acceptable. The Iraqw cultural ideology and ritual practice resulted directly in a territorial expansion that fulfilled simultaneously the Iraqw cultural expectations for spatial and cosmological order, and the British requirements for material production.

Chapter 2

The Cultural Organization of Domestic and Political Space

I will begin the discussion of the Iraqw use and meaning of space with the description of the immediate household environment. I will work outward toward spatial categories of greater inclusiveness, such as the neighborhood, the settled area, and beyond the boundary of the region to the "wilderness" and lands of hostile (or so they are viewed by the Iraqw) outsiders.

The House

The house constitutes a large part of the everyday reality of the person and is the symbol of the group that it houses. In some cases, a symbolic action directed against the house—the physical object—directly affects the people or person it represents. The relationship between the inside of the house and the outside is the same as the relationship between the settled land (the *aya*) and the wilderness outside its borders (the *slaa'*). The boundary between these regions, the threshold of the house, *duxutamo,* and the boundary of the land, *digmu,* are ritually significant; that is, there are specific symbolic acts performed on them and directed to them.

Finally, as with the domestic space of all peoples, the way it is divided and the different uses to which this limited and bounded space is put, is meaningful and emotionally evocative.

It should be noted that this discussion is complicated by the recent moves on the part of the Tanzanian government to "modernize" housing

31

and to require all Tanzanians to live in villages, *vijiji* (singular, *kijiji*), where services may be provided, and education and political indoctrination carried out more efficiently. The required type of house is modeled after the coastal Swahili type of dwelling and, perhaps to a certain extent, on European housing. *De facto* regulations (I do not know if these are in fact set out clearly as national policy) dictate that the "modern" house be square or rectangular, have a peaked ridge-roof of thatch or sheet metal, and have large and ample windows and doors. The customary Iraqw house in Irqwar Da'aw is round with no windows and a small entryway. In spite of these differences, many Iraqw now living in the rectangular houses have attempted to maintain the interior details and construction as it was in the older, round houses in which most of them were born. I shall focus my attention on the round type.

It should be noted at first that the interior and the location of the Iraqw house cannot be discussed simply in terms of areas named and allocated to different tasks. The house is situated in accordance with the landscape and with the cardinal directions. Most houses face west. The single house, too, is always part of a larger unit *maray,* the group of houses of neighbors. There is no word in the language that expresses the concept of a mere collection of houses; that is, there is no single or simple plural of the word *do',* 'house'. The word itself denotes a definite and specific place, the *place* of a domestic unit. The term may be analyzed into two parts: *d-,* the locative particle, and *-o,* a definitive particle, which gives a literal meaning of "the place" or 'a definite and singular location'. It is, specifically, the space of the domestic group that forms an independent economic unit of production and consumption.

It is quite independent of its neighbors. This independence is emphasized by many Iraqw as a distinctive feature of their way of life. It is different, for example, from their Bantu-speaking neighbors who build in villages and share the produce of the fields, or of the Masai who build their shelters in fenced and defensible circles. It is significant that when the Iraqw were most sorely threatened by the marauding warriors of the Masai and other groups, they did not group together for the defense of the group, but instead dug caves and pits in which to hide, each house, *do',* responsible for its own defense and protection (Fosbrooke, 1954). In the face of this threat, too, they built farther and farther apart so as not to attract attention through density of settlement. They feel that the inhabitants of one house ought to be, normatively speaking, quite independent. This notion is reflected in the literal meaning and connotations of the word *do'.*

Like the English term *house, do'* also means the 'grouping of people for whom this place is a residence', the 'domestic group', and in some cases, 'the potential descendants of that domestic group'. In some cases of wrongdoing by a member of the house, the elders may lay their curse against the whole house. When this happens, or when some disaster befalls the residents of the house, they say *"do'os i qwar,"* 'his house is lost', meaning not simply that the house—the physical object—and the people in it are lost to the society of other Iraqw, but that all their descendants shall be as well, unless the curse should be formally lifted (*amahhoma*).

The house is largely the domain of women and children. Although there are no portions of the house specifically associated with male or female activity, the men are usually active outside—either in the field, in the pastures, or with other men. Today men travel long distances in search of grain, to sell tobacco and other produce at distant markets, or for wage employment, and so are absent for long periods of time. By contrast, women rarely travel far and almost never on overnight journeys. They spend a large portion of their day near and in the house, leaving it only to go to the nearby fields or to gather firewood. Children and men are usually responsible for carrying water since this task is both arduous and time-consuming. Thus, it is the women who are found in the house at any time of the day. If a marriage breaks up, if the couple no longer co-habits, it is the woman who remains with the house and the male seeks lodging elsewhere. In a number of cases an older man of influence will build for himself a separate men's house or council chamber, *hularo,* where he will entertain his age-mates (*qaro*) and friends.

The word *hularo*, 'men's house' or 'council chamber', is probably of Tatoga origin. In Tatoga settlements, the men and women always sleep in separate houses. The men's house is called *daghat ghorida hulanda,* which Wilson (1953:36) glosses simply as 'men's house'. The Iraqw term *hularo* appears to derive from the Tatoga word *hulanda.* The Iraqw do not commonly separate men's and women's sleeping quarters, and where they do have a *hularo,* the family is frequently of Tatoga origin or a client of one of the ritual specialists of Tatoga origin. This council chamber of the Iraqw is not called *do',* the word properly speaking for 'house', although this term may be loosely applied as part of expressions such as *bará do,* 'inside the house', when, for example, one calls out a greeting to people inside a council chamber.

The house proper, the original structure on the homestead, *tango,* is the symbol and domain of the domestic group. Even long after a family has moved from a homestead site, they retain rights over it and may return to plant tobacco and pumpkins on their old site. They will not, however, ever build again on a site which has been previously inhabited and subsequently abandoned. The mother of the family, addressed and referred to as *ayordo* (lit., 'mother'—'belonging'—'house'), is ultimately responsible for its care and upkeep. No Iraqw would pass by a house without greeting the woman of the house. She is addressed first upon entering the house, and she may grant or refuse permission to enter her domain.

The house provides shelter for the domestic group and for their domestic animals. The first division of the house that we consider, then, is the division between the space allocated to human habitation and that allocated to the domestic livestock (see Figure 2.1). There is a pen for the goats and sheep to one side of the house underneath the sleeping platform, called *do'ara* ('place of the small stock'), which leads onto the

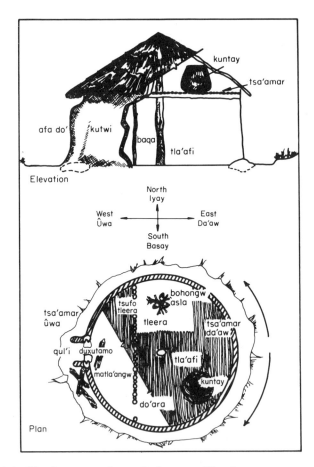

FIGURE 2.1. *The house: its plan and elevation. The diagram represents a type of house that most Iraqw would regard as characteristic of Irqwar Da'aw. Where modernization has required rectangular houses, the same plan is adapted by squaring the curved outline without significantly changing the internal arrangement.*

area immediately inside the door. This area, called *matla'angw*, is where the cattle spend the night and which, during the day, is the "public" portion of the house to which a man and his friends would retire on a rainy or cold day, and above which the older males of the house would sleep. The word may be related to the word for 'middle' or 'center', *tla' angw*, since it is a sort of middle ground between the outside and the private inner portions of the house where women and children live and where most of the cooking, eating, and sleeping is done. From the *matla' angw* we pass through the one solid internal wall (*baqa*) via a small doorway (called *tsufo tlera*) into the *tleera*, the only part of the house with standing headroom. (*Tleera*, the name for this area, evidently derives from *tleer*, 'tall' or 'long'.) The sleeping platform, *tsa'ama*, does not cover the area of the *tleera*, which provides access to the platform itself. This allows room for cooking and for the smoke to rise from the fire pit, *bohongw asla*, on the floor in the center of the *tleera*. The sleeping platform's edge serves as a shelf around three sides of the *tleera*. Facing the center of the house, the portion to the left is reserved especially for gourds of prepared food, cooking utensils, and leftovers. It is called *tsa' amar da'aw* (lit., 'high-place-belonging-east', or 'the east shelf'). This orientation is invariant from house to house since they are oriented in the same direction. On the observer's right is the corresponding *tsa'amar ûwa* or 'west shelf'. Here are stored the general possessions of the family, and the trade goods such as tobacco cakes, pyrethrum, or fat. Immediately in front of the observer is the *tla'afi*, the central portion of the house. On the upper level, the *tsa'amar tla'afi*, the family members sleep among the granary casks formed of withes plastered with dung and clay. On the ground floor, beneath the platform, the family members and friends work and play during the course of the day, and entertain close friends and neighbors around the hearth. A newborn kid or young calf might be tethered here during the night, and excess stores of grain, trade goods, and firewood might also be stored here.

The house is entered through an opening, sometimes including a tunnellike vestibule, *qui'i*. The opening itself is called the *afudo'* or 'mouth of the house' (*afa*, 'mouth' + *do'*, 'house'). There is a log partially buried, or a sill of stones, which forms the actual threshold, *duxutamo*, of the doorway. This opening is closed at night with a set of heavy logs with "keys" or projections carved on either end that fit into a vertical channel in the right and left jamb of the door frame. This doorway is closed securely at night against hyena (who the Iraqw believe will enter a house, especially in the case of were-hyenas inhabited by human witches) and other, smaller vermin such as mongooses.

The area immediately adjacent to the door on the outside is the

FIGURE 2.2. *The house in Irqwar Da'aw. The round house is traditional in the protected Iraqw uplands. This house, in the* aya Kwermusl, *was over 50 years old. Livestock is closed up in the house at night and the manure is scraped up and spread in the courtyard to dry each morning.*

kutwi, which merges with the flat courtyard of beaten earth (*afeni*) in front of the house (see Figure 2.2). This court is usually sunken below the level of the surrounding grassy areas. It is considered to be an integral part of the house-space. Courtesy demands that a visitor to the house stop at the edge of this court and exchange greetings with the residents, proceeding into the court and, if necessary, into the house only on invitation of the resident. There is a specific verb for the act of crossing the court, *ka'afeni,* which, if done without permission, is considered trespass or encroachment. It is believed that only a witch or an evil person would do this without communicating with the residents of the house first. Footsteps heard outside in the night occasion alarm until the person identifies himself or herself. Any person of good intention, when passing nearby a house, will call out a greeting no matter what time of day or night it may be. To pass silently signifies evil intent.

The night is not sacrosanct among the Iraqw. It is not the ultimately private part of the daily cycle as it is among most Europeans and Americans. Whereas we make a profound distinction between the bedroom and the office or the street, frequently acting, speaking, and thinking quite differently in each place, the Iraqw do not make quite so clear a distinction. One must call out a greeting to the people of a house when one passes with good intentions whatever the time of night. The greeting is usually acknowledged from within, if only by sleepy grunts. This is especially true since witches are believed to be abroad and active in the night. Although more dangerous for the innocent, the night is rather more a dark part of the day than a separate thing from it.

The courtyard is the center of activity during the day. Early in the morning, after the men have taken the livestock to pasture, the dung and refuse of the night are swept up inside the house and carried out to the court on small rush mats. There it is spread carefully over a portion of the court to dry in the sun. This dried mixture of dung, straw, dirt, and the refuse of daily life serves two needs. A portion of it is returned to the house in the evening and spread in the livestock enclosures to absorb the next night's dung and urine. The rest is put on a heap in the corner of the court where it composts and is later used as fertilizer in the fields. During harvest times, the courtyard is used to dry and thresh the crop. During the day most of the domestic work of preparing food, weaving mats, and repairing household implements takes place here.

The sides and back of the house are called *papay,* and are not actively useful space, although beer pots and fermenting troughs, spare mats, and firewood are stored here under the wide overlap of the eaves. The word that I translate as 'neighbors', *papahhay,* derives from a compound of the words *papay,* meaning 'back and sides of the house', and *hhay,* the most general term for 'a group of people'. *Papahhay* may be glossed then as 'a group of people in the locus of the back and sides of the house'. The term is a linguistic "shifter" because it is dependent on the context for its precise denotation. It carries some negative connotation. Neighbors are in competition with one another for land, but they must cooperate in the maintenance of cattle pastures and cattle throughways (*tlaqandi*) in cultivated areas that are communally maintained. One's relationship with neighbors is ambiguous. We shall note below that the "back" of a mountain or hill (relative to the house, which faces west), has a negative connotation. In part, the negative connotation attaches to the back of the house as well, with the implication that neighbors are slightly dangerous, albeit necessary. *Neighbors,* then, are defined topologically as the group of people who live in the locus of the back and sides of the house, whose living spaces bound the *papay* of the house of the speaker.

In Irqwar Da'aw the house is situated on the west side of a hill or the slope of a ridge, just below the crest. A terrace on which to build the house and its court is dug back into the face of the slope and the house is

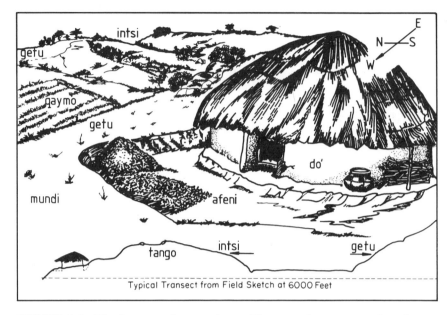

FIGURE 2.3. *The house and its environs. The immediate courtyard and grass sward surrounding the house constitute an integral part of the domestic group's living area.*

built close against the hillside facing outward into the valley below. Immediately around the house and court is a cleared grassy lawn kept short by the family's livestock. This area, not formally bounded and merging with the common pastures of the neighborhood, is the *mundi,* the 'home pastures' where young or sick livestock are pastured close to the house. The *mundi* is actively maintained by weeding it of undesirable grasses and woody forbs. If this were not done the grazing pressure would soon turn the area to unpalatable brush. The fields are in the valley below the house (see Figures 2.3 and 2.4).

In Irqwar Da'aw, the wind blows from the east, gathering force in its sweep across the Masai Steppe before it meets the Rift Valley Escarpment where it is suddenly forced upward into the cooler, higher levels of the atmosphere. From March to August this wind brings rain, but it also brings cold and fog. Most of Irqwar Da'aw lies above 6500 feet, and clothing is rarely adequate against the chill of the nights and the rain. It is largely for these reasons that the houses face the west, away from the prevailing winds. The sleeping platform, a sort of second story above the livestock and fire on the ground floor, is warm even if it is a bit dense with the vapors of cattle urine and smoke. The necessity of providing

FIGURE 2.4. *The house, its home pastures, and fields. Stock paths etch the hillside above the maize fields in the valley. An enclosed pit-toilet (top right) is a recent addition to many homesteads all over the district as adult health education has taken hold.*

warmth and a shelter from the prevailing winds no doubt dictates to a certain extent the common orientation of all Iraqw houses and their thick-walled, two-story construction, but the spaces and areas so delimited have a significance that goes beyond their practical function. The household orientation demonstrates the cultural appropriation of climatic variables into a system of values.

We shall consider the threshold, *duxutamo,* of the Iraqw house. Very early in the history of anthropology, Van Gennep recognized the significance of the threshold as a point of transition, and, using this notion as his fundamental metaphor, he elaborated a theory of *liminal rites* (from the Latin *limen,* 'threshold') which has proved to have a wide and powerful application. Van Gennep noted that "the door is the boundary between the foreign and domestic worlds in the case of an ordinary dwelling" (1960:20). Among the Iraqw the threshold is both the boundary between the domestic world of the inside of the house and the public domain, and in some contexts between the world of man and the world of spirits.

It may be decided by the elders, or by community opinion, that a certain person is evil, or that he or she has engaged in witchcraft or other antisocial activities. Never does the community take action against a felon's person. Control is exercised instead by means of a statement involving the person's house. The entrance to a cursed house is blocked by thorn bushes. In most cases the household is not forced, physically, to move from the place, but they will be scrupulously avoided, will not be allowed to herd cattle with the neighbors' cattle as is usually done, nor will they be greeted or welcomed at anyone else's house. By blocking the doorway—the symbol of continuity between a family's domestic space and the rest of the inhabited area around them—the message is conveyed that they are no longer considered to be part of the community. Under such circumstances, persons dealt with in this manner leave the community and go into the frontier, the unknown and dangerous outside.

Formerly children born with serious defects, or born in unpropitious circumstances, for example, a breach birth, were placed on the threshold in the morning and the cattle were driven over them in order to kill them. Children whose teeth came in on top first, it is said, were also killed or sacrificed in this way. An episode of this is recorded in the story of the prophesy of Saygilo in which a mysterious child is placed on the threshold in order that the cattle might trample him. In the story, the child is not trampled but instead milks the cattle as they pass. This was given as a sign that the child was especially sacred. In these instances the threshold of the house represents the liminal category, the "betwixt and between," which is neither part of the domestic space of the family nor part of the inhabited neighborhood that surrounds the house.

By sacrificing children who are born with defects, who develop abnormally, or who are otherwise anomalous, on the threshold of the house, the Iraqw are performing an action that is the domestic analog of exiling a witch. The exile is sent into the uninhabited bush, the *slaa'*, 'wilderness', which is the no man's land between the areas of Iraqw settlement and that of other ethnic groups that surround them. These actions demonstrate a structural similarity between exile and the killing of anomalous children on the threshold. This similarity is, more specifically, a topological isomorphism of culturally conceptualized spaces: the contiguous spaces represented by the inside of the house, the threshold, and the outside are equivalent to the spaces represented by the settled landscape (*aya*), "the bush," and the lands of other peoples.

The threshold is also the locus of communication with the spirits of the dead, *gii*. The dead are normally not troublesome, but they may occasionally be held responsible for illness of family members. If it is divined that the *gii* are to blame, an ox is sacrificed by the family. Most of the sacrifice is consumed by the family and friends during the day. Beer is brewed and all of the neighbors partake of the sacrifice. But the hide is reserved, and at night it is spread across the doorway over the threshold and several bits of meat are placed on it. In the night hyena always come to the door to carry away their portion of the feast. If they do not, it is held that the problem was misdiagnosed and that the *gii* probably were not responsible in the first place. Such sacrifices are, in any case, uncommon (see Figure 2.5). In this case, the threshold is the boundary between the world of the living and that of the dead. By means of the rite of sacrifice to the *gii,* the Iraqw believe that they also strengthen the boundary between the outside and the interior of the house against hostile influences. It is considered to be primarily a rite of protection, *pa'asamo,* similar to the *masay* ceremony that purifies and protects the land.

The interior space of the house may also become contaminated with

FIGURE 2.5. *The house entrance,* afudo'; *favorite spot for conversation and the site for sacrifice to the* gii.

evil influences that may be expunged by a relatively simple rite of sacrifice. In this rite a wild cucumber is broken open beside the central post of the house. The spirits are exhorted with the phrase *"netlangw ngi gwed,"* 'spirits of the earth, may you be opened, released'. The cucumber is then carried to the door and tossed over the bank. This ceremony of purification of the house, *ma'a'e,* also bears many close resemblances to the ceremony of the purification of the land. What is significant here is the symbolic isomorphism of the house and its surrounds with the inhabited landscape (*aya*).

The Ridge Community

The features of the landscape of Irqwar Da'aw influence to a large degree the size of the immediate neighborhood of any house. The land takes the form of long ridges, branching away from each other and separated by valleys that drain into several rivers and disappear over the edge of the escarpment. These rivers originate in the dense forests that surround Irqwar Da'aw. Springs are found at the heads of most valleys, and the floors of these valleys are frequently boggy and choked by rushes unless they have been artificially drained. Except for a few months of the year, a lack of water is never a problem, but during the rains measures must be taken to protect crops from washouts and to drain fields that would soon become waterlogged. The ridge in turn, with its valleys and slopes, provides a selection of microenvironments that are exploited in different ways to yield the necessities of life. The Iraqw prefer to live along the shoulders of these ridges.

The 'ridge community', *gayemo,* as I shall call the group of people who live in proximity to one another on the ridge, is determined by topography.

The ridge community constitutes an ecological unit, although this is not formally recognized by the Iraqw. In general, homesites are distributed along the shoulder of the ridge that faces most nearly west. As we have noted, each house more or less dominates a margin of grass around it, the *mundi,* which is the special pasture of that domestic group. The rest of the slope of the ridge is devoted to communal pasture, *getu,* or to hillside fields cultivated during the rainy season. Some effort is devoted to these communal pastures, ideally, by all who use them in order to keep them in good condition. Today parts of the ridge slopes have been given over to woodlots since the wattle tree, eucalyptus, graphilea, and cypress trees were introduced to the region during the Colonial era.

The yellow wattle, in particular, has become naturalized and forms monospecific stands along the slopes of many ridges, and in the heads of the valleys. Although this has made firewood and building materials easily available to most residents of Irqwar Da'aw, it was originally greeted with great apprehension, and today considerably reduces the amount of land available for pasture.

These exogenous species have significantly changed the complexion of the landscape in the 40 years since they have been growing there. Indigenous species of trees and shrubs are either especially resistant to the intensive pressures of livestock, cutting, and fires (e.g., the spiny *erithrina abysinica* or the poisonous *euphorbia candelabra*) or they are ritually significant (e.g., *ficus thoningii, ficus sycamorus,* and other *ficus* spp. especially), but even so they are very limited in distribution within the settled area. Before the introduction of wattle trees, graphilea, cypresses, and eucalyptus species by the colonial government, the land must have been much more open and grass-covered than it is today.

Where there are no dense stands of trees, or where the pasture grasses have not been preserved actively by weeding out undesirable vegetation, the ridge slopes are covered with a more or less dense stand of bracken fern (*pteridium* sp.), numerous rough forbs (*hibiscus* spp., *solanum* spp., *labiatae* spp.), and dense tussock grasses (*imperata cylindrica* and others). With the exception of the ferns, and the indigenous trees already mentioned, all vegetation is induced as the result of human activity.

The ridge slopes, in some cases, are separated from the cultivated valley bottoms by channels that run the length of the ridge from the head of the valley to its mouth, which gives onto a large valley or depression. These ditches are dug and maintained to prevent rainwater from the slopes from washing down over the fields in the valley floor. In this capacity they are usually quite effective, although they have encouraged erosion where they disgorge into a river or stream. In many ways, it is worth noting, these channels resemble irrigation ditches since they frequently run from the locale of a spring in the head of the valley, along the valley wall, and into the streams at the end of their course. Were it not for the fact that when irrigation is needed, the springs are dry or too low, it might be thought that these were irrigation ditches instead of drains. I raise the point because this feature closely resembles the "irrigation channels" of the abandoned Engaruka site excavated by L. S. B. Leakey to the north of Irqwar Da'aw along the escarpment, which have been linked to the Iraqw by Leakey and others.

The lower slopes of the valley and the valley bottom are usually cultivated. Sorghum and finger millet are planted, primarily for beer, but maize is the principle food crop. Beans are interplanted in the same field with maize, and hills of pumpkins are planted sporadically about the fields. Sweet potatoes are planted in long running ridges either in the alluvial soils of the valley floor or on the gentler slopes of the valley wall. Today, pyrethrum is planted as an important cash crop, usually in dry fields on the steeper slopes of the valley.

Most houses in Irqwar Da'aw share the hillside on which they are built with several other families. They form a unit defined by the topography of the land, and may interact with each other to a greater degree than with more distant persons, but only as a matter of convenience. The community on a single ridge is not a politically or ritually corporate unit—they are not represented or served by any single ritual specialist or speaker as is the section or the *aya,* but they share work as a matter of practical convenience. But this is not always guaranteed. The inhabitants of the ridge are in direct competition for land and for water, and this fact necessarily creates a certain tension. People are ambivalent, therefore, about neighbors, so neighbors must do their best to get along. The *slufay,* a communal prayer and sermon, ordinarily exhorts such people to love one another, to love one's neighbor, and to cooperate (see Text 1).

In these lines from the *slufay* the speaker exhorts the people to get along with one another and to cooperate "like the hand and the mouth" or "the penis and the vulva" in securing a good life for all of them. It is significant that they are not exhorted, in terms of kinship, to cooperate

---

TEXT 1
Slufay: Cooperation among Neighbors

aten lo' ta wahharaan	truly we grow fat
kar lo' mundi wahhar	the home pastures expand
papahhay ti sla'i	neighbors are appreciated
aten lo' ta sla'aan	we who want one another
ti sla'a sla'aan	we who like one another
tlawu ne danda	[like the] cape and the back
dawa ne afa	the hand and the mouth
ya'e ne ya'ati	the foot and the sandal
ma'ay ne neqwa	the water and the razor
nu'a kar lo' ne nu'a	the penis and the vulva
lo' ta mayegutaan	truly we become strong
hee xororen a femakuun	the person who would harm our people
do'os lo' i qwari	may his house be lost

like brothers and sisters, for example. The models of social relationships put forward here depend for the rhetorical sense on the practical necessity that the members of these pairs be *close to* one another in order for them to work together: The cape must cover and be close to the back if it is to do any good; the hand must come to the mouth if one is to eat; the foot must be in the sandal, and so on. Although the pair penis and vulva (note that the same word, *nu'a,* is used for both terms) might be seen as a reference to marriage, and thus "kinship," in the context of the other pairs of terms, this interpretation seems unlikely. In any case it refers to the lowest common denominator of kinship, and would not be rhetorically relevant in a passage that concerns itself with cooperation on a level beyond the residential group defined by the house and its environs.

The group of neighbors, the *papahhay,* constitutes a spatially defined grouping of people that is similar to the topological definition of the neighborhood. It is this concept of "neighborhood" that defines the ridge community in the relative absence of other relations of kinship or economic cooperation.

The ridge and valley system that provides the immediate environment of the Iraqw household is evaluated in a particular way. The topographic feature has a front, *gene'î,* and a back, *intsi.* The front of the ridge is the sheltered, generally west- or south-facing slope, the back is the 'cold' (*tsaa, tsaqwa*) side exposed to the weather. These distinguished faces are valued as good or bad: the 'back-side', *intsi,* of the ridge is associated with evil and with witchcraft. It is sometimes called *intsi wakuse,* 'the side of evil persons', and in the *slufay* sermon, witches are admonished, "get thee behind our ride."

In fact, this distinction of "good" and "bad" sides of the ridge appears not to influence everyday practical activity. Both sides of the ridge are used for agriculture and pasture. The association of the "back" side

---

TEXT 2
Witchcraft and Space

hee do hee	there is a man among men
gus kikii	who returns among us
gus makuun	who prepares witchcraft against us
hhartos intsi	his stick "behind" the mountain
ka intsiri kwahhi	is thrown behind the mountain
ar wakuse	the place of evil persons
kar mamo'ô	and he herds his cattle there

of the hill with witchcraft is a spatial metaphor that exploits the relative
climatic differences of the different sides. A natural distinction of micro-
climates is appropriated to symbolize a social distinction fundamental to
the Iraqw view of their society: the distinction between good people,
'those who desire goodness', *muk ti hho wa slaa'*, and evil people.

This system of ridgetop settlement, ridge-slope pastures, and valley
cultivation characterizes the ecological setting of the Iraqw household.
This pattern is repeated for all households. Agriculture is carried out by
the domestic group and its products are consumed either directly by
them, or used in trade to obtain clothes, metal utensils, soap, salt, and
other necessities that they do not produce for themselves. Several households may exploit the same ridge-valley system, but they do not cooperate
as a group in any agricultural tasks, and allocation of land resources is
not decided nor are disputes mediated at this level. Since the household
produces and consumes or barters all agricultural produce by and for
itself, the relations of production at this level, in the sphere of agriculture,
do not define a group any larger than the residents of one house. We
must consider a larger unit to discover and analyze the relations that
define larger economic units and which of these units are defined by the
Iraqw themselves as significant social groupings.

The Section

In terms of a phenomenological topology, as one moves from the
interior of the house through the inhabited landscape and beyond into
the lands of other ethnic groups, two significant boundaries are encountered. The first is the boundary of the domestic space located at the
threshold of the house; the second is the boundary of the section, or *aya*.

The section is the smallest territorial unit that is bounded. This
contrasts with the ridge community, which is not formally defined by the
Iraqw, and the unit of space called the *papahhay*, which has no precisely
located boundary. On the other hand, the largest territorial unit, defined
as such by the Iraqw, is the *aya*. The boundaries of the *aya* and of the
section are known and marked, and the area so defined is named. The
very act of naming it, in fact, gives it a value in the cultural structuring
of space.

In saying that the section is the smallest bounded *territorial* unit, a
distinction of scale only is implied. In the cultural system of the Iraqw,
the domestic space of the residential group is as much a part of the order
as the *aya*. In important ways the household space and the surroundings
are analogous to the space defined by the borders of the *aya* and the

lands that surround it. This equation of the boundary of the house with the boundary of the *aya* is made explicit in Text 28 (Chapter 8) in which the speaker uses the word that ordinarily refers to the threshold of the house to refer instead to the border of the *aya*. This relationship can be expressed formally by the proportion:

house (*do'*) : its neighborhood (*papahhay*) :: the *aya* : the lands that surround it (*tumbo*)

We may draw this conclusion because the household and its residents are in many ways like the *aya* and its residents. The household residents create their own shelter, dig their own fields, maintain their home pastures; they create their space out of what would be "useless" bush. So, too, is the *aya* ritually created out of the bush, *slaa'*. The physical structure of the house is 'tied' (*tsegiin*) with tough 'lianas' (*hayri*); when the boundary ritual for the *aya* is performed, the borders of the *aya* are tied with the same types of lianas. Ritual sacrifice for the *aya* or for the household is conducted on the border of each. The close, immediate bonds of sexual reproduction and of commensality, while they do not generate social links between persons outside of the domestic group, are nevertheless used rhetorically in *aya*-level meetings as models for proper conduct.

This symbolic and sentimental equation between the household and the *aya* contradicts the distinction that Fortes has made between the domestic domain and the "politico-jural domain." While this distinction is almost certainly valid for most African societies that, like the Tallensi, have an encompassing ideology of kinship that relates large numbers of persons in terms of marriage, descent, and filiation in the 'politico-jural domain,' where these multiple links become the "rules" in the strategic contest for resources, it is not valid for the Iraqw. In this society the immediate relations of siblingship and marriage are manifested only in the household group, and are conceptually generalized in ritual at the level of the territorial unit—at which level people see themselves as being in some sense "like" the domestic group, or "like" the spider's web (see Text 4, Chapter 3)—but there is no intermediate and shared ideology of lineage membership, marriage, or filiation over the whole *aya*. In ritual, the *aya* and the domestic group are symbolically equated in order that the immediacy of the relationship of cohabitation and siblingship can be used in political rhetoric at the territorial level. Unlike the Tallensi, where descent, marriage, and filiation provide the ideology of association among people, for the Iraqw the *common residence* in the house or the *aya* provides the cultural rationale that unites small-scale residential groups into larger-scale territorial units.

The section emerges as a systematic whole in three ways: as a historical association of people and descendants, as a cooperative association of people, and as a ritually and politically corporate community. Its boundary defines the group of persons within it; or, to put it another way, they define themselves as a group through the use of relations of space rather than through the use of other means, such as kinship.

Again and again, the Iraqw have preferred ritual action to direct forms of action in the mediation or settlement of disputes. This fact has earned them the reputation among neighboring ethnic groups and colonial administrators alike as an unwarlike, passive people. While the Iraqw freely admit that they are not fighters, they feel that they are protected by the effectiveness of the rituals designed to maintain the borders against penetration by hostile outsiders.

The reliance on ritual action demonstrates the nature of the territorial unit in Iraqw thought: It is an explicit symbolic category, generated through ritual performance that is itself governed by the underlying structures of cultural logic. Of course, the territorial unit is also an economic, ecologic, and ethnic entity, objectively observable from others of its features, but for the Iraqw it is defined and maintained by means of symbolic operations in ritual. Their thought about land, and the metaphorical development of other concepts based on the relations of space, is a logical system of thought. The logic of that thought, furthermore, is topological.

The logic is *topological* (in two dimensions), that is, rather than *hierarchic,* as is Indian cultural logic (Dumont, 1970), or the logic of medieval European religious and political organization (Bloch, 1965), or rather than *algebraic,* as is the logic of Australian Aborigines' organization of marriage, or the economic/ritual organization of the Kula ring exchange in the Pacific. Values are expressed in "horizontal metaphors," that is, in the form "east is bad, west is good," rather than in "vertical metaphors," in the form "higher is better," or in "algebraic metaphors," in the form "the giver is superior to the receiver (of the gift, woman, pig, etc.)."

Although the section is a very real, demonstrable entity in the organization of space, there is no general word in Iraqw that describes the "section" as a general class of phenomena, although the word *aya* may at times serve this purpose. The section is a named area, and most sections have as part of their name the term *hhay.* The use of this lexeme in the formation of the word *papahhay,* 'neighbors', has already been noted. It is the most general class-designator in the Iraqw vocabulary and means roughly 'the group of—'. In referring to a particular section, *hhay* is in most cases prefixed to a proper name in forming the name of the particular section, as, for example, *Hhay Loto* or *Hhay Ga'angw*. Were it not for the fact that *hhay* is used in so many different contexts in Iraqw, we might say that it would be an adequate term to refer to the section in general. The use of this term implies that the section, in addition to being a symbolically defined area, is also conceived of as a group; in particular, as a group defined by a territorial unity.

As a group occupying and defined by a particular space, the section necessarily has a past and a historical process of development. I shall consider here the particular case of one section, *Hhay Ga'angw*. I am most familiar with this case since this is where I lived while in Irqwar Da'aw.

Hhay Ga'angw is part of an association of sections that make up the *aya Kwermusl* (see Figure 2.6). *Hhay Ga'angw* and the other eight sections, *Hhay Loto, Hhay Qongo, Hhay Waha, Hhay Ge'ay, Etlawe, Hhay Ombay, Hhay Ali,* and *Kwermusl o Da'aw,* have a history of cooperation in warfare with other sections and associations of sections.

Hhay Ga'angw is composed roughly of four ridge communities (see Figure 2.7). Two of these communities are dominated by agnatic groups which, for the time being, I shall call 'lineages', *tlahhay*. (Again the difficult term *hhay* appears, and we must wait to define this concept more clearly in Chapter 5 on "groups.")

Hhay Ga'angw was among the first to be settled by the people who were to become the Iraqw. The first lineage to establish itself in the area was *Hhay Bayo*. The members of this lineage descend from the eponymous ancester Bayo who was one of the followers of Haymu Tipe, who led the original Iraqw-speaking settlers in Irqwar Da'aw from their previous homeland in *Ma'angwatay*. It is said that Bayo came to *Hhay Ga'angw* to settle after water, which once covered the land, had been caused to rush over the escarpment by the magic of Haymu Tipe. The descendants of Bayo continued to live in *Hhay Ga'angw,* establishing themselves on one ridge and its neighborhood. Shortly thereafter, another person came to join them from someplace below the escarpment. This man, Amo, also came to live in *Hhay Ga'angw,* but on a different ridge. This was not the first place he settled. He and his family, it is said, first established themselves in a place farther south, in the neighboring *aya* called *Muray* which was already settled by the followers of the ritual chief Haymu Tipe, and the family of Amo eventually was forced to move. They moved to the edge of *Hhay Ga'angw* that was most exposed to attacks by the people of *Tsa'ayo,* a neighboring *aya* on that side (see Figure 2.6) which was hostile to the association of which *Hhay Ga'angw* was a part. The original homestead of Amo is today remembered and is marked by a prominent

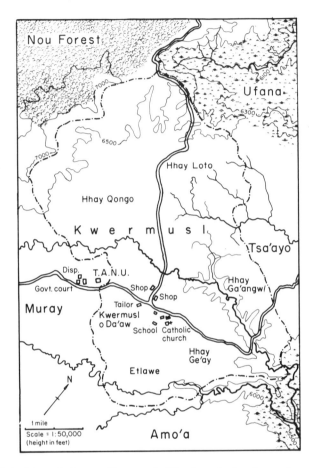

FIGURE 2.6. *Map of the* aya Kwermusl. *The boundaries shown here are not ad-ministratively recognized and differ from the surveyed boundaries of the 'ward' (*Swahili* kata*) *into which the area is also divided. As drawn, they are only approximations of the boundaries that are marked in the* masay *ritual.*

tree. This place is a well-known "meeting place" called *tlahho Amo,* 'the sacred place of Amo', where elders may convene their gatherings to discuss the ritual state of the land.

It appears that the borders and extent of *Hhay Ga'angw* were defined and located by the followers of Bayo who first occupied the land (see Figure 2.8). The person in charge of the ritual maintenance of these borders, the *kahamusmo niina,* or 'junior speaker,' is a member of that lineage today. The residents do not know where the name *Ga'angw* came from, except to say that perhaps it was the name of another man who came with Bayo, or that Bayo discovered that the place was already

FIGURE 2.7. Hhay Ga'angw *in* aya Kwermusl, *looking east toward the Rift Valley Escarpment. Almost all of the trees are Australian species, recently introduced, except for forests on the mountaintops at the edge of the escarpment.*

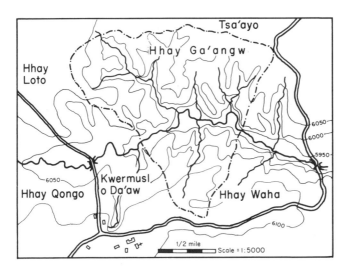

FIGURE 2.8. *Map of Hhay Ga'angw. The boundaries indicated here approximate the customary limits of agricultural and residual land claimed by the section Hhay Ga'angw. Like the* aya Kwermusl *(Figure 2.6), its boundaries are not administratively recognized by the national government.*

51

named when he came. By whom, no one would care to guess, and it is clear that the origins of the name are lost to time. It is known that Amo formed an alliance with Bavo and that Bavo granted him the land, a ridge, on which to settle with his family and followers.

At some time (the chronology is always uncertain), *Hhay Ga'angw* joined with the other section of the *Kwermusl* alliance in a conflict with the neighboring *aya* of *Tsa'ayo*. This story (Text 3) is told about that encounter and its results. As a result of this conflict and the defeat of *Tsa'ayo*, *Hhay Ga'angw* added a considerable piece of land to itself (see Figure 2.6).

This story introduces a feature that is a constant in all Iraqw stories of the past, especially stories of conflict. The defenders of *Tsa'ayo* did not make an attempt to defend their land once the medicine had been taken from them by the trick of the *Kwermusl* elders. So strong is the efficacy of the medicine held to be by both sides that defeat or victory is entirely ascribed to the influence of ritual action. Whether or not there was actually fighting at the time is a moot question and one that does not concern the Iraqw recounter of the past. The fact that the contest was won as a result of possession of the purloined medicine is a point agreed upon by all persons that I talked with about the matter. Naturally, elders have told me, there may well have been fighting because youths are hotheaded and not easily controlled, but this did not influence the outcome of the event once the medicine had been acquired and the sacrifice of the black sheep completed. We note, too, that the boundary was then re-marked by four points. Today this border is reconfirmed yearly during the *masay* ceremony.

The section, then, is a historical association of people who have settled the land and who have marked their claim to it by means of a number of ritual acts of blessing (*masay*) and sacrifice (as in the previous episode). It is also a political entity that seeks to maintain its power over the land thus defined and to expand its claim if possible.

Since conflict is mediated through ritual acts, or—and for our purposes, it amounts to the same thing—incidents of conflict that occurred in the past are remembered as having been mediated by ritual action, it is theoretically useless to distinguish ritual from politics. With this in mind, we can also characterize the section as a politically *or* ritually corporate group.

The corporation is distinguished by the presence of the "corporation sole" who represents it to the outside. In the case of the section, this representative is the *kahamusmo niina,* the 'junior speaker.'

The *kahamusmo niina* has a number of functions that mark his role

---

TEXT 3
The War between *Kwermusl* and *Tsa'ayo*

In this war *Tsa'ayo* was led by Meta Mado. And in that time the ritual expert of *Tsa-ayo* was Ama Surfi ["grandmother Surfi"]. The leaders of *Kwermusl* were Yayaa Hape and Meta Irafay and the ritual experts were Maaray Xombay and Guute. In each country the people customarily took medicine from their own ritual expert. The ritual specialist of *Tsa'ayo*, Ama Surfi, was known for her powers. Now, during this time there was a struggle over the borders between *Kwermusl* and *Tsa'ayo*, and during one of these struggles over land, *Kwermusl* obtained information from some of its youths who had gone to Ama Surfi's house in the night concerning a matter of their spirits [*fuqi*] as was their custom. When the youths had reached her place, they discovered that the elders of *Tsa'ayo* were there talking with the old woman inside. When they heard the voices, they concealed themselves outside and listened very carefully to all that was said. Then the old woman told the elders that on the day when *Kwermusl* came to attack them, they should come immediately to her to fetch medicine, and meanwhile to have ready a black sheep that was pregnant. After the old woman had finished, the elders of *Tsa'ayo* went home and the youths went to their homes. Before they even entered their own houses they told the elders of *Kwermusl* everything that they had heard. With this information, the elders and the youths of *Kwermusl* planned their attack, and decided that they would take the medicine from Ama Surfi before the men of *Tsa'ayo*. When they reached the old woman's place on that day, they deceived her into thinking that they were the elders of *Tsa'ayo* who had come to take the medicine. They cried, "Mother! *Kwermusl* is coming." When she heard this she gave the medicine very quickly and told them "take this axe and throw it on their land, and before doing this you are to slaughter the pregnant black sheep and pass through it." So they took the medicine and did everything they were told, and then they moved on *Tsa'ayo*. Now, when the people of *Tsa'ayo* saw the people of *Kwermusl* approaching, they ran to the old woman. The old woman cried, "Hoyee . . . run and save yourselves! The medicine has already been taken." So they began to run away and to leave their land. They were followed and the axe was thrown on *Mantla*, west of *Tsa'ayo* and they were told, "Come out of the woods!" That is why that spot is called *Tsa'ayo* Woods. *Kwermusl* was able to capture a mile and a half of land in *Tsa'ayo* to the north of *Kwermusl*. The location of the main border markers are *Ayati'ay*, *Awaye*, *Ayakala'e*, and *Hasa'awak*. The old woman was deceived because she was blind.

as representative of the section, both within the section and in relation to the other sections of the *aya* and the rest of the settled lands.

Within the section the *kahamusmo niina* presides as *primus inter pares* among the elders (*barise*) of the section when they meet to mediate disputes. The *kahamusmo niina* presents the facts of the case and guides the discussion, usually by reminding the council of the condition of the people and the lands at the time. The council of elders of the section ordinarily consists of all of the males of the section with grown sons of their own and who are themselves held to be good and honorable men. Other elders who may be visiting at the time also attend. Deliberations of particular cases begin after the *kahamusmo* has delivered a sort of "state of the nation" address in which he reminds those before him of the diseases among the people, the condition of the agriculture, and the state of the rains and soil. All of these things are held to be directly affected by the acts of man that may do violence to the ordinarily quiescent state of the spirits of the earth and the spirit of the sky. Each line of the *kahamusmo's* prologue is answered by one of the assembly with the word *e'it*, 'it is as you have stated it'. The *kahamusmo's* words are expected to guide the council in their undertakings. Having stated the case and provided the "state-of-the-nation address," the *kahamusmo niina* has no other role than to participate with the others in the discussion of the case.

A typical case the elders of the section might meet to discuss concerns a stick fight; for example, the case of a man of *Hhay Ga'angw* who had gone to *Tsa'ayo* to drink beer with some of his friends. He returned late in the evening after drinking all day in *Tsa'ayo* with money that he had earned working on a seed-farm estate in the Rift Valley. His friends had left him to go to another party, so he was alone when a group of youths from *Tsa'ayo* who had seen him drinking waylaid him on the path and relieved him of his money. He fought back and laid open the head of one of his assailants with his stick. Since blood had been spilled, the case was considered serious. The thieves were known to everyone because one of them had been wounded, but everyone also felt that the man who had been robbed had been foolish for flashing his money around so freely at the beer party. The incident had taken place just within the bounds of *Hhay Ga'angw* and therefore endangered that section because blood had been shed within it. Furthermore, the incident had occurred in the valley by the river *Nambis,* which flows through all of Irqwar Da'aw from the high forest of *Noow.* It is held that the spirits of the earth, the *netlangw,* are especially angered by the shedding of blood upon the soil. Furthermore, they are closely associated with water, especially where water comes from the ground in springs or where it cuts through the surface of the soil as in a stream bed. Therefore, the elders were concerned not simply for the condition of the water in *Hhay Ga'angw,* but also for the condition of the water in the river *Nambis.* The elders of *Tsa'ayo,* in addition, were demanding that some restitution be made to the injured man, even though it was known that he had been the assailant! After a number of days of meetings, the man who had been robbed but who had also injured his assailant was fined a sheep by the elders of *Hhay Ga'angw*. The fine was paid and the elders sacrificed it to the *netlangw* and divided the meat among themselves and the elders of *Tsa'ayo*. The thief was ordered to pay back what he had taken, but by then the money had disappeared. It was left up to the man from *Hhay Ga'angw* to collect on the debt as and when he could.

What was at issue in this case was primarily the ritual condition of the section, *Hhay Ga'angw*, which had been endangered by the shedding of blood. The theft was severely disapproved, verbally, but neither required nor motivated ritual action.

The aggrieved still had the option of taking his case to the government court, where witnesses would have been called and the case decided by a government judge. In this case the judge who would have presided was not Iraqw and the ritual aspect of the case would not have come to his attention. But the case was never taken to the government court.

I think this set of actions is understandable in terms of Iraqw thought about boundaries, and the importance of maintaining them. Here three boundaries coincided. The skin is the boundary of the person, and by breaking it, the man, who merely acted in self-defense, endangered the continuity of the boundary of the section near which the incident occurred. The boundary between the world of the *netlangw* and the world of man was also involved. The ritually uncertain status of rivers and springs derives, according to this analysis, from their penetration of the surface of the earth that marks the boundary between man's domain and the domain of the *netlangw*. Blood falling on the earth made a direct connection between the breach of the boundary of the person and the boundary between man and the *netlangw*. Since the incident occurred on the border between *Hhay Ga'angw* and *Tsa'ayo,* it occasioned alarm because this border remains politically uncertain, having been captured from *Tsa'ayo* by means of stolen magic. Thus, in considering the case, thievery was subordinated to the more important issue arising from the symbolic damage that had resulted from the wound. The wound and the loss of blood—an example of the loss of continuity of a boundary, and the spilling of that which belongs inside to the outside—was of concern because it endangered the continuity of two other boundaries by an association with them that was brought about by the proximity of the event to these boundaries.

The incident endangered the whole section as the result of the action of one member of the section on one part of it. This clearly demonstrates the corporate nature of the section with respect to its ritual condition, and with respect to its political relations with the neighboring *Tsa'ayo*. We note, too, the extent to which ritual and politics are indistinguishable among the Iraqw.

The section is corporate in another respect. The *kahamusmo* is responsible for the condition of the crops. Among other duties, he represents the residents of the section to the *qwaslare* (*qwaslarmo*, sing.), individuals who are believed to possess especially powerful medicine against crop disease and losses, and who control the rain. The *kahamusmo* "goes around and talks to the people about their problems and then presents their problems to the *qwaslarmo*, and asks for appropriate medicine" (Mayot Ara, *Kahamusmo niina* of *Kwermusl o Da'aw*).

The *kahamusmo*, then, if he is successful in obtaining medicine from the *qwaslarmo* returns to his section and applies the medicine or executes the prescribed actions on behalf of the whole section. Such medicine may be of two types. One type is applied to the borders: it is called *pa'asamo*, or 'protection', while the other type is applied specifically to the fields and is compounded for specific pests or diseases as the occasion requires. Although the *kahamusmo* may know some charms, and may compound some medicines more or less ad hoc, as the occasion presents itself, his medicines are generally held to be less effective than those of the *qwaslarmo*. Many times the *kahamusmo* will obtain only a specific ingredient from the *qwaslarmo* and then compound the medicine by himself; or he may obtain the details of a specific rite of sacrifice or the characteristics of the victim (whether black or red; monorchid or entire; pregnant or not; sheep, goat, or cow; male or female, etc.) from the *qwaslarmo* who will have learned these things through divination with stones (*tla'e*) or dreams. This type of medicine is called *xumpe awaakur*, or 'the whitening (curing) of disease'.

The office of *kahamusmo* is passed on from father to son. There is no rule of primogeniture or ultimogeniture in inheritance, either of land or of office. In the case of the *kahamusmo*, the father picks one of his sons according to his judgment of their aptitude for the job. Most of the *kahamuse* of the *Kwermusl* alliance remember their lineage of predecessors in the office back eight or so generations to the time of Haymu Tipe. I give the example of Mayot Ara, *kahamusmo niina* of the section from which the *aya* takes its name, *Kwermusl o Da'aw*, or "Kwermusl of the East." Mayot was unsure of whether the first *kahamusmo* of *Kwermusl o Da'aw* came with Haymu Tipe, or whether he came with others at a later time. His lineage, however, goes back eight generations to a man named Sanka, the eponymous founder of the lineage to which Mayot belongs (see Table 2.1).

Mayot is about 60 years old and has held the office since the death

TABLE 2.1
The Ancestors of Mayot Ara, kahamusmo.

Name	Number of generations before the present
Sanka	8
Lohay	7
Amsi	6
Gatlingw	5
Intsangw	4
Gatlingw	3
De'ewasl	2
Ara	1
Mayot	0 (the current *kahamusmo*)

of his father about 10 years ago. If we were to assign an average length of tenure to each of his predecessors of about 20 years, it would appear that Sanka first established himself in *Kwermusl o Da'aw* about 170 years ago. This would give us a date of about 1800 for the establishment of Iraqw control in the area, and this agrees with other evidence that we shall consider later.

Mayot also says that Sanka came with three other "families" named *Hhay Masay, Hhay Fara'ay,* and *Hhay Duway.* Other sources agree that these lineages arrived either with Haymu Tipe or at very nearly the same time. On the basis of this and other evidence that we shall discuss later, the date 1800 represents a good approximation for establishment of this and other sections of the *Kwermusl* alliance.

The sections of *Kwermusl* then have a historical identity. The specific date of arrival that our outsider's speculation might suggest may be generations off the mark, but it is, in any case, irrelevant to the question of identity. What is important is that a link with the past exists. They have a ritual and political unity marked by spatial continuity and by boundaries that surround and define them as a group. Before we move to consider the integration of the sections into the larger unit, the *aya* called *Kwermusl,* we must examine the economic integration of the section.

I have noted that the nature and organization of Iraqw agriculture does not foster economic integration or interdependence within the section. Each family is an independent unit of production and consumption. Those things that they do not grow must be purchased from outside. There is no basis, therefore, for trade in foodstuffs within the section. But no house is self-sufficient in animal husbandry. It is with respect to this economic activity, then, that the section is an integrated economic unit.

In the first place, since animal husbandry is carried on in a restricted area, the pastures must be maintained. Unlike the Masai and other transhumant pastoralists, the Iraqw family does not move with its cattle, but remains in one place. In response to this condition, the residents of the section cooperatively maintain the commons where the herds are grazed. Maintenance activities include burning off dry herbage in order to induce new growth, the active weeding out of unpalatable species of grass and forbs, and the regulation of the amount of land tilled for crops. Before new ground is broken, the individual who wishes to plant a new field must obtain permission from the elders. If they feel that it would significantly reduce the available pasture, the request would be refused. Most people abide closely by such a decision because every house has livestock. Also, communal throughways, *tlaqandi,* are maintained where cattle may cross arable tracts. These are grassy corridors between one pasture and another that are necessary to preserve access for all residents of the section to the common pasture.

Usually, each ridge community will herd its livestock together. Responsibility for the combined herd of the ridge community circulates from one person to another by mutual agreement. At dawn each household drives the cattle from their house out to a meeting place where all of the household herds are joined. They are taken to pasture by the young boys and by some of the men who have agreed to herd that day. In the evening they are all returned, the herds are divided, and the complement of each household returned to their respective places.

Just as the household is the largest economic unit of agriculture production, the section is the largest economic unit of animal husbandry. Whereas the economic relations appropriate to agriculture tend to fragment the community, animal husbandry tends to integrate the community, creating relations of cooperative labor and mutual need. Since the pasture is common and finite, all members of the section stand in exactly the same relation to it: They all invest labor in it and they all receive the benefits by way of their household herd.

This unity is fostered by the fact that livestock is essential to the well-being of the household's practice of agriculture. The animals provide much-needed and much-appreciated warmth for the family. They also provide manure. The Iraqw consider this their most important "natural resource." Again, because the lands of the section are finite, the soil does not retain its fertility for long. They do rotate crops and allow fields to fallow, but no one can afford to let a field fallow for very long. Manure is carefully husbanded and composted on piles near the door of every house. After it has matured, it is carried to the field and worked into the soil together with the stover of the last crop or the "green manure" consisting of the weeds and grasses on a fallow field. Millets, sorghums, and wheat are planted in fertilized fields. Maize is planted in the hills and is thinned and fertilized hill by hill when it is about 12 inches high. Because of this reliance on manure for fertilizer, the agricultural and pastoral sectors of the Iraqw productive economy are closely and organically related. Because of the organic relationship of animal husbandry and agriculture among the Iraqw, the husbanding of animals is carried out in a finite space, requiring in turn the maintenance of pastures. The extensive, ranging nature of animal husbandry, albeit limited to the commons of the section, unites the household units on a higher level of economic organization than would be the case for either agriculture or pastoralism alone. These facts further reinforce the corporate identity and the sense of unity of the residents of the section.

In summary, then, the section is defined historically as an association of people descended from original settlers, as a ritually and politically corporate unit represented by a "speaker" whose office is hereditary in the male line. It is objectively defined as an economic unit. This conflation of features clearly marks the section as a fundamental unit of analysis in Iraqw society, and, to reiterate, it is primarily defined in the minds of its residents in terms of notions of finite space, boundedness, and boundaries.

Chapter 3

The Aya: Territory as Image

The Aya: Boundary and Differentiation of Space

The Iraqw term *aya* is most difficult to gloss with a single English term. Fundamentally, it is a settled tract of land, defined by a boundary, *digmu,* that is drawn and maintained by means of ritual action. The *aya* consists of an alliance of sections whose members cooperate in the ritual that reasserts their common rights to the land, reaffirms its boundedness, and purifies it of dangerous "outside" influences. The existence of a continuous and closed boundary is its distinguishing feature. The term *aya,* however, implies more than this. It is the object of emotional attachment and of communal prayer and blessing. The *aya* is seen as the center of the social universe, surrounded on all sides by either friends or enemies.

Abstractly conceived, the *aya* is the topological equivalent of a closed curve defining a "simply connected" region. The circle is an example of a closed curve and the "disc" it defines is an example of a "simply connected" region.

The notion of a continuous closed boundary implies as well a notion of a continuous boundary region outside the *aya* and enclosing it entirely in a larger region. In other words, the boundary, by definition creates a closed and limited region *inside* and distinguishes it from an open and unlimited region *outside.* Such a region is distinguishable from the 'neighborhood', *papahhay,* which is an open but limited (by the constraint of proximity to the back and sides of the speaker's house) region. In the case of the *aya,* by defining it primarily as a closed and limited region, the notions of inside and outside, of limit and boundedness, then follow of necessity.

61

The existence of a boundary implies a notion of "boundedness." We may examine this concept in the Iraqw context through analysis of a few passages from the *slufay*, a genre of oral performance that communicates some of the premises of the logic of Iraqw culture. The boundary is defined in both thought and action. Actively, it is marked and remarked in the *masay* ceremony of *pa'asamo*, or 'protection'. In this rite the boundary of the *aya* is not only marked on the ground by circumambulation and by fixing a set of points (rocks and trees) that define the line, but it is also manipulated symbolically to effect a closure among the group of people whose homes are circumscribed by the boundary. I shall return to the details of this rite, but first we shall examine some of these concepts as they are manifested in oral performance.

The existence of a boundary does not necessarily imply, in formal terms, that the inside region it defines is continuous. We must introduce the notion that it is also simply connected; that is, it is not divided internally by any other boundaries or cuts. We may define this quality of the region by saying that any point within the region may be connected with every other point without intersecting a boundary. If this condition holds, then we may say that the region defined and limited by the boundary is simply connected. The continuity of the *aya* is also a property that is fundamental to the Iraqw concept.

The word *aya* refers somewhat ambiguously to an area of land, and it carries connotations of wholeness, continuity, and sacredness. When the word is used to apply to the group of sections that cooperates in the ritual protection of their boundary, it is assumed that the sectional boundaries which divide the *aya* into smaller areas in the *ordinary course of events* are all transcended when the larger unit becomes the object of ritual blessings.

The Continuity of Space

In examples of Iraqw *slufay* poetry (see Text 4), we may see how these concepts lie at the root of Iraqw thought about and portrayal of their space at the level of the *aya*.

These examples all express notions of boundary, boundedness, and continuity. It is clear that the property of boundedness, that is, of encirclement and restriction of movement, is essential not only as a means of defining the limits of the region, but also of protecting it from the influence of the outside which is dangerous and threatening.

Consider Example A in Text 4. Here the speaker relates his concept of the *aya* to the "region" of the spider with many young. We can trans-

TEXT 4
Slufay: The Continuity of the *Aya*

Example A

ayaren bar habambi	Our land is like the spiders'
ar daqay yarir	With many young all together
tis af'ura lot	We drive away pestilence
ar amor kum	With many charms
ama hhutlay kur yares	Many knots are tied
hikwaten ham na tlaye'	Now our cattle go forth from the house
siwa matlatle	During the morning time
getu hho ngur tlaye	May they go to good pastures on the hillside
ngur a dafiye'	May they return home
de'emay ngu huweye'	The herdsmen bring them home

Example B

aten ta sla'a sla'aan	We who love one another
Tlawu ne danda	The cape and the back
ya'e ne ya'ati	The foot and the sandal
ma'ay ne danu	Water and honey
tlomi ti yawiye	The mountains protect and encircle us
hayri qwaslare	The lianas of the ritual experts
kar ti yab	Which protect and encircle us
tlomi ti yawiye	The mountains protect and encircle us
itsafo qwaslare	The power of the ritual experts
kar ti oh	Holds us firmly

Example C

O aten hamti	O, now we are
tla'angw u i diriaan	We are in the middle
a gunuû lo'a	In the navel of God
slahhangw ti darfin	The moon comes to us
a kudo lo'a	That one of God
slahhangw ti darfin	The moon comes towards us
tlomi ti yawiye	The mountains protect and enclose us
hayri ir tsegi	The lianas which are tied
aten hayri ir tsegiin	We are tied by lianas
o Haru	From the mountain *Haru*
kar ti itiin	Which prevent us from going, others from entering
Anka ti itiin	The mountain *Anka* prevents passage
tlomi ti yawiye	The mountains protect us
o kar e'it	And that is how it is

late the first lines, *aten bar habambi ar daqay yarir,* as '[*aya*] ours like that of spider having a group-of-young many', or, more freely, as 'our land is like the spider's land with many young all together'. These lines communicate a sense of connectivity and continuity. First of all, in drawing the simile between the *aya* and the spider, the phrase suggests a multiplicity of connections between many points of the region, just as the spider's web is a complex set of paths and connections. The feeling conveyed is reinforced by the word *daqay* which means 'a group of youngsters who are associated for some specific reason or intent'. The word is more than a simple plural since it implies that the collection of girls (*dasi*) and boys (*garma*) that it denotes is greater than the sum of its parts. The children of a certain ridge, or of a section, or a group who are hoeing a field together may be addressed, together, as *daqay*. All of the children in school, for example, or all children in general, or in a crowd, would not be addressed in this way. The phrase in question conveys the notion of connectivity and continuity in two ways.

Lines 3 to 5 of Example A carry the spider's web simile further and indicate that this connectedness is the means by which pestilence is driven from the land. The "many knots" refers as well to the lianas, mentioned in the other two examples, that are tied across paths leading out of the *aya* to mark the boundary. The *hayri,* 'lianas', are any of a number of different trailing fibrous vines that are used to tie beams, posts, and wattles together in the building of the house. Lianas literally tie the house together. In this *slufay,* mention is made of the symbolic use of these same lianas to mark the boundary of the *aya* by tying them across all paths that cross the boundary. The *aya* is thus 'tied' (*tsegiin*) like the house. No one must cross these cordons, and it is believed that any outsider who tried would be tripped by them and prevented from entering. The last five lines express connectivity in a very prosaic way. The cattle go out to pasture and return to the house. The two verbs, *tlay-* and *dafi-,* denote inverse operations. *Tlay-* denotes a movement from a defined point outwards to an undefined but known point. *Dafi-* denotes a movement from an undefined but known point (for example, some place in the pasture) to the house, a definite and known point. These reciprocal motions—out to the pastures and the return home—connect the home with a set of points where cattle might possibly go. Since the cattle complete the motions within the *aya,* the notion of connectivity of the space is conveyed, or rather, may be seen to underlie the surface meaning of the utterance. The set of motions described by the verbs *tlay-* and *dafi-* test the condition for the simply connected region; namely, that any point within the region may be connected with any other point in the region by a path that does not intersect the boundary of the region.

In the second example the connectivity of the *aya* is expressed metaphorically by means of the pairs "cape and back," "foot and sandal," "honey and water." The first two pairs are examples of things that are intimately and closely associated. The third pair, honey and water, a mixture which in solution would be fermented to make honey beer, is an instance of two things so inextricably associated that they cannot be separated. The notions of connectivity implied in these examples expresses in a simile the continuity of the land. And, as we have noted in connection with the notion of neighborhood, such comparisons also express the mutual dependence of neighbors. In this example, the speaker elaborates on the protective property of boundaries, defined by mountains and lianas, and deriving their effectiveness from the power of the ritual experts.

In Example C, the "natural symbol" of the navel, a recurrent symbol of "centerness" in the literature of so many cultures, expresses a characteristic ethnocentrism that appears again and again in the Iraqw world view. This we would expect in view of the significance that concepts like "inside" and "boundary" have for the Iraqw thinker and for his culture. Again, we note the use of lianas and mountains as symbols of the bounded, closed nature of the *aya*.

The Moral Community of the Aya

Perhaps the English word *bailiwick* comes closest to translating the Iraqw term *aya* since it is represented as a corporate territorial unit by the *kahamusmo,* who, like the bailiff of the village in medieval English society, acts as representative to the outside and mediates disputes within the area. Having defined the Iraqw term at length, I shall continue to use it, untranslated, in the rest of the discussion.

The performance of the *slufay* defines the *aya* in another way, for the *aya* is also the object of communal prayer and ritual. In the prologue that always precedes the delivery of the cadenced verses that comprise the *slufay* itself, the speaker lists all the ills and anxieties that beset the inhabitants of the *aya*. The ailments of men, cattle, plants and grasses, and of the earth itself are listed. The spirit of the sky, *lo'a,* and the spirits of the earth, *netlangw,* are beseeched to permit the rain to fall or to drive the illnesses from the land.

The aim of the prologue, according to most of the Iraqw who have recited these for me, is to ensure the unity of the people assembled. The assent of the assembly, representing the different sections of the *aya,* is the condition that, if it is fulfilled, ensures the benevolence of whatever force happens to have caused the problem in the first place. The speaker frequently disclaims any direct knowledge of the agent of harm. He asks that the illness be healed and the harm be undone, "whether from the hand of God (*lo'a*) or from the hand of man."

The *aya,* then, is a moral community. Although it is objectively defined for its inhabitants by physical boundaries and by definite points such as mountains and trees that are known to all, the ultimate welfare of the spatial unit so described depends on the assent—and the unity of purpose that such assent implies—of the people who live on the land and who are addressed by the recitation of the *slufay.* The speaker emphasizes the responsibility of the group for the welfare of the land they inhabit. This feeling of collective responsibility is probably the single most important element of Iraqw morality. The case of the fight on the border between *Hhay Ga'angw* and *Tsa'ayo* is a good example of the moral force of this notion. The wrong perpetrated by the thieves from *Tsa'ayo* became less important to the inhabitants of both places than the responsibility for the land, endangered by the spilling of blood. Although the joint maintenance of pastures is ostensibly economic, it clearly shows evidence of a sense of moral responsibility for the land held in common, for if the conviction were not held that all residents were responsible for the commons, this preeminently economic activity could degenerate into an individualistic tilling of one's own garden. But statements such as the *slufay* prologues presented in Text 5 communicate to the members of the society a clear message of collective, moral responsibility for the land. On this moral unity depends the health of the land and of those who feed on it. The speaker in each case asserts that neither the earth nor the heavens can withhold goodness if the community declares its solidarity. Although the cause of evil is not known, if the people declare their accord, "even heaven must agree." Thus, the moral unity of the community is held to have an active force of its own. Simply by declaring their accord, the forces responsible for the illnesses and evils that exist lose their potency and are persuaded to relent.

Furthermore, the existence of some evil persons in the community may be overlooked in the face of common assent. In the performance of the *slufay* this assent is given by the group after every line in a chorus of *eee--,* 'we agree' and at a number of junctures in the delivery all will repeat a line in a sort of cheer (marked in Text 5 by "*All:*").

These utterances are performatives; that is, are in themselves the act they describe. Thus, a chorus of *i tsa'ur,* 'be it cooled', does not ask that the land be 'cooled'; the very utterance is the act by which this is accom-

TEXT 5
Excerpts from *Slufay* Prologues

Excerpt A

ham dinkwari aga iwitaan	Now we are gathered together
ana kaya	And I say
hami yami i tiqiya'	Now the earth is ill
fala i tiq	The ground is ill
mu i tiqi	People are ill
gewot ki ur	There is much disease
hikwa i tiqiya'	Cattle are ill
ala mu ham bira dinkwari iwitiya'	So if people are together now
ala muruhho gun firiiriin	They ask for good things
yamu kakaâ in firimaan	We beseech this earth
ne doori	And the heavens
iqo axamisiya'	They are hearing us now
asma ham slahhaamayar komaan	Because we have many troubles
gaka baraka'e gewot i der	There is much illness here
mu i tiq	People are ill
kikwa i tiqiya'	Cattle are ill
ala ya'âa	So agree
bara ya'ânde	If you all agree
kar muruwi un firimaan	Then we ask concerning these things
muruwi tlakw	Evil things
tiqitiri ala an firimaan	We pray about this pain
ar slaqw mu nawa hikwawo	In the bodies of people and of cattle
gimse bara ya'ânde ya	Now if you agree
gimse xa gewori bar ar lo'a laqa dakw hee xa i tsa'ur, ya'âmaree	Whether this illness is from God, or from the hand of man, be it cooled; Agree
(All:) i tsa'ur, i tsa'ur . . .	*(All:)* Be it cooled, be it cooled . . .
gim birinde kiî ya gam	As I return to say again
bara ya'ânde	If you all are of one accord
ala doori sleme iqo ya'ânaa'	Even heaven must agree
yamu sleme i ya'ânaa'	Even the earth agrees
asma daxta fala i tiq	Since even the ground is ill
fala i tiq	The ground is ill
mu hami tiq	People are ill
hikwa i tiqiya'	Cattle are ill
an kah ya	I say
bara ya'ânde ka'	If you all are of one accord
falti an tle'eesaan hami	This ground we must husband carefully
asma kunga bara ya'ânde bar kunga'	Because by your agreement it is as if you

slemero guri huw bire ya'âan	All were carrying a burden
ala dori iqo ya'âana ne yamuwo	Then heaven must agree, and the earth
gimse ya'âmaree falti i tsa'ur	Now all agree the ground be cooled
(All:) *i tsa'ur, i tsa'ur . . .*	*(All:)* It is cooled, it is cooled . . .

Excerpt B

ham yamu i tli'a'ina iga andi	Now the earth has gone sour, don't you see?
yamu i slahhahhair aluda	The earth is hurt
muru yarir ki ak ur hamaa'	Many things are overripe (i.e., we endure much)
masok diri burumburitaan lo'a a firimaan	It is good that we should gather together to beseech God
bar lo'a firimaaniya', xa! tiqitir ayaren	If we beseech *lo'a* (God) this illness in our land
xa bara gumuwose i kiî	Returns to whence it came
(All:) gumuwose kiî gan . . .	*(All:)* Return to whence it came! . . .
muk a burumburit intsi ta qo slufiis	People who are gathered together here on the cold (evil) side of the hill we who pray
lo'a ka firiin ne hhapu yamu ga qo axa axaas	God is beseeched and the soil listens also
ala bara ateka' aga burumburitaan diri ale	So we have gathered together here again
is aten ti tlakw	We are evil
aten ti hho'eka	We are not good
muru yarir de'emu ka ilak hhitirumaamiit	Many things are nearly ruined
kungane dir lo'are xwatsir ta anda kar in dero?	Do you think that you can see the staff of God that it exists?
kahh, kahh, iwa kahh, xwatsiros kar aan aleehheemis gam	Nothing, nothing, when there is nothing? the staff of God is to punish
kar ala aten firo a mawaanaka	And yet we do not leave off praying
xa ya ya'amare	Let us agree
bara ya'ande, dinkwari ale	In so agreeing, together again
aten tam ti tlakw	Although we are sinful
daqta karo heko ku hho, bar tsar	From time to time a certain one is good, sometimes two of us
aten tam tsiruwo, lo'a afoda ga ila ot gam	And although we are a hundred, our words are received by God
ar muki ila ûwan nar mukda	Those people (the evil ones) are obscured by the good people
xa ya' ya'amare hami mura ku yarir tam	So let us agree, now these many things—

TEXT 5 (continued)

muruqa ayma tinda hanis, sleme u gera i hhitrumiit	Although these things to eat are given to us by the earth again
a lo'a na nahis, sleme u gera i hhitrumiit	We receive it from *lo'a*, even if it is ruined
slee gera kile a tlawu danduwok oryok	The cow itself has leather on its back, right?
laqa lama?	Or wrong?
tawa tlawu danda bir hhitrumiit	How is it if that clothing of his is destroyed
lo'a sleme a firimaan, xay tiqitir hikwa	Even so we pray to *lo'a*, Ah, the illness of the cattle
ne muko xa kuûwos ngi watl kara	And of people, may it be flung to the wall
hama ga andi siwirihe aang	Now do you see, that time, long ago
tluway ko nina ugwa muka ala slawaan	The little bit of rain that we got
ham kwisliit i kahh	Now we find none
aga andi gar ta dahas sleme ham in kat	We have seen that that which has been planted even now is dry
kuru kwi o maga? o ko'an	This is how many years now? Five!
o gera balangw in dirku'ut bara hhapa	At first the grain rotted in the soil
ûwa wa ale, hikwa nay qo fakir, hikwa nay fakir	Eclipsed again, the cattle started to die, the cattle died
aludada daxta adori na kamamiit	Afterward it continued in the same way
xu'aanaka	We don't know
tam ar dakw hee	Whether from the hand of man
tar ar lo'a, a xu'aanaka	Or from *lo'a*, we don't know
ala aten a munesianaka	And so we despair
kar ma xu'aan har ako kilos una firimaan	And how are we to know? so we ask Father himself
ako lo'a ari un firimaan	Father *lo'a* we ask you
xa, oryok, tluway ado qa ngi koon	I say, may we have rain like this
oryok, xa, i tluwi	Hey! it rains!
(All:) i tluwi, oryok, i tluwi, i tluwi . . .	*(All:)* It rains! Hey! it rains, it rains . . .
gim daxta aang slufay ugwa hhe' eesaan	So at this time we have finished the prayer
muru tlakw ugwa hangesaan ari adorihe	Evil things we have cleared away by doing so.

(The cadenced chant then follows.)

plished. The chorus of *a ya'âan, a ya'âan* (which does not occur in Text 5 examples, but which is common), 'we agree' or 'we are of one accord', both states the fact and accomplishes it. The use of these words in the performative mode is predicated on the notion of the force of moral unity, for the words spoken in chorus are taken as signs of such unity, which, if it exists, lends its force to the utterance so that even heaven and earth must also be affected. The notion of the performative and the moral solidarity behind it are keys to the understanding of the curse (*lo'o*) and of exile in Iraqw culture. These facts will be given more attention in Chapter 6 on social process, as they go beyond the scope of this chapter.

The Meeting

A look at the nature of the situation in which a *slufay* is said also sheds light on the nature of the *aya*. The *slufay* is said at the meeting of people, *kwaslema* or *dogito*. The first term, *kwaslema,* denotes especially the meeting of the elders of the *aya* in order to discuss the state of the land and the execution of ritual, or when they meet to adjudicate disputes. *Kwaslema* is a meeting with a purpose, whereas dogito is simply a meeting of people after work or around the beer pot. In either case a *slufay* might be said, but it is always said as a prologue to the *kwaslema*. The *kwaslema* is the objective practice of moral solidarity. It is the forum in which the moral principles of the society are discussed and acted upon. Although the discussions appropriate to the *kwaslema* are always couched in terms of ritual states and ritual actions, it is the preeminent political body representative of the *aya*. The verb *kwasleemuut* (literally, 'to strike by the meeting') means 'to accuse' or 'to assign guilt or responsibility for an action or state of affairs'. If responsibility can be assigned to someone or something, then direct action can be taken by the group to rid themselves of the harm caused by this agent. If a witch is found and exiled, or if an event that has put the land in danger can be discovered and put to right, so much the better. If it happens that no cause can be discovered, the more indirect and diffuse action of the recitation of the *slufay* may be all that can be done, for, whatever the cause, they "do not leave off praying." Thus, the affixing of responsibility for harm with a thing, individual, or event is one of the fundamental functions of the meeting in the Iraqw view. The meeting represents the whole of the *aya*, or perhaps the whole of the section in some cases. It is composed, minimally, of the elders of each household, or their representatives, and, maximally, of the whole

TABLE 3.1
Words Derived from the Root Tla'

tla'afi	The interior of the house where cooking is done and where the family sleeps at night
tla'angw	The middle, in between
tlahhay	(*a*) The place of the community meeting; (*b*) a windbreak set up to give shelter to a group of people; (*c*) a family, the members of one house sitting in a group telling stories; (*d*) a "kindred," the group of persons descended from a common ancestor
tlahhi	(*a*) The area in a certain direction; e.g., *tlahhi baskwi*, 'the area to the south of here', distinguished from just "south of here"; (*b*) verb, stirring up trouble at a beer party, being quarrelsome with a group of people
tlahho	A sacred place; e.g., *tlahho* Amo, the grove of trees that marks the first settlement of the followers of Amo before they came to *Hhay Ga'angw*
tlatla'angw	Afternoon, midday

population. Usually the meeting is composed of numbers somewhere in between, but it is not limited only to the elders.

The meetings are convened in a few designated places in the *aya* called *tlahhay*. This word, like *aya,* is difficult to gloss in English, but is fundamental to an understanding of Iraqw society. In the context of the meeting, *tlahhay* means a 'meeting place' usually a cleared patch of ground under or near a large tree or grove of trees. It is almost always a sunny place with a good view of the countryside. But the word also means a 'windbreak of any sort that might be constructed to shelter a group of people', and 'a family sitting around telling stories to one another'. Finally, *tlahhay* means 'kindred' ,or 'a group of people descended from a common ancestor'. The reader will immediately note the morpheme *hhay* again, which we have already defined as the most general term meaning 'group'. We may discover, similarly, a root meaning for the morpheme *tla'* by considering a group of words that appear to be related to it (Table 3.1).

All of the words in Table 3.1 have in common a notion of "middle-ness," "focus," "period," or "vicinity" in either time or space. They are all multivocal and ambiguous. All of these words denote concepts that are defined around an imaginary point, or set of points or instances of time, but which have no defined boundaries. In terms of a topological representation they denote, like the *papahhay,* a limited but open region or set. Membership is defined relatively in comparison to an ideal point, thing, or instant. The extent is never finite but always open to include yet another point or element. This is true, for example, of the notions "interior of the house," "middle of the day," "middle" (space), "a sacred place," or "the area in a particular direction." This core meaning helps us to understand why *tlahhay* has such a range of meanings. The first two meanings given in Table 3.1 are closely related; the *tlahhay* is the spatial coordinate of the meeting, which we might further define as a group of people gathered for a purpose or with some intention. The second two meanings are also related to each other; the *tlahhay* here is a group of people defined by the fact that they meet together. The group of story-tellers-and-listeners and the bilateral kindred are defined relative to a common activity (story-telling) or descent from a common ancestor; that is, with respect to some conceptual center. Neither category is a closed group since another may always join the story group and young members of the group are constantly being born.

This in turn helps us to understand the constitution of the meeting. Similar to the core meaning of *tlahhay,* we have already noted that the meeting, *kwaslema,* is minimally a group of elders who represent the *aya* but which may include all persons in the *aya.* In other words, the meeting is defined at its lower limit as a "group which is the 'focus' of" the total community, but which has no upper limit within the universe defined by the boundaries of the *aya.* Again, like *papahhay* and *tlahhay,* the *kwaslema* is a limited but open set, in this case of persons who inhabit that particular *aya.* The *kwaslema* represents the *aya* and is the chief body undertaking collective action. In turn, the *slufay* is the chief oral performance of the meeting. It is both prayer and sermon. As a prayer, it makes the *aya* its object and asks *lo'a* (God) for relief from the ills that beset creation. As a sermon, it sets the mood of the meeting and states the parameters of action, the premises of their cultural logic which, they hold, must govern life. It exhorts the community to solidarity and conveys a sense of moral community among the inhabitants of the *aya.* The collectivity that the meeting represents may undertake ritual actions designed to protect and purify itself (e.g., the *masay* ceremony) and, on occasion, it may take action against individuals by accusing them. We have noted that this action of accusing or "affixing responsibility" is preeminently the function of the meeting. This action usually results in symbolic action directed against the house (*do'*) that, in this instance, represents the individual himself. Eventually, the accused is forced into exile.

Exile for the Iraqw is a moral act of the solidaristic community of the *aya,* but not of the section or *tlahhay,* neither of which is ritually constituted. That it is also clearly an economic act does not detract, for the Iraqw, from its force as a symbolic statement-in-action of the rightfulness of the categories as they are drawn.

As a final note, it is worth emphasizing that the spatial order of the *aya* is quite independent of an ideology of kinship. Four points serve to demonstrate this fact. First, it is notable that there are no references to kin-groups in the *slufay* literature; there are individuals and "social types" (e.g., people who wish ill) as well as age groups. There are no references to the dispersed *tlahhay*. Second, the ritual that defines the *aya* is not derived from the kinship order. It is not, for example, a generalization of a segmentary system that marks out on the ground a sort of mapping of a segmentary lineage. In fact the ritual of demarcation shows every evidence of being historically derived from the elements of a ritual that is observed in other ethnic groups across Tanzania, but which serves quite different functions among them (e.g., praying for rain). For the Iraqw case, this ritual practice, used for the demarcation of land, had been appropriated and revalued so that it might serve the political purpose of encompassing and defining a territory that is not marked in any other way. Third, the use of the similar ritual at both the household level and the territorial level indicates that the ritual itself is separable from either context and is applicable, therefore, wherever the idea "enclosure-means-safety" is appropriate. Fourth, the ritual itself is only by ritual experts to whom everyone else is a client. There is no kin ideology that links the performer with the people for whom it is performed. The people who carry out the rituals that justify and legitimate the use of land are significantly not called "father" (or some other term that would indicate political position in an idiom of kinship), but instead are referred to and addressed as "speaker."

The Contiguous Outside

So far we have seen that the *aya* is a closed, connected region.[1] We have now to consider what lies outside of the boundary of the *aya*. The boundary, and the region it defines, are conceptually separate. We

1. By the definitions of formal topology, a region is a collection of points. The *topgraphical* regions that interest us here are two-dimensional "areas" of physical space defined and evaluated in different ways. They also have different properties. A region is open if there is no boundary included in our definition of it; or closed if its boundary is a bicontinuous image of a circle and is included in the definition of the region. A region is connected if all the points within it can be connected by a path or line that does not intersect the boundary. These definitions appear to be implicit in the Iraqw conceptualization of their space. In fact the formal, mathematical definitions of these concepts are merely attempts to make rigorous statements about what is intuitively known by all humans (Bourbaki, 1966). See Lewin (1936) and Trognon *et al.* (1972:70) for uses of these concepts in discussions of the psychology of personality and the derivation of metaphors in literature.

have already seen how in a number of instances the boundary is not considered to be part of the region it defines (e.g., the sacrifice to the *gii* on the threshold). This is the case with respect to the household space, which does not include its boundary, the threshold. But where the inhabited area of the *aya* meets the uninhabited bush, we must say that the region (*aya*) includes its boundary. The wilderness is, from the Iraqw point of view, an open and unbounded region, distinguished from the settled area by means of borders defined and reinforced in the course of regular ritual observances. It appears that although this wilderness is, strictly speaking, continuous with the *aya,* it is conceptually entirely "outside" since the border separates the two regions but is included in only one of them. The boundary, *digmu,* is a cultural phenomenon belonging, as does the land, to those who create it out of nothing by the explicit act of definition in the *masay* ritual.

The boundary, as we have seen, is the "protection" of the *aya.* It protects it, in Iraqw view, from two sources of danger. First, the wilderness itself is a source of power. Frequently a seer or a man with political power is characterized as "a man who walks in the wilderness." This was said in particular of headmen and chiefs who were appointed to office during the Colonial period since they were required, as part of their duties, to travel outside of Iraqw lands. When they returned they were accorded special status, informally, for having "walked in the wilderness." The history of the Iraqw people shows, too, a special regard for "foreign" medicine. The functions of *qwaslarmo* were taken over at least three times since approximately 1800 by representatives of different ethnic groups.

The power and the danger of the outside is of course not unique to Iraqw culture, but it has a greater significance among the Iraqw and at least some of their neighbors than elsewhere. Mary Douglas (1966:114) cites V. Adam (1963), who worked among the Ihanzu, to the effect that powerful men among this group also were described as men who walked in the wilderness. The walk in the wilderness as a source of power is a recurrent theme in biblical literature as well. There may be, as Mary Douglas suggests, a correlation between such ideas and a strong collective sense of identity and boundary. The boundary and the wilderness would constitute in her terminology "natural symbols."

The second source of danger to the Iraqw is the Masai and Tatoga pastoralists, who, before the imposition of the Pax Britannica, terrorized the Iraqw by raiding them frequently. The Iraqw were powerless to resist them militarily, and were forced to adopt a different strategy in which ritual manipulation and forceful symbols of identification and solidarity played central roles.

The "outside," then, from the point of view of the resident of the *aya* consisted, in the first analysis, of two distinct types of outside: the uninhabited bush, *slaa'*, and the land inhabited by other, hostile peoples, *tumbo*.

Although the territorial boundary where it separates the Iraqw from other ethnic groups is in part an "ethnic boundary," as this term has recently been used, a glance at the literature reveals that the territorial boundaries in themselves are frequently considered to be mere concomitants of groups defined in other ways. For a large part of the ethnographic sample of the world, this does appear to be the case. But here we are concerned specifically with the organization and definition of space, as such, by a group for whom this is an integral part of their ritual and political praxis. Fredrik Barth's recent work, *Ethnic Groups and Boundaries* (1969), does not give much help on this matter: "The boundaries to which we must give attention," says Barth, "are of course social boundaries, though they may have territorial counterparts. . . . Ethnic groups are not merely or necessarily based on the occupation of exclusive territories [p. 15]." While this appears to be true in general, the Iraqw present a case in which territorial boundaries are of paramount, not concomitant, importance.

The Frontier

There is yet another outside region. This is the region created by the historical processes of expansion and exile that have probably been active since the beginning of the century. This region is the *sehha*, the Iraqw frontier, settled by those ejected from the establishment represented by the perduring arrangements of the *aya* and the powers that maintained them. We shall consider the properties of each of these outside spaces in turn: the wilderness or bush (*slaa'*), then the lands of foreigners (*tumbo*), and, finally, the frontier (*sehha*).

In the oral literature, and in conversations and stories, the chief symbol of the bush is the tall tree. Just as the microclimatic distinctions of the warm and cold side of the hill are exploited to make metaphorical statements about the division of people into "those who wish evil" and "those who wish good," the relatively barren aspect of the inhabited landscape is contrasted with the forests of tall trees that surround Irqwar Da'aw as the inside is contrasted with the powerful outside.

G. Calame-Griaule (1970) discusses the theme of the tree in other African literatures. Her discussion is a "typologie des symboles phenomenologiques." In the stories that she considers involving trees (mainly West African), the tree is frequently a symbol in initiation rites, but also in other transitions such as death, birth, succession to office or high status, and so on. As Victor Turner (1967) and others have shown, the tree may be a highly ambiguous and multivocalic symbol, occurring in different contexts with different meanings. Mme Calame-Griaule's partial listing of possible phenomenological sources of symbolisms includes meanings that are also possible in Iraqw contexts:

> through its form, the tree is first of all a link between the underworld into which it plunges its roots, and the sky. . . . By means of its shadow which gives shelter from the sun, and by its leaves . . . and trunk, the tree is a protector and a provider of good things, especially of food. The tree is a living being, maternal and feminine, yet from another point of view it is a phallic image. . . . The apparent ambiguity resolves itself in the characteristic and essential symbolism of the tree [Calame-Griaule, 1970].

Such ambiguity and range of meaning is encountered in Iraqw literature of all types. Here, however, we are only concerned with one limited set of meanings, and do not attempt a full discussion of the symbolism of the tree in Iraqw thought.

The story of Simboya, for example, deals with the fact and the problems of exile. In this story a youth is exiled for disturbing his father's traps. The father takes him to the bush and, by tricking him into climbing a ladder into the branches of a high tree to search for honey, abandons him there. The father removes the ladder, leaving him quite literally up a tree. In this episode the tree symbolizes the bush, reinforcing the message of the story: The removal of the ladder symbolizes his exile from society by depriving him of the means to reach the ground. But the tree is also a spatial metaphor of generational transition from boyhood to adulthood, and of spatial transition from *aya* to the lands of enemies. In sum, the symbolism of the tree is complex and condensed, with a set of meanings clustered around the notion of transition and change between statuses that are not encompassed within the symbolic topography of the landscape. The tree, like rivers that cut the surface of the earth, and springs that come from below the surface of the earth, introduces a third dimension into an otherwise two-dimensional conception of social space. On the ground, differences between ethnic groups, between good and bad, warm and cold, inside and outside, domestic and political, secure and dangerous, can all be referred to as places on the surface of the earth. Differences between generations, between the real world and the world of spirits, and perhaps between the familiar world of traditional life and the unfamiliar world introduced by the colonial administrators, cannot be encompassed by or referred to the conceptual topography. Trees, together with springs and rivers, by introducing an additional dimension, provide spatial metaphors by which such differences can be comprehended. But the differences and transitions that are symbolized in these "vertical metaphors" transcend those that are comprehended in topographical space. They have, therefore, a particular potency, danger, or orectic potential.

In the story, Simboya encounters a Barabaig warrior. He prepares himself for the encounter by cutting a tree and, according to some versions, eating the leaves. Empowered by the unpredictable energy attributed to the bush, the boy easily masters his opponent and steals *his* cattle (for a change!). The use of trees in this manner appears again and again in almost every instance in narrative episodes where an Iraqw meets in a hostile arena with a member of another ethnic group.

Yet, the Iraqw resisted the introduction of the tall, rapid-growing Australian species (eucalyptus, wattle, jacaranda, and others). It has only been in the last 40 years that trees have been an important feature of the settled landscape. An entry by the agricultural officer of Mbulu District, Michael H. F. Cooper, in the pages of the *Agricultural District Book* of 1956 begins to relate the story (see Text 6).

Upon closer examination it is of course quite obvious that there was a shortage of trees in the settled *aya* of Irqwar Da'aw. With the exception of a few sacred locations where the indigenous trees have been protected, virtually all of the trees are exogenous and could not have been there before the 1930s, as Chief Elias states (Text 6). But why did the Iraqw resist the planting of trees so strenuously? Other sources reveal that anyone who attempted to plant trees before Chief Elias' law were scorned by their neighbors and the trees were uprooted or cut in the night.

The wilderness (*slaa'*) is, by the implicit topological definition, a foreign region. That which belongs to one region may not belong to the other. The tree, the symbol of the wilderness, could not be allowed to intrude into the region of the *aya* if these boundaries were to be maintained. The nature of these fears and the thinking that underlies them is clearly shown in Text 7 collected in the *aya* of *Muray*.

The speaker in Text 7 was trying to put the best face on things for my benefit. Many of the Iraqw make no distinction between the colonial government and "Nyerere's government" which has been in power since independence. They fear to criticize either. But the apprehension with which the Iraqw greeted the introduction of trees is clear. The death by lightning of the woman who was in the forest is recalled in illustration of the dangers that the forested wilderness held in store for people who encroached on its domain.

The prophecy of Saigilo alluded to in the first line of Text 7 was also significant. Saigilo was a man of great power and influence who settled with his followers near the present town of Mbulu in the valley of

---

TEXT 6
Agricultural District Book: Trees

"In the 1930s the area of Kainam could be described as practically treeless. Legend has it that the area was originally thick forest similar to the existing *Nou* Forest which, in fact, is all that remains of what was a huge forest area.

"Chief Elias [the District Chief, or *Wawutmo* who assumed his office in 1943] explained that during these years while he was still subchief of the area, the building of a house was a formidable undertaking as each pole and stick had to be cut in the *Nou* Forest and carried to the house site, a distance that could be 12–15 miles. The collection of fuel for the household was the major occupation of the women. They had to walk either to the forest or to the foothills of *Qwam* to cut fuel. . . .

"As far as memory served him, Chief Elias believed that it was during the years 1935–36 that the *Serikali* [government], probably the *Bwana Miti* [forestry officer] pressed for the planting of trees.

"There was, strange to say, an intense opposition to the idea. 'What is the use of planting trees'? the people said. 'They are not food'. However, *Ga'usmo* Elias [subchief], as he was then, saw the advantage of the scheme and he, together with the Forest Department, using forced labor, planted up to 4 or 5 Native Authority plantations of wattle. The wood from these would be sold to the people wanting it. However, long before the trees reached any size really worth cutting, it was found that they were being stolen for fuel by local people. Elias, realizing the value of tree planting for fuel was now appreciated, made his own law that every single household had to plant its own plantation no matter how small, but something had to be planted. Wattle seed was supplied and the law enforced vigorously. Failure to plant was punished by a fine of 5 shillings which in those days was a heavy fine. It soon became obvious that the idea caught on and after a year or so there was no further need to force the people to plant. To look over the Kainam area [i.e., Irqwar Da'aw] today, one would never believe that there had once been a serious shortage of fuel and building materials."

Source: M. H. F. Cooper, agricultural officer, Mbulu district, March 2, 1956; Manuscript in Mbulu, Agricultural Office, Mbulu District (unpublished).

Hharka below the hills that isolate Irqwar Da'aw from the rest of the plateau, around 1890 or later. He made a number of prophecies about the future that have circulated among the Iraqw since that time. His prophecy in general predicted rule by foreigners and the decline of the political and cultural order that then existed. The people of Mbulu district believe that he predicted both the colonial rule and the rule by "a small black man from the west" (i.e., Nyerere, who is from a village on the shores of Lake Victoria in Musoma district). Saigilo himself died near Mbulu and his one

---

TEXT 7
Alqado: Trees

"The prophet Saigilo dreamed and said that 'the thing which I see is that people will not return to the forest. The trees will grow up to a great height. *Funtsar* [a type of forest tree] will be taken beside the house. Trees will grow up to a great height. No trees from the forest. Wood is easily obtained from near the house. The people said 'where will this wood come from? How will it show itself'? Now, the darkness is light [i.e., the meaning of the prophecy is apparent]. If you go to Mbulu these days you may cut wood from beside the road. Even here it is obtainable near our house. No man will return to the forest. Forsooth, these trees were given from the west by White people. Forsooth they came from the west. These trees we must plant them! If you do not you'll be fined. People were told to prepare holes and to put manure in them. If you do not you'll be fined up to 100 shillings! At first we just planted them. And our answer came. Forsooth, the government was going to pull us up! We did not realize it. Now all of the *aya* has woods. . . .

"In the past we go to the forest to bring pieces for sleeping platforms. Even today we go into the forest for some small pieces of roofing poles, firewood. . . . In past days the woman of our home went to collect firewood at noon and returned late in the evening. Sometimes rain and lightning caught her. The woman of our house was killed by rain [i.e., lightning] one day. Then that evening black women went to carry firewood [the meaning of this sentence is not clear]. They carried and carried and carried it. They returned home in the evening. Another day they continued. Even today firewood is in the forest. In our *aya* there is now firewood near the house. In the past if one wanted to brew beer one returned to the forest many times. Women remember how they assisted when the father of the house wanted to brew beer. They agreed to help one another."

Source: Godiye Naman, son of *qwaslarmo* Naman, of *aya Muray* in Irqwar Da'aw. Interview transcript.

---

son was captured and killed by the Germans in 1910. These events were linked with the appearance of trees that, he prophecied, would grow to great height near peoples' houses. Today, his prophecy is still recounted (see Text 8).

This prophecy and the turn of events against Saigilo that symbolized the loss of his power and the seizure of power by the Germans, is associated with the trees that were originally introduced by the Germans. Again, the tree is the symbolic mediator of change. Although the English tried to introduce a different type of tree to Irqwar Da'aw, its meaning was the same to them and was held to be a portend of certain change, probably for the worst.

What we have called the contiguous outside also includes the areas

---

TEXT 8
Alqado: **The Prophesy of Saigilo**

"First, from the country of the Iraqw will sprout a certain tree, which is called *Funtsar.* The day that tree is cut my house is lost. It will be lost because I have one male child. The day that I die the country will be fiercely cold; then a jackal will come to take me and he will eat me. When my son is engaged to be married, he will die before his marriage and that will be the end of my house.

"And so it all happened in the time which he had prophecized."

---

inhabited by other ethnic groups. The surroundings of the inhabited *aya* constitute a sphere of intensive and long-term interaction with other ethnic groups.

The lands of foreigners are called *tumbo* in Iraqw. There are four distinct glosses of the word that we can give in English: (*a*) the land or country of a foreign people; (*b*) an uncircumcised person; (*c*) a long conical and flexible basket used to strain the lees from beer (which resembles an uncircumcised penis); (*d*) the act of playing in the water of a river or stream. Although the fourth gloss (*d*) is apparently unrelated to the others, it is tempting to relate the first and second meanings. Accordingly, "foreigners" are considered to be uncircumcised, and therefore un-Iraqw; by extension, their land is as well. But this association was never suggested as a possibility by Iraqw informants, and they were skeptical when I presented the idea to a few of them.

The Iraqw think of the lands that surround them in two ways. First, as we have said, it is a source of power or danger. They are particularly concerned with the Masai to the north, the Mbugwe in the Rift Valley floor to the east, and the Barabaig to the southwest. Second, these lands are seen as potentially theirs if they are able to capture them. That part of the surrounding land that is potentially Iraqw is called *mumbi*. By expanding into surrounding lands and by successfully settling them, the danger that arises from the enemies, *homo,* is removed from the center of habitation, thereby providing not only more fields and pasture, but a safer homeland as well. No *slufay* performance is ever complete without some prayer that expansion continue, that surrounding lands be "pierced" and captured (Text 9).

Finally, the *sehha* is the third spatial category of the "outside." This is an area settled by exiles, or *émigrés,* from the inhabited and established areas. It appears that the *sehha* was, in its primary sense, a cursed area to which those who had been accused of witchcraft (*da'aluse*) or other social

---

TEXT 9
Slufay: **The Expansion of Territory**

Excerpt A *

kar hu alhheesaan	And we finish what we start
gwa qu hayohaan	It is now captured
o tumbor homo'i	The foreign lands of enemies
kar ka hayohaane	And it is captured
ar manda ka alaan	That of the Mbugwe is ruled over (by us)
walaydamo ku mutaan	The lake Walaydamo (in Mbugwe) is reached
heko hano îya	There is a certain man in the north
heda duwanqwdamo	That man is a Masai warrior
ku tsatay da'ât	With a nasty red knife
tsatay dir sol'oti	The knife is dropped
i bara nanu hu'i	It falls in the wild greens
amenar doren	The women of our house
ngu bara namu wa sles	Find it among the greens
kar gunsang amur sik	And use it to cut pumpkins
o e'it	And that's how it is

Excerpt B

îya kwi difitaan	The North is penetrated
mumbi ngi muuti	The surrounding lands are pierced
bar ar sakweli	Like ostriches (in the way we move across the land)
ar gwar'âya boô	With black spots
sakweli kum	One thousand Ostrich
ar kuma lele	Thousands of thousands

* *Source: Slufay* transcript; aya Kwermusl.

---

wrongs of a lesser nature (*irange*) went. Their sentence of exile, *tleemisu,* was pronounced by the words *sehha keer,* 'get thee to the frontier'. More recently, however, perhaps mainly since the turn of the century, there has developed a directed movement of emigration. Parties of *émigrés* were led into new territories by ritual specialists, who carried with them special medicines designed to protect the new territory from the raids of Masai and Barabaig warriors. They obtained their authority to conduct such rituals from the *qwaslarmo,* who specified the form that the protective ritual was to take in order to ensure its effectiveness. Once a group of Iraqw had settled in an area and broken the sod to plant a crop, the land was rendered useless to pastoralists since a fallow field does not grow palatable species of grass. The *sehha* of the Iraqw, with its limited pas-

FIGURE 3.1. *The edge of Irqwar Da'aw, looking toward the town. The bush and pasture (foreground) separate the* aya *of Irqwar Da'aw from the settled areas of the rest of the plateau.*

tures, soon became useless to pastoralists from whom the land had been taken. If they troubled the settlers at all, it was to steal cattle. Usually, however, they retreated away from the Iraqw *sehha* toward more open pastures (see Figure 3.1).

The *sehha* was demarcated and ritually protected in much the same way as the legitimate *aya*. The ritual was called *masso harwer amor homo*, or 'encirclement medicine in the place of enemies'. Although I have not seen this ceremony carried out, I am told it is the same as the *masay pa'asamo*, or 'protection medicine', carried out for the established *aya*, but with some small variation dictated by the dreams of the *qwaslarmo* or *kahamusmo* who carried them out. Eventually, it was possible to achieve legitimate status for the *sehha*, which became an *aya* with the same structure as every other *aya*. In the traditional view, the categories of bush, enemy lands, and frontier exhaust the region that surrounds the *aya*.

But recently, the Iraqw have had to cope with yet another category of the "outside"—the town. Towns such as Mbulu are entirely surrounded now by the inhabited "legitimate" *aya*. The towns are settled by people of a great many ethnic origins. The language spoken is Swahili, a language with which most Iraqw are neither comfortable nor familiar. The old men and women distrust and fear the town. Young people find it attractive, but since there is virtually no employment offered, there is no reason for large numbers of them to go there except for a day's shopping or to pass through on the way to monthly cattle auctions. The town figures not at all in the elders' conception of the world. To the young, it is a mere curiosity. Economically, the town is significant since it provides a market for some cash crops and a source of metal goods and cloth. Even so, the informal trade in cattle, tobacco, grain, iron, and salt, which relates not at all to the Tanzanian national economy represented by the traders and government officials in the town, consumes a much larger share of the Iraqw surplus production. The town, then, is a sort of "hole" in the Iraqw conceptualization of their land and surroundings.

The Masay *Ritual: Realization of Spatial Categories*

Introduction: "We Are a People in the Middle"

The Iraqw word *masay* refers to a ritual conducted on behalf of the inhabitants of the *aya* both to mark and to resanctify its boundaries, and to purify the land that these boundaries enclose.[1] In its performance we see demonstrated, in overt behavior and speech, a number of the central precepts of the Iraqw's own view of their social predicament.

They say the ritual is necessary simply because *"aten a muk tla'ângw"* —'we are a people in the middle'. This phrase means two things. First, it implies an ethnocentrism that places their own society in the central role as either the leader or the victim in events that they observe in the world around them. Most often, they see themselves as the victims, and this leads us to the second implication of the phrase, which, by paraphrasing it slightly, may be rendered as, "we are a people *caught* in the middle." They see themselves as a people beset with dangers on all sides—from the north, south, east, and west—and feel both enclosed and threatened by their situation. Bearing these meanings in mind, it is then easy to see why the phrase, "we are a people in the middle," constitutes an explanation of this ritual which establishes, in unequivocal terms, a boundary separating them from the threats from the outside and which explicitly encloses them in a sanctified and purified space.

To the outside observer, an understanding of the Iraqw understanding of the event (*verstehen,* in the sociological vocabulary of Max Weber)

1. The Iraqw word *masay* bears no relationship to the name of the ethnic group known as the Masai. The Iraqw call these people *duwangqe.*

85

is an adequate and complete sociological explanation. In the following pages I shall pursue this line of inquiry further, but the ritual may also be viewed "from the outside" as a means of communicating to the members of the society a common social ideology that opposes "potential victims" (themselves) to "potential aggressors" (e.g., the Masai, spirits, disease) as the "inside" to the "outside." This symbolic relation allows us to understand and develop the relations between the explicitly topological symbolism of the ritual itself and the political and cultural meanings expressed in the performance. Yet even so, we must go beyond the meanings expressed in the ritual to its use in a number of social situations in order to give a complete sociological picture of this ritual and its relationship to other aspects of Iraqw social action.

The performance of the *masay* ceremony is the central ritual observance of the Iraqw. The symbols they employ to express a particular view of life derive from their view of the nature of the cosmos. The order of their cosmos is a moral order since it results from their own evaluation of it and orientation with respect to it. For them, order is man-made. The *masay* ritual is one of the means by which this order may be created and maintained. By means of this ritual the *aya* is "created" out of the bush (*slaa'*), which remains outside it so long as the ritual renews the strength of the boundaries that created the inhabited, cultural landscape out of it, and which will engulf it if the work of maintaining it is not kept up. It is an act of creating the *aya* afresh out of the bush each time the ritual is performed that makes it a powerful means of "protection" for the Iraqw, and which gives it its force as a medium of communication.

Religion and Politics

Like the *slufay*, the *masay* is both a religious and a political statement. It is religious, if by *religious* we mean anything that addresses supernatural beings or refers to transcendent knowledge of the cosmos. Such is certainly the case here, for the two sacrifices, dedications, and other aspects of the performance do make reference to the *netlangw*, to *lo'a*, to the sky, *dorí*, and to the earth, *yamu*. The whole is motivated, too, by the sense that ritual utterances and acts can transcend the course of everyday events to create an order that is enduring and that overcomes the chaos inherent in the bush. But the performance of the *masay* ceremony is not religious in the same sense that a Catholic Mass or a Nuer sacrifice to *kwoth* is religious since its primary objective is not communication with the supernatural. Rather, it is directed to the condition of the land, a condition which, though partly resulting from the disposition of the *net-*

langw and *lo'a,* is not entirely due to supernatural causes. The ritual condition of the land is influenced most greatly by the acts of men and the events that involve men. These acts and the events endanger the condition of the land in all respects, interfering not only with the order imposed on it by the performance of the *masay* ritual itself, but also with the fertility, the germination of seeds, the predations of birds, and with the rain itself. The object of the ritual is the land itself.

Of course, land is the primary productive resource of the inhabitants of the *aya,* and the order and control of the land must therefore be political by its very nature. The *masay* ritual is therefore political. Ritual is politics and politics is ritual: These two spheres that are distinct in other societies are scarcely separable in Iraqw life. The performance is political in at least two arenas: within the community of the *aya* itself and within the larger arena of interaction that includes all other Iraqw and all other ethnic groups in the region.

First of all, since the ritual is conducted by the elders and by the *kahamuse* ('the speakers of the community') who are ultimately responsible in disputes over land rights, the ritual legitimates their offices by virtue of the fact that they "create the *aya*" in the first place. The ritual thus reaffirms the political status quo. But since it also draws up boundaries between the inhabitants of the *aya* and other groups, thereby laying claim to a portion of land, the ritual also has an important bearing on the political ecology of the whole region. Where the Iraqw have expanded onto lands formerly grazed, cultivated, or hunted by other peoples, they have used the *masay* rituals as the chief political instrument by which to gain control over land, and to legitimate their claim to it. Once the *masay* ceremony has been performed for a piece of land, "creating" it, as it were, out of the bush, the settlers who inhabit it cling to it in the face of repeated raids and adversity. The *masay* ceremony is in such cases their deed to the land.

The artificial cultural separation of one piece of land from an expanse of what is seen to be undifferentiated bush creates an important political tension. We have seen that the Iraqw ethnic identity entails, among other things, submission to the authority of the *kahamuse* and the elders in whom responsibility for the land is vested. Their power rests on this submission to authority by those who live in the *aya.* In most cases their authority does not rest on the use of violence or even the threat of their resort to violence.

It has frequently been stated that political power, and consequent submission to political power, must ultimately rest on the use or threat of violence. While this is ultimately true, what is unusual about the Iraqw case is that political violence—as opposed to random aggression at beer parties, for instance, which is not directed toward particular social ends —is not in evidence within the *aya* community. Wrongdoing and political transgressions are sanctioned first by resort to symbolic acts against the person or house of the offender. Fines may be levied, but these are paid voluntarily or not at all. Ultimately, wrong behavior is punished by the suspension of all social contact with the offender and eventually by exile into the bush. Once in the bush, beyond the borders of the *aya* where neighbors can warn of approaching danger, the offender is prey both to beasts and to men. It is frequently the case—or at least it is believed to be the case—that the offender is dealt his due by the Barabaig warrior, the Masai raider, or the rampaging buffalo. Thus, political violence is attributed to the outside, beyond the borders of the *aya*. We note that violence is never discussed in the *slufay* or in the *alqado*. On the other hand, consent and attestations of agreement and submission to the social order are very frequently mentioned in Iraqw discourse. It is interesting to note that violence occurs in animal stories, but not in stories in which the characters are human. The two sides of the political coin, violence and submission to violence, are thus separated in the Iraqw view by the *masay* ceremony. This ritual is a key feature in the political ecology of the region.

The Conduct of the Rite

The *masay* ceremony is held, more or less, once a year. It may be conducted more frequently if drought or illness of unusual degree seems to demand it. The rituals are organized and carried out by the *kahamuse* of the various sections that compose the *aya* together with the elders of the *aya*. They choose a number of youths (*masomba*) to serve in the conduct of the ritual.

The *masay* ceremony that I observed took 3 days to complete. It was conducted in three different locations and involved two separate meaning complexes. The first day of the ceremony took place directly on the boundary of the *aya,* and it was concerned primarily with the boundary (*digmu*). The ceremony of the second day was conducted at a place near the center of the *aya* and involved the purification of the land that had been demarcated on the previous day. The third day of the performance consisted not of the performance of ritual acts, but of a meeting and performance of a number of *slufay* in which the events of the previous days' ceremonies were discussed. The *slufay* frequently deals with other rituals and other performances, reanalyzing them and examining in retrospect their conduct and results (see Chapter 6). On this day then, the focus was on neither boundary nor land themselves, but on the ritual—the verbal and social forms by which boundary and land were marked.

The ceremony described was conducted for the *aya Kwermusl* where I lived while conducting this research. This *aya* includes seven sections (*hhay*) named *Hhay Loto, Hhay Qongo, Hhay Ga'angw, Hhay Waha, Hhay Geay, Etlawe,* and *Kwermusl Da'aw*. There are five other corporate *aya* in Irqwar Da'aw called *Hare'abi, Kaynam, Kuta, Amo'a,* and *Muray*.

When I arrived at the site of the first day's activities, the early preparation for the ritual had already begun. I arrived with a group of elders and *kahamuse* from the section in which I lived and others adjacent to it. Others continued to arrive throughout the morning. While the elders and *kahamuse* were slowly arriving, a number of youths had begun to collect firewood for the fire that was soon to be lit. They had cleared a small meeting area near the top of a hill that overlooked the plateau to the west. This spot was located on the boundary of the *aya Kwermusl* and the *aya Imboru* (Mbulu) which neighbored it on the west. Within limits the location of the site was apparently not important so long as it was on the western edge of the *aya* and on the boundary (see Figure 4.1).

On the previous day two youths had been selected to drive the sacrificial victim entirely around the *aya*. They had started from near the site of the ceremony that was now being cleared and had driven a young, black, monorchid ram around the borders of the *aya*. They slept on the way and arrived at the site early in the morning on the day of the sacrifice. The identity of the sacrifice had been "seen" in a prophetic dream by one of the *kahamuse* (I was not able to discover which one) who thereby determined that it be a young ram, that it be entirely black and that it be monorchid. It is said that other types of animals were possible, if that is what the dream revealed, and that the particular features of this one were not determined by tradition.

When the sacrificial animal arrived at the site it was killed. Several young men wrestled the ram to the ground, then sat on it while the young man who had been chosen to conduct the sacrifice grasped the animal tightly around its nose and mouth in order to suffocate it. This was done quietly and without verbal prayers or dedications while others went about other activities.

While the ram was being sacrificed, a number of elders began to light a fire using the traditional friction drill. A lower piece (*dahangw;* lit., 'to plant') was held against the ground in the midst of dry grass, while a stick (*bu'i*) was twirled between the palms of the hands to generate friction. But, as it was a cold, wet day, the fire would not light. Finally, in frustration the fire was lit using a flint lighter. I was told, however, that the fire ought by custom (*getlangw*) to have been lit with rubbing sticks. The fact that it was lit with a manufactured lighter seemed to cause no concern. Meanwhile, other youths who had been gathering firewood from around the site began to bring the wood and to place it on the

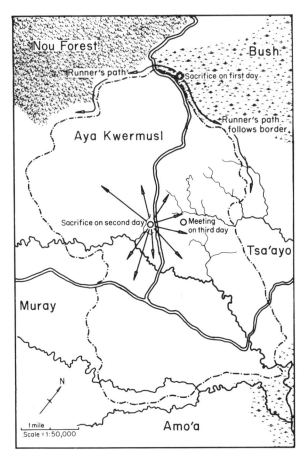

FIGURE 4.1. *Map of the* aya Kwermusl *showing the sites at which the* masay *ceremony was conducted. The opposition of periphery and center that distinguishes the performance on the first day from those of the second and third days is evident.*

small fire that had been lit. The rubbing sticks were allowed to be burned in the fire. More and more wood was added until a roaring bonfire was built. It was left to burn down to a bed of coals.

While the fire burned and while the sacrifice lay on the ground, a meeting was convened at the crest of the hill on its western face. The chief topic of discussion was the absence of a number of elders and one *kahamusmo* (Tarmo from *Hhay Ga'angw,* who had gone to visit his son some 96 km [60 miles] to the north in Mbulumbulu, one of the areas recently settled by the Iraqw). It was decided that these people should be fined one goat apiece. Then two youths were chosen to play an important part in the ceremonies later on. With that, the participants adjourned the meeting to begin the cutting up of the sacrifice. The actual cutting was done by the young man from the section *Kwermusl o Da'aw* who had suffocated the ram. He was assisted by a boy from the section *Hhay Loto.* The proceedings were observed by the chief *kahamusmo* by the name of Siqe, also from *Hhay Loto,* and by other *kahamuse,* although they did not actually take part in the killing or cutting of the sacrifice. All this was delegated to the youths chosen by the consensus of the meeting.

The animal was laid with its head to the east, and with its feet pointing northward, so that the left side of the animal was exposed. The youth who had been chosen to cut up the sacrifice then began his work. He made small incisions around the hoof of each leg. Then, beginning at the throat, he cut a strip of skin off the ventral portion of the animal. This strip included the scrotum; the entire ventral strip was discarded in the bush.

Starting with the left side of the animal, nine strips of skin were cut off and laid on the south side of the carcass. The strips, called *Hhamangw gurta,* were cut off on a diagonal running from the ear across the shoulder and progressing toward the flank and rump. When nine strips had been cut and laid on the side in a pile, half of the carcass had been flayed out from backbone to the ventral mid-line. The carcass was turned over and nine strips were cut from the right side in the same fashion. These were placed in a pile on the north side of the carcass.

Two youths who had been chosen earlier were then called forward. They squatted on each side of the carcass. With the tip of the knife each strip was pierced at one end and the strips were pushed onto the middle finger of the left hand of each youth (see Figure 4.2). Each one received nine strips of skin cut from the side of the ram where they sat; that is, the one who had strips from the left side of the carcass sat to the south of it and the one who had strips cut from the right side of the carcass sat to the north side.

At this juncture, two more youths brought forward several handfuls of broad leaves from a nearby shrub (*crassocephalus* sp.) and laid them out to cover the ground near the stomach of the carcass. The abdominal wall was then slit open and the stomach pierced so the stomach chyme, *sanká,* could be removed. The chyme was divided into two portions and each of the portions was put into "leaf cups" that had been made from the broad leaves of the shrub. The two young men came forward and took the leaf cups containing the chyme from the sacrifice. Each of these youths joined one of the youths who held the strips of skin. Each pair of youths, one carrying nine strips of skin, the other carrying a leaf cup full of chyme, were then taken aside by a small group of elders and *kahamuse*

FIGURE 4.2. *Piercing skin strips,* hhamangw gurta, *to push onto the runners' fingers. The strips cut for the runner on the right lie to one side of the suffocated and flayed ram.*

and advised on the path that they were to follow around the *aya*. They were told to run with the strips of skin and the portion of chyme around the border of the *aya* as quickly as possible (see Figure 4.3). They were told that they had been chosen for their energy and speed. Each pair was sent off running in opposite directions along the *aya* boundary. At nine points along half of the perimeter assigned to each pair of runners, they stopped, placed a strip of skin in the branches of a tree and threw a small portion of chyme at the base of the tree, then ran on to the next designated point and did the same. The two pairs of runners met halfway around the perimeter on the east side of the *aya* later on that afternoon, each pair having placed skin strips and chyme at nine stations along half of the perimeter of the *aya*.

   After the runners had been sent on their way, the remaining participants gathered around the carcass of the sacrifice. The ram was cut up into pieces and laid out on the bed of leaves. The flaying of the carcass and stomach incision had produced almost no blood, but now the blood ran freely into the ground. Every portion of the ram was cut up and only the hooves, the tail, and the ventral strip of skin with the genitals attached

FIGURE 4.3. *Runners prepare to carry the medicine around the border of the* aya. *The* kahamuse *from all sections of the* aya *oversee the activities and consult with the runners.*

were discarded. All of the elders and *kahamuse* came forward and chose pieces of the animal to roast in the coals of the fire. The meat was only barely warmed when they began to eat. All of the internal organs as well as the head and brains were quickly consumed by the elder participants of the ceremony. The two youths who had participated in the cutting of the sacrifice also ate, but all the rest of the youths who had come to watch sat together at a distance talking among themselves. When the sacrifice had been entirely consumed by the elders, they again repaired to the face of the hill to discuss the conduct of the ritual and other events in the *aya*.

From this time until the close of the second day's ceremonies, it was declared that no one must cross the border of the *aya* either to leave or to enter it. This restriction was, in fact, carefully observed by all of the inhabitants of the *aya* including the small group of Christians. It was admitted that nothing could be done to restrict the entry of persons since they could not know that the ceremony had been performed. Furthermore, such observances are strongly disapproved by the Swahili-speaking government officials, who call such observances 'foolishness' (*upuzi* in Swahili) or worse in newspapers, speeches, and school lessons. Formerly, the paths across the boundaries would have been "closed" by tying lianas across them as a sign that no one should enter or depart from the *aya*, but this practice is not seen today. In one instance during colonial times, a trench was dug across the Land Rover track that crossed the border so that government vehicles could not enter. This was inevitably seen as a show of resistance to the government. The trench was immediately refilled, but its trace on the ground is still visible today.

After the meeting in which the absence of several important elders was again decried, the participants drifted away to return home leaving the fire to burn itself out, and the remains of the sacrifice to be eaten by hyenas that night.

The ritual observances of the first day are called *pa'asamo*, 'protection'. They are said to protect the *aya* from all evil things, but most especially from lightning, *kwara'a*, which comes from the heavens, *dorí*, or from the clouds, *tlangú*, which are sent by *lo'a*, the spirit associated with the sky and rain. The ritual of the second day is concerned with driving the evil associated with the earth-dwelling *netlangw* spirits out of the *aya* and flinging it over the border and into the bush (or the next *aya*). The second day is called *xumpe awakur*, 'the whitening of pestilence'.

The ceremonies of the second day begin with a meeting conducted by the elders and *kahamuse*. Again, a number of people were missing or were late in arriving, and this prompted discussion about the state of the world today. There were also not enough young men to carry out the ritual as it should have been done. Eighteen youths were needed, and there were not half that many present. Instead, nine persons were eventually chosen, including one elder who agreed to play the part of one of the youths for the purposes of the ritual. Although most Iraqw will passively observe the restrictions associated with the ritual, few are willing to actively participate in the face of strong government opposition. This matter was discussed by the meeting, but they concluded that nothing could be done except to roundly condemn the apathy of today's youth.

With the meeting over, people dispersed into the surrounding areas to gather firewood while a small group of men set to making a fire with rubbing sticks as they had done on the previous day. This day the sun was shining and they were able to start the fire in the "traditional way" very quickly. Again, they left the fire sticks to burn in the fire. Now the sacrificial victim was brought forward. This time it was a brown goat with two testicles. Its mouth was forced open and a small portion of white, chalky earth that had previously been dug from a secret place within the *aya* and mixed with certain herbs was then forced into the goat's mouth until he was forced to swallow some of it. The goat was then led to a spot near the fire, thrown to the ground and held there by several men while a short dedication prayer was said (Text 10).

A number of men then sat on the goat while its mouth and nose were pinched closed to suffocate it. The same men who had conducted the sacrifice the previous day performed the sacrifice and also did the cutting. Even at the point of sacrifice of the animal there was no hint of solemnity. At all times during the course of the ritual groups of people conversed casually, and only a small number of people showed a mild interest in the sacrifice itself. In fact, when the man performing the sacrifice saw that my tape recorder had malfunctioned during the dedication prayer, he offered to say it again, waiting until the machine was running and taking care to speak clearly into the microphone.

As soon as the animal was dead, it was oriented as the sacrifice on the previous day had been oriented. Instead of carefully cutting strips from the carcass one by one, this time the whole carcass was flayed in two halves. The left half was placed to the south of the carcass and the right was placed on the north.

The body of the carcass was still entire, and almost no blood had been shed in the flaying operation. The stomach was then carefully slit open and the chyme was carefully drawn out from inside. This was placed in nine leaf cups made from the broad leaves of a nearby shrub (*ricinis*). The packet of ritually prepared white earth that had been fed previously to the goat was brought forward and the remainder was divided into nine portions that were thrust into the center of each small parcel of chyme that lay beside the sacrifice.

The nine people who had been chosen at the meeting then approached and each was given a packet of chyme. Nine strips were cut

---

TEXT 10
"Xumpe Awaakur": Dedication of the Sacrifice

xumpe awaakur	Disease be white [i.e., be made pure, be cured]
gwa slaqwa muko	In the bodies of these people
ne laqloro ne hikwawo	And the children and the cattle
xumpe awaakur	Disease be white
ki awaakur, ki awaakur, awaakur, awaakur . . .	It is whitened, it is whitened, whitened, whitened . . .
gawa hikwa slemero	Among all the cattle
ne bara xoror ayarene	And in the people of our *aya*
xumpe awaakur	Disease be made white

from each half of the hide more or less at random, and these were left in two piles on either side of the carcass. Nine strips were chosen from the two piles (four from one, five from the other) and these were pierced and pushed onto the middle fingers of each of the nine men. (Ordinarily, there should have been 18 men.) These men removed their capes and tied them round their waists in order to begin running.

Starting at the site of the sacrifice, the nine men began to run outward toward the boundary that had been demarcated the day before. They ran in nine different directions, ideally reaching every inhabited house in the _aya_. At each house they stopped to drive out the spirits, sweeping them toward the perimeter as they went. Upon reaching a house, the runner stopped by the door, swung the strip about his head while saying, _"netlangw wa gweer"_ (Text 11). He then threw a small pinch of chyme inside the house and ran on to the next house where he repeated the formula. Every house in the _aya_ was treated in this way, beginning at the center near the site of the sacrifice and working out toward the periphery. When the border was reached, the strip of skin and any remaining chyme were thrown over the border. The evil spirits that they had swept before them as they ran from house to house were thereby flung out of the _aya_ with the skin and chyme.

I did not witness the blessing of the house, but my wife, who remained in our hut that afternoon, reports that she was quite startled when a young man suddenly ran up to the doorway, swinging a strip of rawhide over his head and muttering, and then disappearing just as suddenly as he had come. All buildings in the _aya_ were treated this way, including the Catholic church, the rectory, other parish buildings, the post office, and the few shops that lay within the borders.

While the runners visited each building in turn, the elders who remained at the site of the sacrifice cut up the animal, roasted it, and quickly consumed it among themselves. Finally, after a short meeting in which it was agreed that everything had gone smoothly, the party broke up and everyone went home.

On the third day, the elders and _kahamuse_ held a meeting under a

---

TEXT 11
"Netlangw Wa Gweer . . ."

netlangw wa gweer	Evil spirits of the earth be gone [lit., 'be open']
netlangw wa gweer	Evil spirits be gone
netlangw wa gweer . . .	Evil spirits be gone . . .

large fig tree (*ficus thoningii,* called *tiita* in Iraqw and are ritually significant wherever they occur). A number of *slufay* were recited by several
elders. The value of consent to the order to the land, the responsibility for
maintaining its fertility, the state of the soil and of the rains, and the
possibility of Masai raids—some Masai youths suspected of being scouts
had been seen recently—were all discussed. Most of all the formulas of
agreement and consent were in evidence. On this day, too, the two youths
who had done the sacrifice and cutting of the skin and meat were placed
in confinement for 2 weeks. They were in a state of pollution or ritual
danger, *metar tsere* (lit., 'blood residue'), because they had spilled the
blood of the sacrifice—quite unavoidably—onto the ground. They remained inside their houses for the 2-week period. It was decided that
the borders of the *aya* were now open again. With that, the ceremony was
at an end.

The Cultural Creation of Space

The ceremony is concerned with the two primary organizational foci
of Iraqw society: the *aya* and the household. In fact, what amounts to a
small-scale replication of the same ritual is conducted for the household
group. This would be performed in cases of severe or chronic sickness
among members of the household. In this case, the sacrificial animal is
identified in a prophetic dream by the elder male of the household. The
animal is led around the house while the phrase *"gewer i paâ' "* ('it is a
shield against plague') is repeated. The animal is killed by suffocation
inside the house beside the central post. The belly is slit so that the chyme
may be obtained without spilling the blood on the floor. A thin strip of
skin is cut from the hide—apparently it does not matter from where.
This strip of skin is whirled about the head and portions of the chyme
are thrown in all directions toward the walls from beside the center post.
Then the skin and the chyme are pitched out the door. The animal is
roasted and eaten by the domestic group.

If an animal is not available, or if the seriousness of the situation
does not warrant an animal sacrifice, the same ritual may be carried out
using a common wild cucumber, which has a tough, yellow, leathery skin
and a blood-red interior. This fruit is broken open at the center of the
house, turned inside out, and thrown out of the house with the words
"netlangw wa gweer" ('evil spirits be gone').

The rituals performed for the household and for the *aya* are near
equivalents. They may both be called *masay,* 'medicine', or *pa'asamo,* 'protection', and the symbolism involved in both is the same. The house and

the *aya* are implicitly equated, too, when the norms of peace and solidarity that pertain most particularly to the domestic group are held up as examples of the way neighbors and common residents of the *aya* should behave toward one another. The household space and the space of the *aya* are, in this instance, conceptualized as images of each other.

There is, however, a very important difference that this symbolic equation obfuscates: The residents of the *aya* are not integrated as an economic unit. Quite to the contrary; the residents of the *aya* are in competition with one another for land and pasture. On the other hand, the household unit holds and exploits its agricultural land as a resource that is common to all of the members of the group.

The symbolic equivalences that are drawn in Iraqw ideology and in the practice of ritual serve to conceal and obfuscate the objective economic differences between the organization of the *aya* and of the household group. The solidarity of the household is based on its exploitation of a resource—the land. The application of the *masay* ritual to the household group reflects an objective economic solidarity that derives from their relationship to productive resources. By drawing a parallel between the territorial group and the domestic group, the solidarity of the smaller unit is projected onto the higher level of organization where it becomes the principal metaphor of organization for a grouping that is not based on direct and simple productive relations.

The same ritual forms at different levels of social organization may either reflect or generate social forms, and the distinction must be clearly drawn here between ritual that is a statement that reflects social reality, and ritual as a social instrument that generates social organization. At the level of the household, the *masay* ritual reflects a determinate social organization for production. At the level of the *aya,* it generates a social organization for protection and control of the productive resources. The *masay* ritual, performed for the *aya,* is necessarily a political instrument that imposes an organizational structure on a group of people.

For the Iraqw themselves, of course, the distinctions we have just drawn do not exist, which means that for them, the *aya* and the household are, in a metaphysical sense, the same. The political nature of the organization of the *aya* is obfuscated by its obviously (to them) metaphysical nature. The *masay* ritual at the level of the *aya* is believed to control the metaphysical factors of production for the *aya* as a whole— that is, the benevolence of the spirits and of belligerent ethnic groups who take on some metaphysical aspect in Iraqw ideology—just as the same ritual, performed for the household, controls disease which most clearly affects the productive potential of the group. In this light it becomes clear why *homa* may refer in different contexts to either hostile aliens or to disease of the body. At both levels the ritual is believed to offer protection from the unpredictable violence that is characteristic of the outside.

The Manipulation of Spatial Relations

In this ritual we see an abstraction and manipulation of relationships that derive from the fundamental concepts of space. In view of the fact that these relations are abstracted from the objective world in which they have their basis, we shall call them topological, to distinguish the relations and manipulations of thought from the topographic, kinesthetic relations of behavior. On the first day of the ritual in its very first act, an identity is established between the boundary of the *aya* and the sacrificial animal by leading the animal entirely around the *aya*. The same identity is established in the household version by leading the animal around the perimeter of the house. The killing of the sacrifice is done by suffocation; that is, it is killed by being sealed up tight. Since the sacrifice is symbolically equated with the boundary in the first operation of the ritual, this sealing up of the air passages also, metaphorically, seals the borders of the *aya*. At this point, and until the end of the ritual, no one is allowed to cross the boundary or the medicine will be ruined. This exactly parallels the rationale behind the suffocation of the victim instead of killing it with a knife. Text 12 contains the words of the men who carried out the sacrifice I have just described. The sacrifice accomplishes in symbolic terms the closure of an area of space. The identity between the boundary and the sacrificial victim is then further strengthened by redistributing the skin of the victim—that is, its own boundary—around the boundary of the *aya*. The very fact that the sacrifice takes place directly on the boundary serves to establish an identity between the *aya* and the victim metonymically as well as metaphorically. By means of these operations, the sacrificial animal is placed in relation to the *aya*: The animal stands for the *aya* as a small-scale representation of it. This allows the topological

---

TEXT 12
"If the Ram Is Cut with a Knife . . ."

"If the ram is cut by a knife, the medicine will have no strength; it will not exist *[masay i kahh]*. If the ram is smothered, the blood returns to the body. The chyme *[sanká]* must be taken out first or the sacrifice is ruined."

operation of closure to be expressed kinesthetically by operating directly
on the animal, which is the concrete representation of the *aya*. The animal's body is simply a model that objectifies the cultural idea of the *aya*.

In a second operation, the inside of the sacrificial animal is brought
to the outside. The contents of the stomach, which are the center
(*tla'angw*) of the organism, are brought directly to the outside and distributed around the boundary of the *aya*. In this operation the body of the
sacrifice is symbolically inverted: the inside becomes the outside, and the
inside and the outside are distributed about the perimeter to the territory.
In terms of an apt analogy, the whole operation is like turning one's
pockets inside out to dump out the accumulated dirt and lint. In the
masay ritual the sacrificial victim is turned inside out to entirely empty it
of its power. It is the power resulting from the symbolic pocket-shaking
that is applied then to the border of the *aya* in the form of the skin and
the chyme.

What is left, incidental to all of this, is the meat that is neither the
center nor the periphery. The life force of the animal has been used in
closing the boundary of the *aya*. In the commensal feast enjoyed by the
elders and *kahamuse* from all of the sections of the *aya,* the unity of the
people is reaffirmed. Eating together is a symbol of unity at this level because it stands for the solidarity of the household. The members of the
household consume the product of their labors together in peace. In eating the sacrifice together the elders say again, in effect, that the *aya* is like
the household. Yet, unlike many other instances in which political solidarity is expressed in terms of domestic solidarity, the Iraqw draw their
metaphors from the relations of space rather than of kinship. In the Iraqw
view the *aya* is like the household by virtue of their common boundedness,
discreteness, and closure, not by virtue of brotherhood, descent from a
common ancestor, or familiality.

On the second day, the sacrifice, which resembles that of the first
day in many respects, is done at a point that represents the center of the
aya. Here the sacrificial victim is identified with the land, not the border,
by feeding it earth dug from within the *aya*. Again, the victim is killed
by suffocation. The symbolism of closure is continued into the second day
as well. This, however, marks the turning point. The boundary has been
sealed, and now the site of the ritual has been withdrawn to the center.
The sacrifice is identified with the land, that is with "being in the middle," both by its location at the center and by its eating the earth. At this
point the ritual begins to express an opening out, an ejection, a movement
away from the center to the periphery. The skin is quickly removed, to be
cut up later. The chyme is removed and the ritual operations focus on
it—the symbol of the center—while it is further identified with the earth

by placing some of the ritually prepared earth into the center of each parcel of chyme. The cutting of the skin strips appears on the second day to be haphazard by contrast. Whereas the ritual of the previous day concentrated on the skin of the animal, that of the second day focuses on the chyme. The subsequent actions—running from the center to the periphery driving the spirits before the onslaught—and the verbal formulas— "opening" the evil that has been shut in the *aya* and in the houses—represents a cleansing and purification of the land.

Just as the sacrifice is "inverted" by bringing its center to the outside, the whole *aya* is in effect turned inside out and the "dirt"—the evil influences of the *netlangw*—is shaken out over the border and into the bush. The movement of the runners who sweep from the center to the periphery parallels the operation performed upon the body of the sacrifice. A topological operation on a symbolically generated space, the *aya,* is expressed kinesthetically in ritual. The topological metaphors of Iraqw social thought are objectified in behavior.

The Realization of Culture in Political Reality

Up to this point, it perhaps has not been clear why, and how, the *aya* exists at all as a corporate group in Iraqw society. There is no consistent leadership or hierarchy among the elders and *kahamuse* who exercise moral power over, and accept moral responsibility for, the inhabitants of the *aya.* The existence of the *aya* community does not derive from the material relations of production. In fact, the existence of the *aya* cannot be explained at all if we are forced to explain it with reference to the purely "objective" social relations that are contained within it.

We must look beyond the borders of the *aya* to the political ecology of the region to explain its existence. In this way we see that the *aya,* generated by the *masay* ritual, is a means of legitimating control over and access to land. The Iraqw are surrounded by other peoples. In this competitive environment the *masay* ritual is an adaptive institution that defines the limits of the territory that a given group exploits. It also serves, especially in this century, as an organization for predatory expansion into already occupied ecological niches. In this sense, the *aya* (and the ideology that sustains it) is analogous to the segmentary lineage organizations of the Tiv and Nuer, which, in both cases, are organizations of predatory expansion in competitive environments (Sahlins, 1963:323). But since the organization of the *aya* is based on an idiom of spatial relations rather than on kinship relations, there are profound differences in these two modes of organization, even though both function as successful organizations for the capture and retention of control over more and more land. Spatial ideas are pervasive in Iraqw thought about time, history, and society, and it is therefore not surprising that we should find that the central political and ritual instrument of the Iraqw is concerned with topological relations and manipulations. The focus on space ideally suits this ritual form for the adaptive role it has come to play. The effectiveness of the *masay* ritual, both as a means of predatory expansion and tool of internal social control, must be explained, however, in terms of the way social thought is related to social practice, and this relationship must be developed at the level of the regional political ecology.

In the light of the foregoing discussion, then, we turn to reexamine the nature of political violence.

The elders never resort to physical force or coercion in the enforcement of their power, but they do have control of the symbolic means of coercion: the curse and the arousal of public sentiment in the meeting that may be used to "accuse" (*kwasleemuut*) an offender. These means are primarily moral, and if they fail, there is rarely any recourse except exile. Thus, in effect, by the use of exile, and by their performance of the *masay* ritual which "protects" the *aya,* the elders claim to control the violence they see to be inherent in the external environment and use their control over external violence to their own ends.

In most cases, one thinks that a political organization of a scale similar to that of the *aya* would normally direct aggression outward, and that there would normally exist judicial means for dealing with interpersonal strife. In the Iraqw case, however, this does not appear to hold true. In part, the judicial institutions of the society have, no doubt, atrophied since the colonial government and now the independent government of Tanzania has taken over judicial functions. But the lack of judicial institutions goes beyond this. There are many fights and long-standing feuds among neighbors, in spite of the constantly reiterated call for neighborly relations in Iraqw discourse of all types. Yet, these conflicts are not seriously controlled by the contemporary Iraqw politico-jural organization. Instead, the elders attempt to control aggression directed at them from the outside.

The Iraqw have attempted to exploit the violence of the interethnic relations beyond the borders of the *aya,* and have in large part succeeded. Notably, the Iraqw have taken advantage of the British colonial use of violence to subdue the Masai and Barabaig. It is this use of violence by the colonial governments against the pastoralists that permitted the Iraqw to expand in the first place by limiting the raiding of the Masai and Barabaig warriors against Iraqw settlements on the fringes of their land.

They have also made use of the violence done to them by the pastoralists as an effective sanction in the maintenance of internal social control.

In the competition for land, ritual forms, which were at first directed at controlling natural forces affecting the productive potential of the land, were now redirected with the aim of controlling the social forces that affected Iraqw access to the land. What originally was meant to prevent lightning and to bring rain now prevented Masai attack as well, and could be used to bring more land under Iraqw control. That is, a ritual form that functioned as an instrument in agricultural magic became the key instrument in a social praxis that the Iraqw were able to work to their advantage, but only in the presence of the external force of the colonial government.

To themselves, they represent their reasons for conducting the ritual as a means—practically their only means—of protection. This endeavor is reasonable in the context of their society, which exists, in their view, by ritual and verbal fiat. In their view, it is only necessary, and completely sufficient, to say "let there be an *aya,*" and there is one. This political act of expropriation of land is fully conditioned by cultural concepts that govern and generate the specific techniques, or praxis, by which it is accomplished. Because the *masay* ritual is a political instrument, it has historical force; it is not merely the expression or communication of cultural or mythical concept. A historical analysis of ritual is demanded in this case and it is to this task that Chapter 8 is devoted.

Chapter 5

The Definition and Evaluation of Groups

I have discussed the Iraqw cultural representation and creation of space, and I have tried to show how these representations are the underlying forms that govern the organization of land ritual, residence, and their general orientation to the environment. Some of these representations also underlie the formation and definition of social groups that partition the population into subsets defined by area of residence, age, or sex. Beyond this division of Iraqw society into discrete groupings of people, there is also the partition of members of other ethnic groups into discrete categories. These ethnic categories are defined according to different criteria: by type of interaction, degree of competition or cooperation, and degree of danger they present to the Iraqw. The Iraqw stereotypes of the ethnic groups that surround them in turn influence the way they are treated in narrative and in ritual, which is designed either to ameliorate their dangerous influence or to influence the outcome of interactions with them. The way in which different ethnic groups are perceived and evaluated by the Iraqw is closely related to the way in which they perceive themselves. It is commonly noted that the stereotypes a people may have about another ethnic group tell us more about themselves than they do about the group so described. The Iraqw are no exception. In the latter part of this chapter, the relationship between self-identity and the definition and evaluation of other ethnic groups is explored. To provide an analytical basis for this, however, the nature of social groups within Iraqw society must be considered first.

There are two types of social groupings in Iraqw society: those defined by the cultural topology of space, and those defined by other criteria. The domestic group, the ridge community, the *aya* community and, to a

105

certain extent, other ethnic groups are defined with respect to space. Age and sex categories are not. The genealogical group, the *tlahhay*, is as we have seen, closely related to the spatial group.

The Domestic Group and the Ridge Community

The domestic group is defined by common residence. It is not necessarily a group of people related by blood, or necessarily even by fictions of blood relationship. Many Iraqw couples, especially if they are young and without many children of their own, will take into their household other peoples' children to raise. These children will be fed by their "adopted" parents and will be expected to work as members of the domestic group to which they now belong. The adoption is not formal, nor is it permanent, and the child may go back to its family whenever the arrangement is no longer comfortable or useful. Usually the adopted child will come from a distant *aya* or perhaps another section of the same *aya*, but may be a close neighbor as well. In several instances that I observed, a child had been acquired from another ethnic group, usually in exchange for agricultural products, cattle, or tobacco. Although this is apparently no longer practiced today (it is outlawed by the government), as recently as two decades ago it was still an important form of exchange of population between the Iraqw and their neighbors. A number of Iraqw wives have come into Iraqw society in this way, when, after having been acquired in trade from non-Iraqw parents, they have later married Iraqw-born men. Conversely, many Iraqw girls have been forced to leave for reasons of ritual impurity or have been traded out during famine years for foodstuffs or livestock. Consequently, the domestic group frequently includes some members who were neither born into it nor married into it.

The domestic group, *muk o do'*, 'people of one house', divide work among themselves according to ability and the cultural stereotypes of labor befitting their age and sex. All members of the domestic group work together during planting to prepare the furrows, carry manure, carry water, break clods, and do all the other tasks involved in planting maize, beans, and pumpkins in the family field. Young and adult men are frequently absent nowadays, travelling some distance in search of wage labor or remaining away indefinitely for schooling or permanent employment. Those who remain work in the fields doing the heavy tilling and weeding and hauling of firewood or harvest. Today, political youth groups such as the T.A.N.U. Youth League (TYL), or other government volunteer labor, involve a great deal of time. Young women do the cooking, cutting of firewood, and minding of the young animals left home when the main herd goes to pasture. They also are increasingly absorbed in government-related volunteer work projects that attempt to provide some community services such as adult education centers and clinics. Children carry water from the valley streams to the ridge tops where the houses are located. They also do most of the picking of pyrethrum flowers which, when dried, are the principle cash crop for most domestic groups in Irqwar Da'aw. Older men, when not engaged in meetings and ritual affairs, generally herd the cattle, sheep, and goats, and assist in agricultural work. The produce obtained from herds and lands that the domestic group manages is shared within the group. There is no wider group defined by the relations of agricultural production.

The ridge community (*gayemo*) has already been discussed in Chapter 2. This group shows some specialization of labor among its members. In general, there is someone recognized as a superior roof-thatcher, an excellent hoe-handle maker, a good circumciser, a good beer-maker, a good honey-finder, and so on; and members of the community will rely on these persons for these tasks, generally paying them in kind, but also with money. The ridge community is a set of persons defined by a geographic feature, and it is roughly congruent to the neighborhood (*papahhay*). The boundaries of either may be indistinct, but neither includes people beyond the boundary of the *aya*.

Both the ridge community and the neighborhood define groups of people whose reciprocity is restricted to specific and specialized services that they perform for one another. At the level of the section, reciprocity is even more limited and encompasses only the sharing of labor necessary to maintain the pastures for the cattle belonging to residents of the section. At the level of the *aya*, there is only very limited reciprocity, and it is usually limited to ritual services. From the outsider's viewpoint one sees a gradual attenuation of the range and generally of reciprocal relation from the domestic group, where it includes all goods and services, to the neighborhood and ridge community, where it includes some specified services and goods, to the section, where it includes only those relations arising from maintenance of pastures, to the level of the *aya*, where reciprocity is restricted to ritual matters. On a different scale the whole *aya*, an analogue of the household, may be viewed as an individual group in opposition to the cosmos. The ritual that defines the extent and membership of the *aya* is, in part, the means by which the Iraqw deal with their surroundings.

In a survey sample of 40 domestic units distributed among four ridge communities, I found the average number of persons residing together to be six. The actual numbers living in one unit, however, ranged from 11 (five cases) to 1 single person (six cases, all male). The num-

ber of unmarried, younger children living in the same domestic group
with their parents was four for the entire sample. There was a considerable range in this figure, too, from a maximum of 10 living children in
one household to some households that had none. There were only two
cases in which grandparents were living in the same household with their
married children. In both of these cases, the grandparents had previously
lived separately and had only come to live with their children in old age,
when they were no longer able to look after themselves.

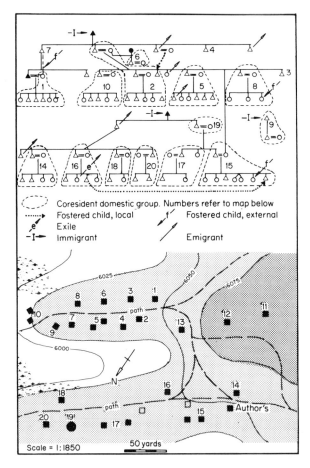

FIGURE 5.1. *Residence and kinship. This shows the spatial proximity of small
groups of kin with no more encompassing genealogical relationship. The exchange
of children with other groups, motivated by famine or ritual pollution, is also shown.*

The settlement pattern is exclusively neolocal after marriage. Moreover, there are a number of instances in which a young man has set up a household entirely by himself. It is not unusual, although not common, for a single woman to do the same. In such cases, the young person begs land to cultivate from the *kahamusmo* of his or her section and builds a house, courtyard, and private pasture (*mundi*) for his- or herself. In the sample of 40 households mentioned above, this pattern of single-person households accounted for three of the total of six single-person households. Of the remaining three, one was an elderly widower, and two were constructed by older married men who wished to get away from their wives and children. In all cases of single-person households, the pattern of construction and meanings that defined the household for the Iraqw was the same.

The largest domestic units consisted of one or both parents and their children. It appears that the size of the domestic group has changed little over one generation. The average family size for 31 parents in the sample of 40 households was only slightly lower at 5.75 than the current average size of 6.

These quantitative data do little to convey the nature of the domestic group itself, and of the ridge community of which it is a part. Consider the case of one ridge community. Figure 5.1 gives a brief indication of the genealogical and other relationships that exist among the principle householders on this ridge. There are 10 domestic units in this example. The number of residents in each domestic unit ranges from one (two cases) to nine persons (see Figure 5.2).

The core of the ridge settlement is a group of brothers: Bo'ay, Leonardi (a Christian), Tluway, Derabe, and Stefano. Of these only Bo'ay, Leonardi, and Derabe have remained in residence on the ridge. The youngest, Stefano, converted to Christianity with Leonardi, his older brother, and left soon afterward. Today he is employed on a government farm near Kilimanjaro. Tluway, far from converting to Christianity, obtained 'protection' (*pa'asamo*) medicine from a *qwaslarmo* and led a settlement expedition of other youths into the pastures of the Barabaig in the 1940s. He continues to live there today even though, since the establishment of the independent government under Nyerere, he has had no recognized powers there. Derabe never married but set up his household independently on the ridge near Leonardi and Bo'ay. Most of the other households on the ridge are those of Leonardi's or Bo'ay's children.

If we examine the constitution of each household, a number of interesting features emerges. In the house labeled *1* in Figure 5.1 lives a widow. She was born in Singida district (to the southwest) of Nyaturu

FIGURE 5.2. *The ridge community. The houses of independent domestic groups share a ridgetop. Although fields are cultivated by their owners alone, cattle are herded together on common pastures.*

parents. She was traded for agricultural produce (probably maize) to Tluway who brought her to live in his household. She came when she was very young and does not remember her parents. She appears to be about 40 years old today, so this must have taken place in the late 1930s. She was married to one of Bo'ay's children and set up a household with him. Her husband was killed a number of years ago doing day labor on a European farm in Oldeani (near Ngorongoro) and since then she has lived alone with their six children. Although she is not Iraqw by birth, she speaks only Iraqw, and is for all intents and purposes entirely Iraqw by any of her neighbors' reckoning.

Household number 2 in Figure 5.1 consists of Leonardi's wife who lives with her daughter-in-law (the wife of Andrea, one of Leonardi's children) and her children. One son of the absent Tluway lives with them occasionally. Although old Leonardi occasionally sleeps in this house with his wife and daughter-in-law, he prefers to live with his bachelor brother Derabe next door. Households number *1* and 2 have no male head.

On the other hand, households 3 and *4* consist of single males, one son and one brother of Leonardi. John, in number 3, sometimes eats with his mother in her house, but prefers to be thought of as independent and spends most of his time in his own house and surrounding land.

Households numbered 5, 8, and 10 are those of three more of Leonardi's sons, Paskal, Kasmiri, and Boniface. They each live together with their wives and children. One of these domestic groups (8) includes a child that was adopted from another Iraqw-speaking family living near Mbulu (outside of the *aya* of which the ridge is a part). The child was "adopted" in exchange for a gift of grain to her family at a time when they had none. Although the child is not bound to stay with her new family forever—that is, she was not "purchased" with the grain—she will continue to live with them until the situation improves with her natal family. The rights and obligations in such exchanges are not explicitly stated so far as I was able to determine, but negotiated more or less ad hoc. So long as the girl continues to reside with her "adopted" family she is fully a member of that domestic group.

Bo'ay, Leonardi's brother, has lived alone in number 7 since the death of his wife. Shortly after my survey of these houses, however, one of Bo'ay's sons returned from the Ngorongoro National Park where he worked as a game scout. He brought with him his Chagga wife to live with his father since he had difficulty supporting his family on his salary as a game scout. She also would look after the old man who was becoming increasingly infirm.

The remaining households, number 6 and 9, are only distantly related to the core of brothers and sons that compose most of the ridge's population. Salustiani, in number 6, has some genealogical relationship to Leonardi's wife, but either he could not or would not specify exactly what this relationship was. Household number 9 consisted of a very old man named Bo'ay (not the same as Leonardi's brother), his son, Hhando, together with his wife and three children. The old Bo'ay of this household was from the Gorowa group whose language is similar to the Iraqw, but who apparently separated from the Iraqw stock several hundred years ago. He had come to settle in Irqwar Da'aw with Leonardi's father who was also a Gorowa. They had both been given land on the ridge by the *kahamusmo* of *Kwermusl* when they had arrived there (c. 1910?). Old Bo'ay had one son, Hhando, who remained with him, bringing his wife to live in the same household. These "immigrants" were only slightly more recent than most other households in Irqwar Da'aw. They are counted as fully Iraqw.

There is, then, a considerable variety in the composition of Iraqw domestic groups. One notable feature is the incorporation of women from other ethnic groups. In two cases, young girls had come into the ridge community through the exchange of goods. Another woman, not Iraqw-born, had been brought into the group through marriage. A simple "ethnic chauvinism" plays no part in the definition of domestic groups or their feelings of solidarity.

In all cases the single most important identifying feature of a domestic unit—one that produced for itself and that was considered a unit by its residents and others around it—depended not on the composition of the people who resided there, but on the existence of a house, its courtyard, and private grazing land around it. Thus, a single person and a family of 10 had approximately the same conceptual status; each constituted a 'house' or *do'*.

The Genealogical Group (*Tlahhay*)

As the membership of these spatial units becomes more inclusive, the quality and quantity of social relations is attenuated in a direct proportion. The *tlahhay,* however, represents a social grouping that is not a necessarily tied to location. It appears to have little practical significance except in the regulation of marriage. The *tlahhay,* or 'clan', appears to be based originally on the local group (see Chapter 2), although its membership is usually spatially dispersed. The *tlahhay* is a bilaterally reckoned "kindred" that includes both males and females, and which consists of the descendents of its eponymous ancestor. In Irqwar Da'aw today, the time depth of these *tlahhay* is various. Each *tlahhay* originated with the settlement of a new settler from outside on the lands of the *aya,* who thereby formed new *tlahhay* as his descendents multiplied. In *Hhay Ga'angw,* one of the oldest *tlahhay* is *Hhay Amo,* named after the man Amo who is said to have accompanied Haymu Tipe, the ritual expert who claimed the land from the mythical lake and tree that guarded it. Another *tlahhay* in *Hhay Ga'angw,* called *Hhay Gorowa* is named after a man who came from the ethnic group of that name only three generations ago. Since the Iraqw rarely count generations between the present and the founder of the *tlahhay,* there is no way to discover the age or length of residence of a particular *tlahhay.* As the result of movements and migrations, there are a great number of named *tlahhay* in Irqwar Da'aw and they are spatially dispersed over all of the areas today occupied by the Iraqw.

A person is prohibited from marrying a member of the *tlahhay* of all of his grandparents. The *tlahhay* appears to have no other social function. It never serves to mobilize labor or resources of any kind. Other than the mention of the *tlahhay Hhay Bo'ok* in Text 22, they rarely figure in the narrative tradition of the Iraqw. It can be observed too, in examining that same Text, that the narrator is quite vague when questioned for specifics about the *tlahhay*. I expect, however, that there is much more that could be learned about the nature of this group in Iraqw society, but it goes beyond the scope and aims of this research.

Age and Sex

Of much greater significance than the *tlahhay* are groupings arising from distinctions of sex and age. The age categories for men are different from those of women and do not parallel them; the systems are quite independent. Today, however, the age categories of women have atrophied to a considerable extent since the primary initiation ritual was banned in 1931 by Michael Ahho, a colonially appointed chief bent on reform (see pp. 218–222).

All Iraqw males are divided into three groups. The youngest 'boys' (*daqay*) remain close to home and have very little part to play in agriculture, politics, or ritual. Male children remain *daqay* until after circumcision at the age of 8 to 10 years. From this age until they have children of their own, they will belong to the group called *masomba* (sing., *masomo*), 'youths'. Not until after they have children who are old enough to marry will they be considered elders, *barise*. These groups are informally defined by consensus and are in no way similar to "age sets" or "age grades" that are found among the Masai, for example.

For one thing, circumcision is a very relaxed, informal affair unattended by elaborate ritual observances. When it is generally felt among the members of the ridge community or among a group of neighbors that there are young boys to justify a circumcision, then it is held. Beer is brewed in the ordinary way as if for a work party or for sale. No ritual or ceremonial is involved in its preparation. In the evening, when the beer is ready, one man who is known among his neighbors as a good circumcisor, then sharpens a knife and cuts the foreskin off the young boys. This is done in an area away from the house, usually in a bushy piece of waste ground nearby. The foreskins are flung away. The area is not ritually prepared in any way, nor are the boys instructed in any secret lore. The men accompanying the boys, usually a collection of their fathers and fathers' brothers (but also other possibly unrelated males), spread honey on the circumcision wounds and the boys are helped back to the house. They remain inside for two weeks recuperating by the hearth. Meanwhile, that evening the men drink the beer they have prepared. Except for the brief act of circumcision itself, the undertaking resembles any other beer party and quite likely will end with as many rowdy drunks.

The informality with which the Iraqw treat life's temporal passings stands in marked contrast to the elaboration of ritual directed to the maintenance and protection of spatial boundaries. It is as if they would wish to deny the flow of time, to ignore it, or at least to pay it as little attention as possible. In view of the degree of pain inflicted on the boys whose wounds almost invariably become septic, and the apparent dearth of symbolic meaning, one wonders why they even bother. But, once the boy has been initiated, he passes into the group of youths, *masomba,* and is expected to shoulder a greater burden both of work and of social responsibility. He becomes, in effect, a member of the community.

A male remains a youth, then, for most of his life. And again, the passage into the next stage of elderhood appears to be informally arranged once other elders judge a certain person to be eligible. As far as I have yet been able to determine, there are no special rituals or ceremonials associated with becoming an elder. Once a person has children who are married, he will be considered by his peers to be a member of the *barise.*

The *barise* are responsible, together with the *kahamusmo,* for the organization of ritual, adjudication of disputes, and the fixing of boundaries. They are responsible, too, for holding meetings in which the community welfare is discussed, and in which blame is assigned in the event of transgressions of the political and moral order of the community. The *kahamusmo* stands among the *barise* as merely the first among equals. At a meeting or assembly convened for carrying out ritual land ceremonies, the *kahamusmo* has the first word but he rarely has the last. The *kahamusmo* in his capacity as "speaker" is the mediator and "chairman" of the *barise.* Decisions are reached by consensus, however long that may take, for time is of much less importance than ultimate unity of purpose, which has a mystical force all its own among them.

The *masomba* on the other hand do most of the heavy work. They are generally responsible for herding the livestock, managing the planting, and harvesting the fields. They are directly in contact with the production of food and other material resources. This fact gives them a certain counterbalancing power: They may refuse to work, they may leave the *aya,* or, worse, they may take with them the herds or produce of the domestic unit. It is this rebelliousness of youth against the elders that led, in their view, to their migration out of the lands they previously occupied to the south and into Irqwar Da'aw (Text 27, lines 1–17). Also, in this century, it was groups of youths who led the settlement of most of the areas to the west and north of Irqwar Da'aw.

The distinction between the *barise* and the *masomba* is constituted as a political polarity. But, it is the polarity that exists between the settled *aya* and the hostile outside that is the dialectic that drives the political process. The *barise* are simply opposed to the *masomba*. There is no further elaboration of political hierarchy outside of this dichotomy; that is, there are no series of grades or ranks within the system. The existence of hierarchy entails the presence of a number of groups (three or more) and a cultural basis for evaluation that orders these groups into a fixed series. The two "age groups" of the Iraqw are *not,* therefore, hierarchical, but simply dual and opposed, and in structural balance with one another.

The political roles of the *masomba* and *barise* are stereotyped in ways that must be familiar to all mankind: "the wisdom of age" against "the folly of youth," or, from a different perspective, the vigor of youth against the undue caution of age. These stereotypical views of *masomba* and *barise* are reflected in the *alqado,* 'received tradition'. The polarity is seen, too, in the differences between the dance, the forum of the youths, and the meetings where the elders preside. The *masomba* gather together at their monthly dances that are traditionally held on moonless nights. These may be convened in direct opposition to the elders' authority (see Text 22, lines 179–185).

In addition to the dichotomous groupings based on age, there are informal groups of friends of approximately the same age. These are called *qaro,* and are informal associations of men close in age who live near one another and interact frequently with one another. The *qaro* will persist throughout the lifetime of its members and will provide mutual assistance for each of them in work or in the case of disputes. The *qaro* are important as factions within the age categories, but they are not ranked in any way as age sets are among Nilotic peoples. Among the Iraqw these groups are not organized hierarchically on the basis of age or any other form of time scale. The legitimation of the authority of the elders arises not from the fact of their age, but from their control of ritual and of the community forum where political issues are discussed and decided.

My use of the word *faction* to describe informal groups of coevals called *qaro* is meant to suggest that the divisions are ad hoc and informal, within a structure that does not explicitly recognize them, and whose relation to power is adventitious or historical rather than structural. In using this word, I am trying to distinguish between the Iraqw use of age distinctions in political structure from the use made of age distinctions by the Masai. In contrast to highly formal, eminently *structural* categories and hierarchies of age that exist among the Masai (Eisenstadt, 1965; Prins, 1953) the Iraqw age organization is indeed very informal. This is especially true of the groups of coevals—friends—that are called *qaro.* The situation is much more difficult to describe and to analyze with re-

spect to the division between the *barise* and the *masomba* who are represented in many contexts as structurally opposed groups and which are not,
therefore, "factions." This involves immediately the question of structure
versus history. The terms for age categories in Iraqw have cognates in the
languages of surrounding peoples. *Qaro* is clearly derived from similar informal groups among the Tatoga peoples. *Basumba* means 'youth' among
the Sukuma, and the Iraqw word, if not the idea and practice, is clearly
"borrowed" from this direction. *Barise* appears to be cognate with *baraza,*
which means 'council of elders' in Tanzanian Bantu languages including
Swahili. In the face of a lack of any real historical data on whether or not,
and how, the terms and the structured oppositions entered or developed
within Iraqw society, we must admit that the issue is not resolvable. (In
any case, see Chapter 8 for the historical result of this opposition.)

Women have a different set of age categories. Today, however, women are extremely secretive about this matter. Questions about it were
frequently greeted with shocked silence, or laughter and then silence.
Although the initiation rites are supposed to have been banned for some
40 years, the strength of conviction with which women guard the traditional secrets suggests that the institution is not dead but hidden from
the public eye. Roughly, there appear to be four categories: young uncircumcised girls, circumcised girls (*dasi*), initiated girls (*dena*), and
married women (*tlaway*). Girls are circumcised, as are boys, around the
age of 8–10 years. There is little ceremony and the arrangements are
similar to those for boys. The circumcised girls return to their houses for
a seclusion of about two weeks. This act seems to have little bearing on
their status. Formerly, at around the age of 14, girls were inducted into
the *marmo* ceremony that constituted a formal initiation into marriageable
status. Today, this ceremony and seclusion of up to a year that accompanied it are no longer practiced, but there is some suggestion that some
form of initiation is still practiced. After marriage, *duxo,* a woman becomes an active member of the community of neighbors. The group of
married women, *tlaway,* appears also to have some corporate identity as a
group and have some political power vis á vis the males. There are also
female ritual specialists, *âbo,* who formerly presided over the *marmo*
initiation ceremony and who today retain some degree of status.

Definition and Evaluation of Ethnic Groups

The social and ethnic environment of the Iraqw is unusually complex. Whatever the origins of this diversity, it has a number of implications for the Iraqw who must cope with this diversity of culture, language,
and mode of economic exploitation. For one thing it means that the

society had to develop controls that allowed it to live in a relatively restricted land area, or it had to expand at the expense of other people's land. In many other parts of Africa, cultural groups have been able to expand at least in some direction with little or no opposition until very recently. This has not been true on the Mbulu Plateau. The Iraqw have frequently been under attack by the Masai, when their expansion has placed them in direct competition with them for pasture land.

Interactions along the ethnic boundaries are frequently hostile, but not always so. I insert the proviso "but not always" since one of the most significant problems that has confronted me in the understanding of this ethnic diversity is why one type of interaction is hostile, another not; or why clear boundaries should be formed in one instance, whereas a peaceful merging and assimilation of different peoples has characterized another. The answer, it seems now, has much to do with the social and ideological processes that have contributed to the context of confrontation of one ethnic group by another. In the presence of such diversity, it is useful, too, to point out that all of the cultures that interact here are influenced to some degree by all of the others. The problem immediately arises of how we are to identify any *one* ethnic group. The criteria that we might choose—dress, language, economic mode, political integration, etc.—all yield overlapping categories of people. It is difficult to distinguish, let alone study, any one "ethnic group" in isolation. Objective criteria fail consistently to distinguish one group from another, and if we turn to their own means of self-identification, we discover, not surprisingly, that their own criteria are different. For the Iraqw, it is the land they occupy that most clearly identifies them as Iraqw. For the Masai, it is the dependence on cattle. For the Bantu-speaking peoples, it appears that their genealogical relationship to others most clearly identifies them to themselves and to others as members of a particular group. Adequate description of ways of defining one's self-identity and the identity of one's group are essential to an understanding of what has taken place in the interaction of one group with another in the complexity of this social environment.

In this discussion of ethnic differences, it is important to point out that we are not dealing simply with ethnic units defined and differentiated under the same set of criteria (e.g., descent from a pair of brothers), but we are dealing instead with *different logics* of identity.

THE IRAQW ETHNIC SELF–IDENTITY

From the Iraqw point of view their society is quite open to other peoples. Roughly speaking, Iraqw is as Iraqw does. In other words, any one may become "Iraqw" by behaving like one and living within the bounds of the land inhabited by other Iraqw. I never heard any suggestion that it was necessary to be born into the society in order to be considered a member of it. Such a doctrine as this would contradict the reality of the situation as the Iraqw perceive it, since they are fully aware that throughout their life as a group they have absorbed peoples of diverse ethnic origins, and have as well "exported" some of their own population into the other ethnic groups that surround them. Territorial boundaries and social behavior are the criteria of membership, not birth, or even language.

To behave as an Iraqw entails a number of beliefs and practices. First of all one must accept and participate in the communal regulation of the pastoral sector of the economy by the ridge community and the section, and must agree to follow the customary rules and to abide by the decisions of the *barise* regarding disputes over pasturing rights. Second, one must practice agriculture in the way that is deemed appropriate; that is, by planting on ridges and by using manure from the family livestock in one's fields. In the *slufay* recitations, all Iraqw are exhorted to care for the land in these ways and through the use of medicines prepared by the *kahamuse* according to the directions of the ritual experts (*qwaslare*). Finally, the Iraqw person accepts the authority of the ritual experts, the *kahamuse,* and the *barise* in the regulation of ritual and cosmological control of the rain, the sun, and the land.

The small domestic groups and individuals that compose Iraqw society are, practically speaking, clients to the *qwaslare, kahamuse,* and certain of the other *barise* who are particularly competent in ritual performance or oration. This ritual control over the land and the elements is what gives them legitimate rights over these things. If a person accepts these tenets of the culture and behaves according to the rules that regulate ritual and economic behavior in the *aya,* then he or she is, for all practical purposes, an Iraqw. I stress the word *practical* because it is the instrumental character of the Iraqw ritual that makes it more than an expression of social organization based on other principles, and that makes it, therefore, a means of political integration that gives rise to "ethnic identity." Thus, in contrast to the "closed" nature of the ideology of classification and perception of space and time, their practical view of the nature of "ethnic" groups is quite "open." This fact has allowed the absorption of peoples of many different ethnic groups into Iraqw society. An understanding of this practical definition of identity—Iraqw is as Iraqw does— gives us a partial answer to the question, posed earlier in this chapter, about interactions across boundaries that may lead sometimes to peaceful assimilation, sometimes to hostilities.

We turn now to consider the way in which the Iraqw characterize and stereotype the principle ethnic groups with whom they have frequent interactions: the Tatoga, the Masai, and the Bantu agriculturalists (the Iramba, Irangi, Wambugwe, and others).

THE TATOGA

Of all of the ethnic groups near them, the Iraqw probably have the greatest amount of interaction with the Tatoga peoples. The Tatoga peoples are themselves organized in a number of "subtribes" (called *eimojik* in their language) that are named and autonomous, although they all share elements of culture and a common language. Among these *eimojik*, the Barabaig are today the most important to the Iraqw. The Iraqw call all of the Tatoga groups *tara* (singular, *tarmo*). Many Iraqw stories, *alqado*, and songs deal with the multiple facets of their relationships. There is, first of all, a great deal of intermarriage between them. S. Wada (1971) has collected some genealogies of Iraqw and Tatoga families in the Mangola area and these show a consistently high number of intermarriages between the Iraqw settlers and the Tatoga living there. There are also a large number of domestic groups in Irqwar Da'aw who claim Tatoga origins. Tarmo is a popular personal name in Iraqw, although it does not always indicate that the person so named is of Tatoga origins. Although I was not able to collect any statistical evidence on the degree of Iraqw and Tatoga interaction, it is apparent everywhere and is commonly attested by both groups of people. At this time it seems that most of the areas formerly occupied by the Tatoga have been successfully settled by Iraqw and large numbers of the Tatoga now speak Iraqw as a second, and increasingly a first, language. Young people today are more likely to speak only Iraqw whereas older men usually speak some Tatoga as well. There are numerous similarities in vocabulary that indicate that the Iraqw and Tatoga have been in contact for a considerable length of time (e.g., Ehret, 1974 gives a list of loan words).

In appearance there are also many similarities. Among both groups, men wear shorts and a cape made of cotton denim or calico. All men carry meter-long parrying sticks and, when traveling in the bush, spears of exactly similar construction. Women wear cotton skirts and a cape of cotton like those of the men. In general the Iraqw wear plaids and bright colors while the Tatoga wear black or dark colors. (The Masai wear red and ochre colors.) Before the introduction of cotton, men of both groups wore long goatskin capes from their shoulders to their knees. Women wore goatskin skirts and short capes. Today goatskin clothing is seen only among very old women among the Iraqw, but many more young Tatoga women continue to wear the leather garments. These diacritics of dress serve to distinguish each group. Recently the government rounded up all

---

TEXT 13
Alqado: Language

In those days the clans of the Iraqw were not many. They became numerous later. People came from many places such as Irangi *[Irangamo]*, Alawa *[Alawamo]*, Mangatti *[Tarmo]* and [?] Sandawe *[Sarwadamo]*. Many people followed each other. This man called Haymu, they met him here. They spoke Iraqw with his man [undistinguishable]. In that world of long ago *[bara yamu ang;* literally, 'in down before'], Kiswahili was spoken by the Mangatti. A very easy thing [is Kiswahili]. It is spoken where people gather together. In those first days when white people came Kiswahili was unknown. Our "Kiswahili" [i.e., our common language] was Barabaig. The people from Singida area speak Barabaig to us. Irangi know Barabaig. Wambugwe [Manda Da'aw] speak Barabaig to us. Speaking Barabaig is easy. It is the speech of people gathered together because a stranger if he comes already speaks Barabaig. The thing they speak, their Barabaig speech is known in our place. It is the Kiswahili of black people. Later Kiswahili of black people. Later kiswahili was easy [to learn] from the white people. They wanted black people who got together to already know Kiswahili of white people. Kiswahili is spoken now and it is very easy. Each area *[ayamo]* speaks differently. They speak differently in Mbugwe, differently in Singida. Differently in Iraqw. Differently in Mangatti. White people speak differently. The place they gather, together, however, they speak Kiswahili. The days when we all speak Kiswahili when we get together are not yet here. The speaking of Barabaig is not lost.

---

of the Barabaig (a subtribe, or *eimojik,* of the Tatoga) for internment after a group of Iramba (Bantu-speaking) agriculturalists were attacked by a group of Barabaig warriors. The soldiers used these clothing features to identify Barabaig along the roads and in the bush.

In their physical features, the Tatoga and Iraqw appear very similar. In the past they used each other's language as well. In Text 13 the speaker has in effect set forth his theory of language communities. He clearly associates language with the 'place' (*ayamo*) in which it is spoken. In addition he discusses two languages that are used "when people are gathered together." The evidence of this Text shows that the languages of the Mangatti and Barabaig—the informant used them interchangeably— formed a *lingua-franca* among themselves and the Iraqw, and apparently between other peoples as well. This role is increasingly being assumed by Swahili under the joint influences of the government's campaign to teach Swahili and the absorption of more and more Mangatti (i.e., various Tatoga *eimojik*) into Iraqw-speaking areas. The speaker in Text 13 has formulated a "rule of use" of languages, to the effect that language *use* is determined by *place*. In an inhabited place (*ayamo*) the language of the people who live there is spoken; in a meeting or gathering of people, a common language such as Barabaig or Swahili is spoken.

The wide knowledge of each other's languages and the existence of rules that determine which language to use where, has come about as the result of constant exchange and intermixture of population. But one thing that has always kept them apart and feuding is their different approaches to making a living from the land. The Iraqw believe that this should be done carefully, according to the consensus of the community, but always by the domestic group. The areas where agriculture is practiced and where cattle are herded are carefully demarcated and the boundaries are scrupulously maintained. Ritual observances and the use of various medicines are believed to be essential to the success of the undertaking. In contrast, the Iraqw feel that the Barabaig are somewhat lax about these matters. They point to the seeming disorder with which the Barabaig graze their cattle, wandering here and there in search of better pastures instead of remaining on and maintaining a fixed and smaller pasture. The Barabaig, in common with other pastoralists of east Africa, do graze freely over large tracts of land held as common pasture by the *eimojik* to which the herdsman belongs. This practice disturbs the Iraqw in a way that should be familiar to many Europeans who view the free-ranging pastoral practices of such people in a similar way.

This conflict very nearly erupted into fighting when a large group of so-called Mangatti from the Mangola area to the north decided to move with their herds into the Dareda area to the south and below the escarpment. This move required that they cross Irqwar Da'aw. The Iraqw were upset by the ill-disciplined Mangatti cattle that were moved through Iraqw farmland without regard for the established pathways (*tlaqandi*) and pastures especially laid aside for cattle. The matter was brought up during a public meeting attended in this case by a member of Parliament for Mbulu district, himself an Iraqw. It was eventually concluded that nothing could be done because now the "Mangatti" were "Tanzanians just like the Iraqw." The ethnic animosities were transcended in this case by an appeal to nationalism. What rankled most, however, was the disregard for the order of the land.

In their expansion, one of the goals of the Iraqw is to impose their order on the land of the Mangatti (Barabaig). In Text 14 this desire is expressed. This passage encapsulates, too, the range of interaction among the two peoples from the Iraqw viewpoint: The Iraqw settle the land of the Barabaig and marry their women. By consequence, they also fight with

---

TEXT 14
Slufay: **Barabaig**

1. *dir ka hano basa*	There is a place in the south
2. *o dida dima?*	Where is that place?
3. *o dida barbaydu*	There among the Barabaig
4. *tlaqandida a met*	The cattle thoroughfares remaining between the fields
5. *ham ga qo mak fakaan*	Now even these are finished (by us)
6. *gim kaa alhheesaane*	Like this we shall finish it all
7. *amenar barbaydu*	The Barabaig women
8. *o e'it*	Oh yes
9. *kari xupu*	Shall stoop
10. *kurema doren ngi ot*	To take our hoes in their hands
11. *amena toren*	Our women
12. *sepiida ngi ot*	Take the milk gourd in their hands
13. *awa barbaydu*	Those of the Barabaig
14. *kar ngi lotiin*	The cattle are milked
15. *kar siximoda*	And the bangles
16. *o amenar barbaydu*	Of the Barabaig women
17. *kari solo'oti*	They fall
18. *amenar doren*	The women of our house
19. *ngu bara nanuwa sles*	Discover them among the wild greens
20. *kar u matler hamahaan*	As they cook them in the morning
21. *mu ti slaa slaa*	People love one another
22. *gimay kar a adori ala*	And so it is like this

---

them. They depend on the Barabaig, however, for milk (Lines 11–14) and also for metal work (Lines 15–19, "bangles"). Other *alqado* indicate that the Iraqw obtained cattle from the Barabaig and even today they depend on Barabaig smiths to provide their hoes and other implements and bangles made of brass (*siximo*) or iron (*qoturmo*). It is a dominant theme in Iraqw characterization of a discussion about the Barabaig that they will eventually become Iraqw, that their women will be put to work with hoes, that the Iraqw shall possess their cattle and farm their land. First, the colonial government and now the independent government of Tanzania have played a large role in encouraging agriculture over pastoralism since agriculture can be more easily regulated and taxed. The Iraqw have consistently taken advantage of this government policy.

Against this determination in organized expansion, the free-ranging Barabaig have consistently lost out as they move their herds farther from the Iraqw settlements or give up their ways to live as Iraqw. Those who move can only go so far, and recently they have reached their limit.

This has resulted in hostilities more than once, although today the Tanzanian government has taken strong measures to pacify them and settle them as agriculturalists. This move will no doubt convert the rest of them to Iraqw modes of livelihood, if not to Iraqw speech.

THE MASAI

The Iraqw interaction with the Masai has been long, but it has produced a different set of stereotypes, and has developed differently from the Iraqw interaction with the Tatoga peoples. Masai warriors have raided the Iraqw for cattle for as long as they can remember. Before the beginning of colonial rule and the imposition of the Pax Britannica, the Iraqw were constantly victimized by these raids (Fosbrooke, 1954). The Iraqw, unable to organize effective defense, retreated to underground shelters and houses dug into the face of hillsides with their entrances below ground level. These underground houses were mainly confined to the areas around the periphery of Irqwar Da'aw. In Irqwar Da'aw itself, the high, thatched round houses remained, but many people dug caves and pits under these houses in which to hide during the raids of the Masai. The constant pressure of Masai raids drove domestic groups apart from each other, reinforcing their isolation and insularity. Although the frequency and ferocity of these raids abated under the colonial government, and since independence, under the controls of well-organized police patrols, they have never been entirely stopped. The Masai still raid and occasionally kill the Iraqw agriculturalists in order to steal their cattle. In one well-organized raid in 1976 on an Ujamaa village in the northern part of the district, Masai youths managed to drive off several hundred head of cattle and killed seven Iraqw men who tried to pursue them.

The Iraqw credit the success of the Masai raids to their advance reconnaissance. They claim that the Masai youths hide in the hills overlooking the Iraqw homesteads while they wait their chance. A Masai raid has the air of a natural disaster, a force which, like the rain, can only be controlled by magical means. At least one ritual specialist made his reputation on medicine that was meant to control the Masai. Be'a, a member of the Manda clan of ritual specialists, is believed to have halted the spread of the ritual and political influence of Saigilo, a rival Tatoga ritual specialist and political leader of much reknown even today. Be'a is believed to have used his medicine to cause a Masai raid on Saigilo's homestead near Daudi (about 15 kilometers north of Mbulu town). Saigilo was wounded in the encounter.

The Iraqw have characteristically dealt with the Masai by means of magic and ruse. They believe that a large part of the reason that the colonial government opened up large tracts of land in the northern part of the district for Iraqw settlement depended on the clever trick of Michael Ahho, an appointed chief of the Iraqw. The colonial government, of course, had other reasons for moving Iraqw into the area that had previously been grazed by Masai pastorialists. They believed the Iraqw to be more tractable, and they were agriculturalists, which meant they could be relied upon to produce cash crops. During 1937–1938, the government selected men from Irqwar Da'aw and the area surrounding Mbulu town to go to settle newly designated Iraqw tracts in the fertile area of volcanic soils just south of Ngorongoro Crater. They at first permitted only cattle "ranching" and no agriculture in these newly opened areas. The scheme was abandoned, however, in the next year because of tsetse fly and East Coast Fever which killed many of the cattle brought by the first settlers, and because of constant raids by the Masai who carried off what cattle remained.[1] The Iraqw continued to push for settlement of the area by Iraqw cultivators. The settlement of the area by cultivators meant, for the Iraqw, that land would be apportioned and that land rituals to mark and protect the borders could be performed. They believed the essential difference between themselves and the Masai to be agriculture. Thus, it is said, Michael Ahho loaded a truck with grindstones one night and partially buried them in a number of places all over the newly gazetted areas. Some days later, after the first settlement scheme had failed, he was asked to provide the government agricultural officer with justification for the Iraqw settlement of the land. He said nothing, so the story goes, but took the agricultural officer on a jaunt through the northern areas. He took him past every grindstone he had buried there and pointed it out, commenting that everyone knew the Masai never ground corn. At the end of the trip, Ahho ingenuously remarked with surprise that the Iraqw, who did grind corn, had obviously settled these areas long before the Masai had stolen it from them—witness the partially buried grindstones! The Iraqw elders today recite this story with obvious glee. They hold that it was this ruse that successfully manipulated the British settlement policy in their favor.

In the *slufay* recitation, the Masai threat is mocked. The elders reassure themselves and affirm that the Iraqw shall eventually win out over the Masai. They credit their success, now, to their practice of agriculture which they feel, correctly, has enriched them and driven the Masai from their former rich pastures in the north. That this could only have been accomplished in cooperation with the colonial government is acknowledged, but most old men today believe that it was the medicine of the

---

1. Agricultural District Book, entry of December 5, 1955, by M. H. F. Cooper, Agricultural Officer of Mbulu District.

TEXT 15
Slufay: Masai

Example A

1. *homo ko hano iya*	A certain enemy is in the north
2. *hanose iya*	A certain one in the north
3. *is a duwanqedamo*	He is a Masai warrior
4. *tsatay a wiriwiri*	His knife is nothing but a little worm
5. *xa, ngu kurmo tlehhi*	Ah, may hoes be made from it

Example B

1. *heko hano iya*	There is a certain man in the north
2. *heeda duwanqedamo*	That man is a Masai
3. *ku tsatay da'at*	With a red knife
4. *tsatay di soloti*	The knife falls
5. *i bara nanu hi'i*	It is flung into the wild greens
6. *amenar doren*	The women of our place
7. *ngu bara nanu wa sles*	Will find it in the vegetables
8. *kar gunsang amur sik*	It will cut up pumpkins
9. *o e'it*	And that's how it is

---

qwaslare that influenced the government in this way. In the Text 15 excerpts from a *slufay*, we note the stereotypical image of the Masai "with a red knife." This refers to the ochre with which the Masai paint all their possessions, but also to the bloodshed that their weapons cause. Again, we note that the Masai, like the Barabaig and the Bantu, are associated with a cardinal direction; in this case, north.

The Iraqw regard the Masai as a sort of natural force, one of the dangers inherent in the outside, that can be controlled and dealt with by ritual, magical means. The Iraqw and Masai do not intermarry. This is in contrast to the frequent intermarriages among Iraqw and Tatoga or Bantu-speaking people. Contacts among Iraqw and Masai men at cattle auctions are marked by formality and distance. There is very little economic exchange with the Masai (unless, of course, we regard cattle theft as a nonreciprocal exchange).

BANTU AGRICULTURALISTS

The relations between the Iraqw and the Bantu-speaking agriculturalists with whom they have contact are generally much less hostile. This is largely because there arises no conflict involving cattle. Since the Iraqw perceive actively cultivated land as "occupied," unlike open pastureland that they perceive as "empty," they have not encroached upon these lands. There has been a large and continual exchange of population among the Iraqw and the Bantu-speaking peoples, such as the Iramba, Isanzu, Wanyaturu, and the Wambugwe.

Robert Gray (1974) reports that Iraqw infants are commonly adopted by Wambugwe when these infants have been "polluted" by some circumstance of their birth or their parents' ritual condition. P. Pender-Cudlipp (1975), who has done fieldwork with Iramba, reports that the Iramba depend on the Iraqw for food during famines and have from time to time traded their own infants to the Iraqw for foodstuffs. In the small sample of population cited in the first part of this chapter, I found two women who came by trade from other ethnic groups (Wanyaturu and Gorowa) during famines. Exchange of population in this way is motivated among the Iraqw by the practice of exile and by their ideology of pollution, but also for economic reasons. For the Bantu-speaking peoples, the exchange is motivated primarily by economic necessity.

Trade in salt, metal, tools, jewelry, maize, and tobacco is common and well-established among the Iraqw and the Wambugwe, Iramba, and Wanyaturu. This trade is motivated by the natural difference in the productive potential of the different areas where each people reside, and by the shifting patterns of famine and plenty that are often strongly localized and unpredictable. This trade is carried out informally as occasion demands by groups of men from one domestic group or by a group of neighbors who travel with their goods loaded on donkeys until they find a suitable location or trading partner. Men will often travel hundreds of miles with their donkeys and empty sacks in search of grain to buy in times of famine, or will carry grain to places where they may sell it. Today there is a government cooperative that is required by law to take over all such trade, but it is frequently bypassed in the patterns of trade already long established in the region. This trade serves to bring the Iraqw into close contact with their agriculturalist neighbors.

Just as they evaluate and stereotype the Barabaig and Masai, the Iraqw evaluate and stereotype the Iramba, Wanyaturu, and Wambugwe. They divide these peoples into two groups: the *Manda'aw* and the *Manda uwa*. *Manda* is the name used to refer to Bantu-speaking peoples. This word is modified by a word denoting cardinal direction to give *Manda'aw* (a contraction of *Manda*, 'Bantu-speaking' and *da'aw*, 'east'; that is, the 'Bantu-speaking agriculturalists of the east'), and *Manda uwa* ('Bantu-speaking agriculturalists of the west'). *Manda'aw*, in ethnographic terms, are the Wambugwe who inhabit the salt pans and groundwater woodlands below the escarpment to the east of Irqwar Da'aw. *Manda uwa*, in turn, are the peoples known in the literature as the Iramba, Wanyaturu, Isanzu, and some other groups who live to the west of Irqwar Da'aw.

The *Manda uwa* are generally viewed as benevolent. Virtually all of the trade and interaction that the Iraqw carry on with other ethnic groups is with these people to the west, and with the Barabaig. The Iraqw view their interactions with these people as ordinary events that occasion very little comment, and reference to the *Manda uwa* is largely lacking in the *alqado, slufay,* songs, and stories. The *Manda'aw* (Mbugwe), on the other hand, are feared and frequently discussed as witches.

The Iraqw believe that the *Manda'aw* have medicines and magic that outdo their own. This was especially true during the period of this field research. Formerly the Iraqw put great faith in a *qwaslarmo* (ritual specialist) by the name of Nade Be'a, whose medicine was highly effective, but since his death in 1967, they have felt vulnerable and unprotected. Three sons have claimed rights to his powers and medicines, but they have not proved themselves capable, and many Iraqw remain skeptical. And so their estimation of the power and danger of the Wambugwe has risen. Text 16 was collected from an old *kahamusmo* in the Mbulu area. It discusses these fears.

In Text 16, the speaker makes the point that the Wambugwe are troubled by the same menace, but that the Wambugwe are better equipped to deal with the raids of the Masai. Their medicine is simply stronger and they do not fear the Masai warriors. Unfortunately for the Iraqw, the Wambugwe would refuse, according to this informant, to reciprocate with powerful medicine the gift of a cow given to them. Such a trade would be the normally expected behavior were the same gift to be made to a ritual expert of the *Manda uwa* (Iramba, Wanyaturu, Isanzu, etc.) or the Barabaig. In fact the Iraqw frequently participate in the rituals of the Barabaig and the Bantu agriculturalists to the west where they happen to live in proximity with them. But this is not the case with the Wambugwe. Although there is an exchange of population among the Iraqw and the Wambugwe, only ritually polluted infants and exiled youths go to live among the Wambugwe. I have not recorded a case where a Mbugwe person was accepted into Iraqw society. Although there is no direct hostility among them, the Iraqw and the Wambugwe generally keep their distance.

We observe, then, that the Iraqw divide the "foreign" peoples who live around them into four groups: the Masai, the Barabaig (or Tatoga), the western Bantu, and the eastern Bantu. This division does not reflect the natural political and territorial division of the people. In fact, there are many subdivisions of the Tatoga people, there are strongly marked differences of language and culture among the peoples whom the Iraqw call the "western Bantu," and they include the pastoral Sukuma in their category that I have glossed as 'Masai'. They ignore entirely the smaller hunting and gathering groups such as the Hadza and the Sandawe. They are more or less included in the *Manda uwa* classification.

TEXT 16
Alqado: **Mbugwe**

The Masai and the Wambugwe. The Masai don't mess around with the Wambugwe. They make a big commotion. The Masai herds his own cattle. They who cry out are the Wambugwe. They grind their tobacco in peace. The Masai herds his own cattle. And if a Masai approaches, they cry out loudly to one another, "eee! eee! eeeee!" They go to get their shields and their spears and sing [a battle chant]. . . . Their medicine is already prepared. It is passed over [the path]. The pathways are white [i.e., protected]. And when the Masai come to raid, the Wambugwe give it to them in their bodies. It enters the body of the Masai who comes to attack them. And the Masai return to them the cattle they have taken because of their magic. And their tongues loll out of their mouths. They die on the pathways, their tongues loll out of their mouths and they are finished completely. They die every which way. And for this reason the Masai fear them. The Iraqw do not know how to do this well. The Iraqw are cowards. They hide in holes. . . .

And if our elders take a cow [as a gift] to that big man of the Wambugwe, to give him, the *quaslarmo* will not agree. He says, "Is there nothing in your own *aya?* Look to your own *aya."* Now if a Masai appears, if we take him something, he will not agree to help. If the Wambugwe are troubled, a thing [gift] is taken. If they are troubled, the next day they return home. The thing which they take to the *qwaslarmo* is a calf. The safe house is that house which does that. Today, now, the cattle of the safe house is the house of the Wambugwe.

It will be noted, however, that although their classification clearly does not reflect the "objective" differences of culture and language among the people who neighbor them, their classification is strongly associated with the four cardinal directions. The Masai are always spoken of as being in the north (Lines 1–2 of Excerpt B, Text 15; Line 1 of Excerpt A, Text 15). The Barabaig are always "in the south" (Line 1, Text 14). The other two classifications are obviously based on direction.

Projective Space and Reciprocity:
Cultural Evaluation and Economic Action

The means by which the Iraqw classify other peoples is again based on a spatial metaphor. The axes of the cardinal directions yield a practical means by which foreign peoples may be categorized. This categorization by spatial axes is a *practical* categorization since it does not rely on an abstraction of spatial principles (as, for example, does our own terminology of kinship when we speak of *descent,* which clearly partakes of the spatial metaphor). The projective space of cardinal directions is part of what Poincare has called the "system of axes linked unalterably to our bodies, and carried about with us wherever we go" (Bourdieu, 1977:2).

This is not, however, the first order of classification. They first of all divide their own land and fellows from the land of other "foreign" peoples. The first principle of classification is this fundamental division into "self" and "other." Beyond this, another means of ordering their experience is required. The ethnocentric system of cardinal directions serves this function. It also allows them to form evaluative stereotypes of the peoples whom they so classify. We have noted already that among the Iraqw the east is considered dangerous, the place of witches. Consequently, the Wambugwe are seen as witches, as ritually and magically powerful people. The mere "facts" of the objective situation do not intrude: A brief review of police records reveals that the Wambugwe are quite as much the victims of Masai raids as are the Iraqw. On the other side, the Bantu of the west are dealt with quite directly and in a normal manner. The reciprocation of gifts and normal trade is held to be a possibility with these peoples and they, too, trade extensively with the Iraqw. With the Wambugwe, normal relations of reciprocity are not expected, and they are not received. The prejudice based on the evaluation of the polar coordinates of orientation rationalizes itself. By Iraqw reckoning, the Wambugwe do not trade with them because they are "behind" (*intsi*) them. The cultural evaluation of space, therefore, partially governs the movement of goods in space. Ritual encompasses economics; we have already seen that it encompasses politics.

In addition to the evaluation of the cardinal directions east and west, there is also a negative evaluation of the outside, whether east or west. Foreign people are called *homa.* The word is difficult to gloss succinctly because it also means an outside substance that causes disease in the body. Thus, *homa* figures as agents in the etiology of disease and other feelings of anxiety or lack of well being. There is a metaphorical relationship between the land of the Iraqw people and the body of the Iraqw person. This relationship is especially clearly marked in the women's initiation rite. *Marmo,* as this rite is called, involved the seclusion of young women for periods of up to a year. During this time, their ritual condition was especially vulnerable, and the boundaries that marked their confinement were carefully guarded. At the ceremony that marked their coming out, they were carefully questioned and scrutinized by an elder for any signs of "strangeness" or "outside influence"; that is, for the dangerous penetration of *homa.* Text 17 describes this procedure.

TEXT 17
Alqado: Homa **Disease**

[He lists the months of confiinement by naming them in order.] "Then they start to release them from confinement. The year is finished, you see. Now, they can't be allowed to pass out until they have gone to see the elder. And so they continue *marmo* until they are taken to this elder. They speak together in order to discover if there is any 'enemy' *[homa]* which will come out, or disease, or disorder of any sort that they may meet with. What they look for is that thing which is already inside. They prepare medicine to remove it, it is *ma'a'e* [the general term for purification medicines]. The *ma'a'e* of the whole country [i.e., like that used to bless the *aya*], they prepare it. Then they return again to the elder, they prepare *ma'a'e*, they prepare it. Afterward they are told, 'Begin to come out.' "

In Text 17 we see an explicit parallel drawn between the body of the initiate and the land of the *aya.* The *ma'a'e* medicine is designed to purify both of the influences of the outside. In both instances it is used where the identity and corporateness of the group is to be defined and affirmed. In the case of land ritual, it is the identity and corporateness of the territorial unit of the *aya.* In the case of the *marmo* rites, it is the identity and corporateness of women's bodies that is affirmed. There is no parallel ritual for men, and no parallel concern for the dangerous penetration of *homa.* Since the *marmo* ('coming out') signaled a woman's eligibility for marriage and for sexual relations, the metaphorical comparison of the woman's body with the *aya,* vulnerable to penetration under attack by outsiders, appears to arise naturally from practical experience.

M. Sahlins (1972) proposes a conceptual model that is especially interesting in consideration of the Iraqw data. He postulates a continuum of reciprocity beginning with "generalized reciprocity, the solidary extreme $(A \rightleftarrows B)$" through "balanced reciprocity, the midpoint $(A \rightleftarrows B)$" to "negative reciprocity, the unsociable extreme $(A \rightleftharpoons B)$." In his conception, *generalized reciprocity* is the altruistic mode of giving without necessarily expecting or getting a return; *balanced reciprocity* is direct exchange in which objects of like value are exchanged; *negative reciprocity* is "the attempt to get something for nothing, with impunity." He then proposes that this continuum of reciprocity is related to kinship distance, such that the household group is characterized by generalized reciprocity among its members. Balanced reciprocity is observed in interactions among those of greater kinship distance (or other socially defined "distances"), while negative reciprocity is observed in interactions that involve people with the extreme of "distance" between them. On first sight this fits very well the observations of Iraqw interactions within the domestic group, the section, the *aya,* and beyond. But it is not exactly right. Sahlins (1972:198) states his position as follows:

> Kinship–residential groupings from this perspective comprise ever widening comembership spheres: the household, the local lineage, perhaps the village, the subtribe, tribe, other tribes—the particular plan of course varies. The structure is a hierarchy of levels of integration, but from the inside and on the ground it is a series of concentric circles. Social relations of each circle have a specific quality—household relations, lineage relations, and so on—and except as the sectoral divisions be cut through by other organizations of kinship solidarity—say nonlocalized clans or personal kindreds—relations within each sphere are more solidary than relations of the next, more inclusive sector. Reciprocity accordingly inclines toward balance and chicane in proportion to sectoral distance. In each sector, certain modes of reciprocity are characteristic or dominant: Generalized modes are dominant in the narrowest spheres and play out in wider spheres, balanced reciprocity is characteristic of intermediate sectors, chicane of the most peripheral spheres. In brief, a general model of the play of reciprocity may be developed by superimposing the society's sectoral plan upon the reciprocity continuum.

In the Iraqw case, this relationship between the quality of reciprocity and distance holds for the household, the neighborhood, the section, and the *aya,* but beyond this the relationship partly breaks down since the valuation of the cardinal directions intrudes. The model would lead us to expect that relations between the *aya* and the outside—the extreme of social distance, would be characterized by negative reciprocity; that is, by theft, chicanery, and deceit. This is certainly true for the relations between the Iraqw and the Barabaig, and between the Iraqw and the Masai. These two people are seen as living to the right (north) and to the left (south) of the primary valued axes of orientation, the east–west axis. Here we see that the spatial ideology of the Iraqw interferes with the expected relationship between the Iraqw and the western Bantu and eastern Bantu. We should see negative reciprocity between them. Instead, we see relations of balanced reciprocity betwen the Iraqw and their neighbors to the (positively valued) west, and the utter denial of relationships with their neighbors to the (negatively valued) east. The valuation of the east–west axis skews the patterns of social relations that we would expect both from the Iraqw's own "theory" of social order and value, and from Sahlins' model of the continuum of reciprocity.

The cultural values associated with the cardinal directions east, west, north, and south—that is, with projective space that takes the human body as its ultimate referent—clearly interacts with purely economic motivations and factors (e.g., localized famines) and with other aspects of Iraqw ideology (notably the ideology of pollution and exile). The projective coordinates provide the base metaphor for classification of surrounding ethnic groups. The spatial polarities implicit in this ordering are appropriated into a cultural system of values. These values then act directly on the patterns of trade and of demographic exchange.

In contrast to the valued polarity of ethnic categories, we note the absence of such evaluations within Iraqw society itself. Economically productive social units are organized segmentally and defined on the basis of the land they occupy and use. Age- and sex-based categories cut across the whole and provide the means for mobilizing larger groups of people for ritual activity (and today for government projects). These categories are organized as simple moieties: youth (*masomba*) and elders (*barise*), men and women. Economic activity, exchange of goods, services, and of persons between age- and sex-groups and among households within one *aya* are generalized and diffuse. Beyond the borders of the *aya,* exchanges of all sorts are balanced and reciprocal or hostile according to the disposition of trading partners with respect to the culturally valued spatial coordinates.

Chapter 6

Social Order and Social Control

Ideology and Politics

The chief political divisions within Iraqw society are those that exist between the elders and the youth, and between the bounded, inside region of the *aya* and the hostile outside. It is more easily appreciated that the division between age and youth should be political, in this case, than that the division between the inside and the outside should be so, since the politics of elders and youths is *the* politics of many African societies. Where distinctions of inside–outside have been described as being characteristic of one society or another, the dichotomy is demonstrated in the context of discussions of their "world view" or "symbolism." It is not at first obvious that this fundamental spatial—or topological—distinction should be considered as a political feature of the society. In this chapter, as in Chapter 4 on the *masay* ritual, I begin to show that the relations of space—which are represented as insideness or "middleness" as opposed to outsideness or "wilderness"—are, in practice, political relations.

This is true because the sides of insideness and outsideness (which are put into practice in the performance of the *masay* ritual or in the use of exile as a moral sanction exercised by the community) are "usable" ideas, not simply expressive ideas. They are "usable" in that they are cultural appropriations of portions of the landscape or physical environment. Appropriation is an act of definition: The definition or delineation of a space is a cultural appropriation of that space. And, any appropriation of space, of land in particular—but also of more abstract spaces such as the sky (*dori*) from which rain comes and where spirits reside—must be considered as a political act since it involves power over persons and

133

over the productive resources of the society. We must be careful not to confuse the cultural definition (and thus, appropriation) of the landscape with what might be called the material conditions or ecological factors. I am not concerned here with the relation between the *ideology* of a culture and the *material base* of society in the way these terms have come to be used (e.g., in Terray, 1972 or Godelier, 1977). Although I shall be talking indirectly about the appropriation of material resources in this chapter and in Chapter 7, I do not take the view that the relations of production determine the ideology of the society. In fact, I take quite the opposite view: It is my aim to show that the cultural formulations of the Iraqw, conceived and executed in a particular social and cultural environment, determine not only the form and practice of politics in the society, but also determine the direction of its history. As we have already seen, the fundamental cultural formulations of the Iraqw are definitions (i.e., appropriations) of bounded and closed spaces by means of verbal and ritual action.

My primary premise is that speech and ritual are *not* simply *expressions* of world view or reflections of the structures of social relations (although they may also be these). In this analysis speech and ritual are *practical* activities, motivated by a need for social control and performed for the purpose of organizing other activities in comprehensible and meaningful ways. In Iraqw society, the political functions of speech and ritual are perhaps all the more obvious since there is, in fact, no separation—in their own terms and in ours—of the practice of politics and the practice of ritual.

The Fundamental Cultural and Political Oppositions

There are three sets of terms that we must attend to. First, the fundamental *social* (and temporal) *opposition* between elders (*barise*) and youths (*masomba*); secondly, the *spatial opposition* between the inside and the outside in its various levels and manifestations; and finally, the *evaluative opposition* between the good and the evil in all things and persons. These latter evaluative distinctions also apply to space and society. There are good and evil persons as there are good and evil sides of a hill, directions, or areas. The social and spatial distinctions interact with each other in more complex ways, but it should be clear to the reader that neither can be understood without reference to the other.

It is the elders as a group who exercise legitimate power. This means that it is the elders who exercise control over the sources of power and the political instruments of social control. In the Iraqw social praxis, power derives not from resort to physical force or the threat of their resort to physical force, but on the "force" of their speech and the power and danger of the outside. The power of the word, in this case, is not the magical power of the word in itself, but the performative force of the word in its utterance by a person, or persons, with authority. The power that the elders wield against their juniors is the power of the curse, *lo'o*, and of the accusation (*kwasleemuut*) in meetings over which they preside. This power rests in turn on the shared belief of everyone concerned that the elders' course *is* powerful and that it *is* legitimate. These beliefs are communicated and reinforced in the Iraqw oral literature. The ultimate sanction available to the community is exile. This depends for its effectiveness on the solidarity of the community in the face of social transgressions, on the consistent expression of disapprobation toward the offenders by all of the community, and on the idea that there exists a dangerous and inherently punishing "outside" into which the offender may be sent. Thus, the ultimate political sanction that the elders may apply rests not on anything physical, but on the cultural definition of the environment in which they live, and on the effective communication of these cultural precepts. And, in the scheme of things, it is the elders who exile, the youth who are exiled.

This cultural division between the inside and the outside has important political implications on two levels. Since the exiled youth must necessarily go into the lands that surround the constituted *aya,* and since if one is to survive one must begin to cultivate in previously uncultivated land that is usually the pastureland of the pastoral peoples surrounding the Iraqw, the practice of exile plays a central role in the social ecology of the region. In fact, exile, and the subsequent expansion movement to which it led, is an appropriation of land in a process of territorial expansion. But this appropriation of external land in the process of territorial expansion is only one aspect of the cultural appropriation that is involved in the practice of exile. The other is the cultural appropriation of external violence in the internal maintenance of social order. The cultural definition of the *aya*—which creates, by the fact of its existence, a peaceful and secure inside, and a violent and dangerous outside—is what makes exile an effective sanction. The elders' power thus derives, in part, from their control over the danger inherent in the outside that is used as an effective threat in the maintenance of social order within the *aya* itself. The culturally defined inside and the outside result in appropriation on two levels: the appropriation of the land in the process of expansion, and appropriation of external violence in the internal maintenance of social control.

The pervasive distinction between the inside and outside in Iraqw culture is analogous to the distinction between the household and the domain of the whole *aya* which is outside of it. We have already seen in what respects this opposition is analogous to the opposition of the *aya* to the wilderness (*slaa'*), but we shall see also how this organizational opposition plays a part in the maintenance of social order in the *aya*. Just as the danger of the outside is appropriated by the elders as a source of political power by using it as a sanction for social transgressions, the verbal instruments by which they exercise their power—the curse and the accusation—are also associated with the public, political domain of the *aya* which contrasts with the interior and private domain of the household.

But in order to carry the discussion of Iraqw politics and rituals substantially further, it is first necessary to discuss the evaluation of social acts and roles. We have already noted the Iraqw concept of good and evil. The idea of goodness is associated with the unity of the solidarity of the community, while the idea of evil is associated, in contrast, with individual action that, in their view, is more than likely to be witchcraft, sorcery, or sinful behavior. It is in these evaluative notions, and in the act of judging individual persons as sinful (*irange*) or as witches (*da' alusamo*), that we can see most clearly how it is that cultural concepts are applied in the attempt to achieve and maintain social order in an egalitarian society.

I shall first of all discuss the Iraqw concepts of witchcraft, sin, and personal pollution as the best means of illustrating the practice of politics in Iraqw society. It is notable that the concepts of 'sin', *irange,* and 'personal pollution', *meta,* are peculiarly Iraqw concepts that are not shared by their neighbors. In the following discussion of sin and personal pollution, I attempt to show how these concepts are conditioned by the political opposition of elders to youth, and by their concepts of the spatial order of their environment. Since I have not maintained that these ideas are merely representations of underlying and determining social or material reality, I show how cultural ideas are submitted to practice in the political arena. I do not wish to suggest, however, that cultural forms are static: I therefore turn, in the final section of this chapter, to a discussion of the creative and generative aspects of Iraqw culture that allow it to adapt to the changing ecology of the region, and in adapting, to change itself in a process of self-regulation.

The Idea of Witchcraft

Although the idea of sin and personal pollution may be unusual in Africa, what is common to much of Africa are a set of varied beliefs and practices that have been called sorcery and witchcraft. Evans-Pritchard, in his study of the Azande, drew a definitional distinction between the *sorcerer* who willed his victim's demise or misfortune and accomplished these ends by magical means, and the *witch,* who caused death or misfortune because of some innate and unavoidable disposition or evil capacity of which even the witch might remain ignorant (Evans-Pritchard, 1936). Both of these beliefs, for the Azande, were predicated on the notion of an ineluctable net that bound all of creation together in its multiple forms and influences. These ideas have had wide currency in the literature, and indeed seem to be well distributed throughout Africa. The Iraqw are no exception, and have a full complement of beliefs concerning sorcery, witchcraft, and the mutual influences between men and the unquiet dead, as well as beliefs about were-hyena, were-leopard, and the evil eye. All of these beliefs exist in addition to beliefs about what I have chosen to translate as "sin" and "pollution." I shall contrast the ideas of sin and pollution with ideas of sorcery and witchcraft. This gives some assurance that what I translate as "sin" and "pollution," some other ethnographer would not translate as "witchcraft" and "sorcery." The ideas are clearly distinguished in Iraqw thought, speech, and action.

The witch and the sorcerer are distinguished among the Iraqw much as Evans-Pritchard tells us they are distinguished among the Azande: the one active, the other a passive agent of evil. The 'sorcerer', *da'alusamo* (or *da'âlusamo*—the words are phonologically different but their meanings converge) is a person who "wishes evil" on his neighbors. Alternately, the sorcerer may be said to prepare medicines and charms with which his neighbors are injured or ruined. Such a person may be anyone. He (or she) is frequently described as a 'man among men' (*hée do hée*) or a 'man in the house of men'. Iraqw sermons and moral injunctions, of which there are a number of types, frequently list specific fates that "men who wish good" wish to befall "men who wish evil." They say, "If it is a grandfather, his council chamber should fall (on him)"; "If it is a grandmother, better she should die"; "If it is a young man, he should meet with misfortune in the hunt or be killed in a raid, his weapons carried home without him by his friends"; "If it is a young mother, better she should die in childbirth"; and, so on for a number of other social and family roles from which such evil manifestations might from time to time be expected. The list of fates of the sorcerer and the witch is specific, so that if anyone should come to the end so described, it is held up as proof of his or her ill-intent or some other evil or impure quality. In contrast to the sorcerer, who actively contrives or wishes evil, we must consider the witch, *wakusamo,* who is conceived as an evil presence in a person who is otherwise good. In a moment we shall consider this balance of good and evil in the world according to the Iraqw view, but here I will only mention that this evil may be quite unintentional, although it may be unavoidable.

I have recorded two slight variants of the word for *sorcerer*:

da'alusamo and *da'âlusamo.* The â sound is significant in Iraqw, and the
two words are related to different sets of words. The first, *da'alusamo*
(without the pharyngealized second vowel) is semantically related to the
verb *da'a,* 'to pierce'. It may also bear a relationship to *dá'aye,* 'liver', although the tone of the latter is different. (This may or may not be significant since the tone pattern, and its relationship either to syntax or meaning in Iraqw, has not yet been worked out.) The second variant of the
word *sorcerer, da'âlusamo,* is related to the words *da'â,* 'to burn or scorch
or parch something', *da'âra,* 'ashes', and *da'ât,* 'to be red; the color red'.
The set of meanings comprised by these related words would appear to us
diverse and possibly without pattern, but it is really quite a typical constellation of associations in many other African cultures. Among the
Ndembu studied by Victor Turner (1967), the color red is clearly associated with witchcraft, especially with the blood that witchcraft in its
necrophagous aspect is believed to expose. In a number of instances the
liver is associated with sorcery and witchcraft, and is often considered to
be the "organ" in which such antisocial propensity exists in a physical
form. Both witches and sorcerers are said to either burn, *da'â,* or pierce,
da'a, their victim. I suspect that this particular constellation of meanings
has resulted from the fortuitous similarity of sound between *da'â* and *da'a*
in Iraqw, and from the influence of a set of ideas and associations concerning witchcraft and sorcery that are widespread in eastern and southern African cultures. The Iraqw have in fact absorbed many people of
diverse ethnic and linguistic origins, and such interference of sound and
meaning is only to be expected. The elder Iraqw say that witchcraft and
sorcery are un-Iraqw, having been introduced among them by immigrant
peoples, especially Bantu people such as the Iramba or the Nyaturu. The
Nyamwezi are frequently said to be especially good thieves as well as
witches and sorcerers. Furthermore, witchcraft and sorcery may cause
their harm through the introduction of a substance or quality called *homo,*
a word that also means 'enemy' or 'outsider'.

   The word for witchcraft, *wake,* and its agent *wakusamo,* are more
difficult to gloss since I have not discovered any related sets of words.
They appear, however, to be more general terms, and the sorcerer may be
subsumed under this heading. The *wakusamo,* quite simply, is a man who
causes evil. It also is associated with outsiders.

The Ideas of Sin and Personal Pollution

   I have elaborated on the range of meanings associated with the concepts of witchcraft and sorcery to be able to contrast them to the concepts
of pollution, *metimami* or *meta,* and to the concept of 'sin', *irange.* The

first category is a metaphysical *quality* of impurity and danger, the second is an *act* against the moral order that places its perpetrator in moral and political danger from the community that this act has harmed. Both conditions are evil. In the case of pollution the condition may result through no intentional fault, and frequently results from accidents. *Irange*, 'sin', on the other hand, is quite clearly an intentional act for which the "sinner" either cannot or refuses to repent.

All of the things of which I have spoken are, for the Iraqw, evil or bad things. In narrative and verse, a number of words are used to characterize these conditions and actions. They are called evil (*tlakw* or *tlakwema*), and they result in dirt or defilement (*tsuma*). They are spoken of as 'hateful things' and 'abominations' (*waqasi*). The latter term is related to the verb *wagaas*, 'to cause hate or to be dispicable', and to *waqat*, an obscene word meaning 'guts' or 'offal' as opposed to the more polite *durumi*, 'entrails' or 'intestines'. In contrast to all of these things are 'good things', *muru hhó* or *tlahhó*, and 'men who wish good', *muk a hhó slaa*.

This contrast between good and bad is extremely important in the world view of the Iraqw. In the world there is inevitably some good and some bad, and all people are either good people or bad. A person may not know whether he is "good" or "bad" until some event occurs or some sign is seen that brings out this unseen characteristic.

At this juncture, let us review a number of central theological and cosmological concepts, which will make the exposition of Iraqw ideas of pollution more easily comprehensible. The first of these is the idea of the moral unity of the community, the group of inhabitants of a ritually and politically defined territory. The community so defined is a morally corporate body; that is, the evil or good of any of its members affects the whole lot. This moral unity has a power in and of itself that is expressed in virtually all forms of verbal performance. In the performance of the *slufay*, for example, the audience is exhorted to agree, to affirm its mutual accord. The phrase "it is as if you were carrying a burden, then the heavens and earth must agree" (Text 5A), for example, asserts the moral force of mutual accord which, if completely and fully accomplished, will necessarily set things to right. It is asserted that the goodness of a few shall obscure the evil of the many in the view of *lo'a*. This pervading dichotomy of good and evil has its analogue with the heavens (*dorí*) and the sky; *lo'a* is believed to be good, but may cause harm as well. The *netlangw* are the spirits of the earth who live below the surface of the earth. They are especially associated with evil. This dichotomy is also symbolized in the Iraqw evaluation of their environment: The west side of hills, or the west-facing slope of a valley is the good side; the other side, the evil or cold side. In oral performances such as the *slufay*, witches, sorcerers, the impure, and sinful are admonished to "get behind the mountain, [to stay] on the 'back side' of the hill." In drawing these distinctions and in evaluating them, the features of the landscape are appropriated as cultural symbols.

Finally, I would like to mention again the concept of the "unknown cause." It can never be fully ascertained, they hold, whether evil is from "the hand of man" or "the hand of God." Understanding these concepts, we are in a position to understand the concept of personal pollution: It is the evil from the hand of God that most often leads to such a state, whereas sorcery and witchcraft are the evils of the "hand of man."

Pollutions: Definitions and Implications

Pollutions, *meta,* result from unfortunate events or accidents and generally require a sacrifice and a period of confinement before they are said to be wiped away or "cooled." The verb from which it is derived, *met-,* means 'to be left over, to remain'. The word for 'harvest', *metangw,* is related to it, and means more precisely, the 'result' or 'residuum' of the harvest—what is left over when the chaff and straw have been removed. Pollution, then, for the Iraqw is the evil residuum of an unfortunate event. *Metiim-,* a word we may gloss as 'to be impure; to be in a ritually unclean state', expresses an idea of the residual essence of evil that derives from the event. What's more, this evil may affect the whole of the community since to ignore it will anger either the *netlangw* or *lo'a* and bring misfortune upon everyone. The person or persons in the state of *meta* are excluded from all human company for varying lengths of time.

There are at least 10 sorts of pollution:

1. *meta xawir dirang*—resulting from the death of an elder male or female member of the household
2. *meta xawir masmo*—resulting from the death of an unmarried youth in the household
3. *meta xawir na'áy*—resulting from the death of a babe in arms
4. *meta hare* or *hotay*—resulting from the spontaneous abortion of a fetus, or from a "stuck pregnancy," one that they say "refuses to grow"
5. *meta doroway*—resulting from the birth of a child out of wedlock in the house of the girl's parents
6. *meta soroh*—resulting from the breach birth of a child, or from one born with teeth, or from one whose teeth come in in the wrong order

7. *metar tsixitu makita'o*—resulting from being clawed by a leopard or
   other wild animal and so shedding blood on the ground
8. *metar muqsli*—resulting from being cut with iron so that blood is
   shed on the ground
9. *metar dori* or *metar tlafi*—resulting from death as the result of being
   struck by lightning
10. *metar tsere*—resulting from the shedding of blood in a sacrifice

Different action is taken in each case to "cool" the pollution. In the
first case, that resulting from the death of an elder male or female of
the household, an animal is sacrificed in the center of the house after the
deceased and all of his possessions have been either buried or destroyed.
The sacrificial victim is immediately split open, the contents of the
stomach removed, and the house and all of its implements are blessed by
sprinkling them with some of the chyme. The members of the household
then endure an isolation of up to a year's time. In the case of the death
of a youth, or of a babe in arms, the sacrifice is roughly the same, but the
period of seclusion is shorter. The pollutions resulting from a spontaneous abortion of the fetus, or from a "stuck pregnancy" (whatever that
may be!), place the woman in ritual danger until she conceives again
or until the fetus starts to grow again, in which case the pollution is over
and she may interact freely with others. The pollution of death from
lightning pertains in particular to the place where this has occurred, rendering it strictly taboo. The survivors of a lightning strike must sacrifice
an animal and remain in seclusion for up to a year. If a house is struck,
it is immediately abandoned. The pollutions resulting from the shedding
of blood, whether as the result of being clawed by an animal of the wild,
being cut by iron, or in the course of legitimate sacrifice in some other
connection requires a period of seclusion of two weeks to several months,
according to the prescription of the ritual specialist.

I would like to comment more fully on the pollutions resulting from
the birth out of wedlock of a child in the parents' house, the breach birth
of a child, and the birth of a child in other unpropitious circumstances.
Such events are common, despite the apparent strength of the sanctions.
If a girl were to give birth to a child in her own house having not been
married, that house is abandoned and the family is forced to leave. In
most cases the girl goes outside to give birth, but she must not keep the
child. Such children are called *doroway* and are described as children
with neither mother nor father. They are given away to people of another
ethnic group, or they are killed by placing them on the threshold of the
doorway and driving the cattle out over them in the morning. The same
is done for breach-birth children, children who are born with teeth (I do

not know of any instance in which this has actually happened, but like
the "stuck pregnancy," the Iraqw believe it happens), and children whose
teeth come in abnormally. If the child is not given away, then the mother
herself is driven away. Whatever the case, the rest of her household must
remain in forced seclusion for up to a year. None of their neighbors will
greet them. They must not approach streams, springs, or wells (water is
brought to them by a neighbor's child and left at the edge of the courtyard
in front of the house). If they are approached by one who does not know
of their condition, they call out *"aten a metimaan,"* " 'we are in a state of
pollution'." (The word *metimani,* by which Swahili-speakers or people of
other ethnic groups describe these customs, derives from this phrase.) In
all cases of pollution, the period of enforced seclusion is difficult to endure, and in fact, no one attempts to endure it unless there is much at
stake that would be lost should they choose exile over seclusion.

The Iraqw today are generally quick to assure the outsider that
metimani is no longer practiced. Nevertheless, I recorded four cases of its
practice in the village where I lived, and heard of many more. One of
these involved a young girl who was made pregnant at a dance, by a boy
from a distant territory. Proceedings were immediately begun to effect the
marriage of this girl to the young man before the birth of the child. It
looked as if everything was going smoothly when about half way through
her pregnancy the girl refused to be married. She could not be convinced.
The negotiations were dropped and the girl moved to the town of Mbulu
which constitutes a sort of hole in the Iraqw territorial constitution. She
stayed there with a woman who had left for the same reason (pregnancy)
and who was related to her mother (the exact relationship was never
clear). She stayed in the town until, only a few weeks before the birth,
she inexplicably returned home to visit her mother. When she began
having pains one night, pandemonium broke loose. The girl and her
mother came to my hut at one o'clock in the morning on a pitch black
night, both of them in a terrible emotional state, howling pitiful prayers
to *lo'a* and the *metlangw,* and begging to be taken immediately to the
hospital in Mbulu 12 miles away down a mountain road scarcely passable
in daylight. It was clear that the girl would be forced to have her baby in
the bush if I did not take her, and so I capitulated and took her down the
mountain. As it turned out she was only having gas pains: The child was
not born until a week later. Nevertheless, her family was put in a state of
metimani and remained so 6 months later when I left. The girl never
returned. She went to live near the Ngorongoro reserve on the very edges
of the Iraqw settlement and did day labor on some of the seed farms there.
All knowledge of her and the child was disclaimed by the members of her
family, except for her young brother who spilled the beans for a ride in

the car. In another similar case, the girl was allowed to stay, provided she lived in a small isolated house in a bushy ravine and did not approach water. She remained in the house for about 6 months while water and food were brought to her by a child. Another instance involved pollution resulting from sacrifice. This particular man had been chosen to carry out the sacrifice in the *masay* ceremony. In this case no blood was shed in the sacrifice itself since the victim was smothered instead of killed with a knife. Blood was shed, however, in the butchering of the animal for the feast. The sacrifice was secluded for a two-week period in this case, the period being prescribed by the ritual expert in charge of the ceremony.

During the 15 months I was in Irqwar Da'aw, I did not witness the death of any older persons, but when the child of a Christian family died of measles, the father, a good Catholic who denied following the custom of *metimani,* cancelled a long-planned trip to Arusha for work and went into partial seclusion with his wife.

Despite denials, belief in pollutions such as the ones I have mentioned are apparently held by most of the Iraqw. Recent theorists who have dealt with the problem of pollution agree that the beliefs and practices associated with it are meant to reassert the rightful order in the face of impending chaos (Douglas, 1970). Ideas of pollution are used, as Mary Douglas says, "to express a view of the social order" (Douglas, 1966:3). Among the Iraqw the boundaries of the person, of the space of the domestic group, and of the territory are ever emphasized in myriad aspects of their ritual and their oral literature. It is clear that the condition of *meta* results from circumstances that involve a breach of boundary, a passing, or transgression. The person is bounded and defined in space and time by birth, death, and while alive, by his or her skin. All of the types of pollution involve a breach of these boundaries. The shedding of blood is most dangerous where it is brought about by some agent of the outside. Wild animals symbolize the uninhabited wilds; iron, the attack of enemies of other ethnic groups. (The Iraqw do not make iron, but acquire it from outside, from those in fact whom they most fear, the Masai and Tatoga pastoralists.) The sacrifice, and death by lightning, put man in direct contact with the powerful and dangerous realm of the heavens. Incidently, the killing of the impure child on the threshold places this dangerous act neither in the house nor in the land; it takes place in the interstice which is neither here nor there, and so the death of the polluted child occasions no pollution in itself.

In the face of the death of a member of the domestic group, the seclusion reasserts their unity, their boundedness, in spite of their loss. Again quoting Mary Douglas, "ideas about separating, purifying, demarcating, and punishing transgressions have as their main function to impose system on an inherently untidy experience. It is only by exaggerating the difference between within and without, above and below, male and female, with and against, that a semblance of order is created." Pollution is believed to seriously threaten the moral unity of the whole community. By asserting the unity of the domestic group in its misfortune, through seclusion and overemphasis of boundary, or by reinforcing the boundary of the person whose boundaries have been breached, again, by seclusion, the Iraqw express their view of the importance of unity and boundary.

'Sin', *irange,* is a transgression of a different, probably less serious type. The community of the territory holds collectively the responsibility for its spiritual and economic well-being. *Irange* is a willful wrong perpetrated against the community, or against one's elders (who represent the will of the community). Such offenses as extending one's field into the public thoroughfares, sexual impropriety, refusal to accept the judgments of the elders or to participate in community work projects are all counted as *irange.* Theft or fighting, although strongly disapproved, are not *irange* since they are offenses against another person, not against the community.

Irange is generally punished by the levying of a fine, say, of a few chickens, goats, or cattle, depending on the severity of the offense and the judgment of the elders who meet to consider the case. In really severe cases, the felon is exiled to that area beyond the borders of the territory and the neighboring ethnic groups—a sort of no-man's land that has until recently surrounded the Iraqw homelands. If the person is unable or unwilling to pay the fine, he or she is exiled.

Pollution, the residual evil of an unfortunate event, and sin, the intentional breach of public law and morality, have in common that they offend against the established order. Sin and sorcery are directly perpetrated wrongs, but sin, unlike sorcery which offends against another individual, offends against the community. Pollution and witchcraft are passively acquired essences both dangerous and powerful, but pollution results from the breach of the cosmological order, the definition of the "person" and the "domestic group," while witchcraft is merely the evil side of man's character that balances the good. The witch, the sorcerer, and the person who commits *irange* are subject to exile. The person in the condition of *meta* is secluded in a place for a period of time by way of reinforcing boundaries that have been imperiled. The polluted person may also choose exile if he or she has nothing to lose by doing so. These beliefs and the means of coping with the conditions in which they result has created a powerful social pump that continually forces people without high stakes in the establishment to the periphery and into contact with their neighbors.

The Practice of Exile

The continual trickle of people out of the hills and valleys of Irqwar Da'aw is, in fact, just the sort of control that is essential if the Iraqw are to remain as they were, a small and isolated group of people in the highlands along the Rift Valley Escarpment.

The occasions that result in pollution among the Iraqw are also dealt with ritually in other cultures of Africa. What provokes comment, however, is the particular form it has taken among the Iraqw. Wherever pollution beliefs are significant, we usually also note that social boundaries are strongly and clearly marked. These boundaries may be between hierarchically arranged castes as in South Asia, between economic specialists such as blacksmiths in parts of West Africa, or between ethnic and territorial units as on the Mbulu Plateau. In my estimation the cultural emphasis on boundaries, and the ideas of pollution and sin that reinforce these boundaries, have come about as the result of their process of adjustment to the exigencies presented by the complex ethnic environment in which they live. Paradoxically, these notions created the conditions under which large numbers of Iraqw could move outward without confronting such social boundaries. The ones who were exiled were, in effect, men, women, and children without countries. Robert Gray, who had done some fieldwork with the Wambugwe, a Bantu-speaking group of people who live below Irqwar Da'aw in the bottom of the Rift Valley, tells me that he "discovered that a number of Wambugwe had been born to Iraqw parents but were adopted by Mbugwe foster parents as newborn infants because the circumstances of their birth contaminated them with inexpungeable pollution" (Gray, 1974). On the other side of the Iraqw, George Klima (1970) reports that the Barabaig, a subtribe of the Tatoga pastoralists, frequently have wives who were originally Iraqw but who have been forced to move out of Iraqw land as the result of their pollutions. The same thing has been observed and reported among all of the people who surround the Iraqw, with the possible exception of the Masai, about whom there is very little information regarding this.

The act of exile removed from those who went into the frontier their Iraqw-ness. The boundary of Iraqw land and Iraqw culture was permeable to those who had suffered pollution or who had committed some wrong against the established order. These practices both expressed a view of the social order and provided the ideological justification for its enforcement: Personal pollution constituted a danger to the productive potential of the land. Its effectiveness as a political sanction, however, depended on the political use that was made of the real potential for violence that did in fact exist beyond the borders of the *aya.* We shall return to the use of "external violence" in the Iraqw political life in Chapter 7.

The Iraqw notions of pollution, *meta,* the residuum of the event that threatens in some way the conceptual boundaries of life; of sin, *irange,* the intentional act that directly transgresses upon the constituted social and economic order; and, the practice of either seclusion or exile in response to pollution and sin, have far-reaching ethnological and historical implications.

Historically, we see that by the 1930s the continuous process of forced emigration into the frontier between the established territory of the "morally upright" Iraqw and the lands of the other peoples had created a large peripheral area that was inhabited by polluted and sinful Iraqw. This region was, we might say, incipiently Iraqw territory. At this time the British government successfully squelched the raids of the pastoralist peoples against the agriculturalists such as the Iraqw. Greatly benefiting from this British colonial policy, which favored agriculture over pastoralism, the Iraqw took advantage of this peace. A number of *kahamuse* led a movement whereby they carried medicines and rituals to these incipient areas. By performing the *masay* rituals, these areas were reintegrated into the fabric of moral society. Men who did this were able to transform their roles as ritual functionaries into outright political chiefs in the areas that they had "rescued" from ignominy by means of their ritual performances. At this point the territory inhabited by the Iraqw expanded explosively.

Their rapid expansion into the whole of the Mbulu Plateau was permitted by the colonially imposed peace and by colonially directed campaigns against sleeping sickness, but this very process of expansion has brought with it a tremendous degree of social disorganization and the loss or weakening of some of the institutional social controls that we have so far discussed. Yet they have maintained a high degree of cohesiveness and sense of purpose through it all. Directly as a result of their history of social disintegration and migration, Iraqw culture is a culture very much engaged in the act of creating itself.

The Control of Social Production and Reproduction

Whereas up to now we have talked about the maintenance of social order within society, we must now turn to a different problem of social control, that of the production and reproduction of cultural and social forms. In the analysis of political society, we are most often content to consider only the control exercised over material production and over the distribution of its products. The necessary control over the production of social forms is frequently neglected. In a well-regulated, slowly changing society, this aspect may be less important than it is in the Iraqw case where new cultural and social forms constantly have to be created in response to changing conditions, especially in this century. In Chapter 8 we shall turn to the history of this century to examine these changes more carefully, but here we shall examine the production of new cultural and social forms in a more or less synchronic frame.

In my experience with the Iraqw, one thing that frequently struck me was the apparently ad hoc nature of many of their rites and rituals. When a group of elders failed to light a ritual fire by the "traditional method," by rubbing sticks together, they unhesitatingly pitched them away as someone produced a lighter from his pocket and lit the fire in an instant. Or, when the Tanzanian government insisted that the Iraqw and the Masai make up and be friends, a group of ritual experts got together and invented a ritual that involved a Masai and an Iraqw woman exchanging infants and suckling them at each other's breast. There were contradictions in their beliefs and practices. For example, a rite that was designed to expunge the pollution resulting from death created pollution itself through the sacrifice of the animal.

In fact, the Iraqw culture is very ad hoc. Its history has deprived it of historical depth and of well-established traditions. Although one sees resemblances in many of its aspects to beliefs and institutions of neighboring ethnic groups, these are combined in ways that are characteristically Iraqw. Migrations and assimilations of people from many different cultural backgrounds have presented a store of content to which the people who call themselves Iraqw have given form. To accomplish this process, there must be both communication of that content and communication about cultural content. In the enterprise of creating culture, the *slufay*, as a legitimate and routine way of communicating about culture in certain specified contexts, plays a central, creative role. It is the spatially and ritually defined group for whom the *slufay* is useful and meaningful. Certain types of discourse are associated with or appropriate to either the household or the *aya*, but usually not both. This distinction is fundamental to the way in which discourse functions as a creative institution in this society, and to the way the limits of creativity are set in social practice.

There are roughly four types of oral literature distinguished by the Iraqw: the *alqado*, 'traditional or received wisdom'; the *ti'ita*, 'stories', with either human or animal characters; the *da'angw*, 'songs' and 'singing conversations'; and the *slufay*, a 'prayer' or 'sermon'. Each of these differs from the others in form, content, and the context in which it is appropriate.

The *alqado* is normally a narrative by an elder about events of the past or about those he has witnessed or heard about. It may be a narrative about prophecy and its fulfillment, or an explanation of some aspect of ritual, religion, or other matter. Its content is most general of all; its form most informal of all. It is delivered by an old man in his own household or among close friends and neighbors.

The *ti'ita* is a story told for amusement and edification. Anyone may tell it and all listen. It is performed together with short songs at night around the fire in one's own house. Many *ti'ita* are animal fables that resemble animal fables told all over the African continent. Others are stories that deal with contemporary concerns in story form. One such story, "*Simboyá*," for example, deals with sin and the practice of exile; another, "*Ari*," with jealousy among siblings. Their themes are frequently serious, but the little ditties and songs sung with them make them entertaining as well as instructive.

Da'angw, 'songs,' is a cover term for a number of different types of songs sung for dances or at beer parties (see Figure 6.1). They are performed in public and consist largely of brief, obscure references to per-

FIGURE 6.1. *Dance performed to a song, da'angw. When Iraqw stand or dance together they maintain close physical contact and move in unison. Here they dance for a woman of the aya who has just joined a Roman Catholic religious order.*

sons, ritual experts, or other leaders, or to places in the landscape. The reference may be laudatory or pejorative, but they always depend for their interpretation on a body of shared knowledge communicated by *alqado* and stories. In the context of a beer party, these songs may take the form of a sort of singing conversation. One man will begin a song while everyone chants and hums a refrain. The singer will eventually cede the floor to another who picks up the song or who sings a rebuttal to the first singer's song. Lively singing arguments result, with the audience chanting a rhythmic refrain that becomes louder and more insistent until the point is dropped or a new song subject is broached. Then the singers begin singing on a different topic with perhaps a different refrain for the audience. Although all comers may participate in the song, it is always performed in the courtyard, *afeni,* or in the public portion of the house, *matla'angw,* where singers and audience sit shoulder to shoulder swaying in time as a single unit.

Finally, the *slufay* is a form of oral verse delivered primarily outdoors at public meetings, but also at beer parties, ceremonies for the ritual blessing of the land, traditional and Christian weddings, and on Tanzanian national holidays. Of all forms of discourse, the formal constraints on performance of the *slufay* are most rigid.

In addition to these named formal modes of discourse, there are also formal curses and invocations. These are not forms of discourse but are verbal performatives that are used to accomplish specific social and political ends. Cursing is the primary political tool of the elders, *barise,* who in concert represent formal authority in the territorial unit called the *aya,* and who are responsible for the ritual observances that maintain the fertility of the land, the coming of the rain, and the ritual condition of both land and people. The curse, when used legitimately—that is, by the assembly of elders in pursuit of an agreed upon end—is performed publicly. Individuals may use the curse, but their use of this form is illegitimate and private.

The individual's curse is usually accompanied by some form of "inversion." For example, a mother may curse her children by flaunting herself naked before them. This is regarded as a particularly potent curse. Another effective way of delivering a curse is to utter it while standing on a high termite mound with one's cloak and other garments worn upside down. If an individual's use of the curse is discovered, its perpetrator is liable to fines of livestock levied by the elders and consumed by them, or by exile into the bush.

ORAL PERFORMANCE AND POLITICAL LEGITIMACY

Now, the four forms of discourse and the several types of verbal performatives, such as the curse and invocation, can be divided into two classes: public and private. The *alqado* and *ti'ita* are appropriate to the private forum of the household unit. They communicate most directly aspects of culture, world view, the norms of behavior, of language, and of other expressive modes. In particular, the *alqado* communicate a cultural ideology through narratives about certain stereotyped events and activities. In most narratives of this type, a set of conditions is described, then a means of dealing with those conditions is detailed, and finally, the outcome is related to an audience who accepts these narrative events as evidence of the effectiveness of a particular means of accomplishing particular ends. For example, when the narrator talks about an instance in which insubordinate youths were punished by a curse that brought 9 years of famine, hearing the narration of the event is as good as witnessing the event itself for an audience who sees this as perfectly good evidence that the elder's curse is potent and that it is right. In another story, the leader of the Iraqw groups who first settled Irqwar Da'aw discovered the land, but found it covered with water and guarded by a mighty tree. He poured the lake over the escarpment and killed the tree through the power of his medicine and prophecy. The lake, Manyara, lying today at the bottom of the Rift Valley, is believed to have been moved there from its former location at the top of the escarpment. Its presence, and the testimony of the *alqado,* are seen as evidence of the effectiveness of magic. Furthermore, it justifies the Iraqw's possession of the land, since it was their leader who reclaimed it from the lake. Up to this point, the *alqado* and the *ti'ita* might be viewed as "charter myths," much like Malinowski's description of the origin myths of the Trobriands; but, the Iraqw myths are not the legalistic buttresses of the status quo that the Trobriand myths would appear to be. They legitimate not a social *structure,* but social *instruments* such as the curse, prophecy, or other symbolic means of acting in response to social conditions.

The *slufay* and *da'angw* are, in turn, legitimate means of reflecting on the use of these social instruments. Both the *slufay* and the *da'angw* communicate about the content of *alqado* and stories. They provide a controlled means of creatively reworking their cultural representations of themselves and of external social reality as they perceive it. They are to be seen as metacommunicative acts—as derived forms of discourse—that deal with the cultural representations of the real world that are conveyed in the corpus of narratives told in a private setting. The *slufay* and *da'angw* are performed in public forums.

CONTEXTS AND FUNCTIONS OF ORAL PERFORMANCE

There is, as we have seen, a strong correlation between spatial organization and types of discourse. Communication of cultural content occurs in the domain of the individual household. Communication *about* communication takes place in the public forums of the meeting, beer party, or other similar setting. It is in the public forum, too, that creative elaboration or discussion of ritual curses and other expressive instrumental symbolic activity takes place. Otherwise, such discussion is deemed inappropriate and dangerous.

The primary context of use of the *slufay* is the meeting that represents the territorially based corporate group inhabiting one *aya*. Maximally, the meeting, called *kwasleema,* is the assembly of all of the inhabitants of the *aya;* minimally, and more realistically, it is the assembly of representative elders of the households who take a particular interest in public politics of the *aya.* The meeting is led by the 'speaker' (*kahamusmo*), whose position is hereditary, but whose status is that of first among equals. It is not always the speaker who delivers the *slufay,* but instead it may be anyone who is good at it. If there are several people who are good at performing the *slufay,* then several will be performed.

Ostensibly, the only topic of discussion is the ritual condition of the land, but since it is the social activities and speech of the inhabitants of the land that affect its ritual condition, it can be seen that the idea of "the ritual condition of the land" is an indirect, metaphorical way of talking about politics. The function of the meeting is to affix blame and to punish by fines or exile persons who have endangered the condition of the land either intentionally through sinful behavior (*irange*) or inadvertently through events that result in pollutions (*meta*). The word "to accuse," that is, to affix blame for these things, is *kwasleemuut,* literally, 'to strike by the meeting.' The power of the meeting is applied symbolically, either verbally by the legitimate use of the curse, or by nonverbal means, such as blocking an accused person's house with a thorn bush placed on the threshold of the doorway, itself the symbol of the boundary between the private domain of the household and the public domain of the *aya.* Political process is thus conducted and perceived in terms of symbolic representations and symbolic acts. In the context of the meeting, we see most clearly the merging of ritual and political spheres in the use of ritual and linguistic forms as practical tools in the conduct of political affairs.

It is in this context, then, that the *slufay* serves to communicate about political and symbolic communications. It is also performed in other contexts, but where this occurs, the *slufay* is really a representation of itself. The song is the metacommunicative form appropriate to the informal gathering, while the *slufay,* performed as a *slufay,* is appropriate to the formal meeting that represents the *aya.* Where the *slufay* is performed at a wedding, for instance, it is performed as an example of the *slufay* performed at the meeting, its appropriate context. In a different context its meaning is entirely different. Expropriated from the political context in which it is a metacommunicative act, the *slufay* performed at a wedding is a symbolic token that serves to legitimate the gathering since its referent is the *slufay* performed in the legitimate meeting representative of the corporate territorial unit. When the form of the *slufay* is used in this way, its content is not important. The entire *slufay* becomes in itself a symbol of legitimacy and as such may be used as an instrument for conferring legitimacy on an undertaking. In this way the *slufay* is a symbol like the American flag or the National Anthem that may be *used* in a wide variety of contexts. The Iraqw have creatively applied this form to new ceremonies of all types including Christian weddings, the celebration of national holidays, the investiture of Catholic priests, and the opening of schools. In these contexts, however, it has been transformed from a means of talking about political symbols into a political symbol itself.

The performance of the *slufay* is part of the message. It is delivered in two parts, distinguished by differences of rhythm and voice quality. The prologue serves to focus the attention of the audience on the performance of the *slufay*. The performer begins by listing the ills of the people and of the land. He appeals to his listeners to show their unity. He invariably instances the fact that they are gathered together as evidence of their unity before the spirits of the sky and of the earth. This is especially important since the unity of the people is the condition upon which the well-being of the land depends. The audience signifies its accord with the speaker after every cadenced phrase by saying, *"e'it,"* 'it is so'. At intervals in the prologue, the speaker will raise his voice in a sort of cheer saying, "let us agree, let us agree," and he is joined by all of the audience in this display of unity. Then he begins the poetic chant of the *slufay* itself. At this juncture a small bundle of grass is taken in the right hand and the speaker dips it into a gourd of beer that has been placed before him. Using the bundle of grass, he then asperses the assembly before him, dipping the grass into the beer several times and shaking it out over the heads of the audience. He asks, *"hho ng komaane,"* 'may we have goodness', and all the audience responds, *"eee,"* after each line of the recitation. This interaction of the speaker and audience symbolizes their mutual accord and unity. The second part of the *slufay* is much more stereotyped in its content and form but still allows for creativity and free commentary by the speaker within stylistic limits. It is addressed to *lo'a*, the spirit of the cosmos that is especially associated with the sun and air, and to the *netlangw*, spirits associated with the ground.

The *slufay*, then, is addressed to two audiences, the world of spirits and the cosmos in general, and to the human audience who hears it and responds to it. For the Iraqw, the participation of both man and the

---

TEXT 18
Slufay: **Exile to Harar**

For life is ruined
By those of bad birth [i.e., the youths]
They shall go to the bush
In the past it was Harar
Our fathers cast their curse on it
That curse is now forgiven
And that's how it is
And they gave birth there at Harar
They have children
Now the young men
Rub shoulders with one another

---

spirits is essential, since the benevolence of the spirits depends on the unity of people. It is this duality of address that gives the *slufay* a dual character as sermon and as prayer.

COMMUNICATION AND METACOMMUNICATION

Directed at the audience, the *slufay* as sermon exhorts the members of the gathering to moral action and mentions precedents as models for such action. The *slufay* is a commentary about the use of curses and ritual forms in the past, or about witchcraft among members of the household or of the *aya*. In talking about these things, which are symbolic forms in themselves, the *slufay* is a metacommunicative act that is also a political act since it is used by the elders, the senior members of the assembly, to effect social control among their juniors. In one example of this, the speaker talks about an instance of exile in which some young men moved to a place called Harar (Text 18). In another place in his performance the speaker talks about witchcraft among members of the household. He lists the appropriate fates that ought to befall a person guilty of bewitching those around him (see Text 19).

The *slufay* is also a representation of their social condition to themselves. The speaker may refer to their own ethnocentric view of themselves: to the ritual tying of lianas across the pathways, for example, to mark boundaries, and to offer ritual protection. This ritual in itself is the communication of an identity (Text 20).

We can see that the *slufay* is not phrased in the second or third person, but in the first person plural, *we.* The speaker includes in his use of *we* both himself and his audience. They ask, "May our land be full,"

TEXT 19
Slufay: **Witchcraft and Wrongdoing**

He who looks at peoples' houses [i.e., the witch]
If it is the grandfather
Let his council chamber
Fall to ruins
If it is the old woman
Raising her grandchildren
Let them be left behind
The children are left behind
If it is the old woman
The stilled-fetus shall kill her
That of women
If it be the young wife
She dies in childbirth
She dies inside
If it is the youth
May his weapons be returned from the field where he falls
Oh, yes
A cry shall break forth.
Even if it is a little girl
Only her beads shall be seen in the swamp
In the fallow field
And so it is

"May we have goodness," "May our bulls and the francolins feed in the pasture together," or "We are like the ostrich of the plains." The *slufay* helps to create and to reinforce their own images of themselves as a people. Its role in the creation of an identity out of the debris of a tumultuous past can easily be appreciated.

TEXT 20
Slufay: **Navel of God (Lo'a)**

Oh, now we are in the middle
In the navel of God . . .
We are surrounded by mountains
The lianas are tied
We are tied by the lianas
The lianas of the mountain Haru
They protect us

TEXT 21
Slufay: Expansion in Dulen

Let us continue northward
May our place have abundance
Other countries shall know us
We are in that place
That place is Dulen [an area presently grazed by Masai]
Shall we capture it?
We have already captured it
The girls of Dulen
Are ours
They shall become ghost-wives
In the homestead of Dulen. . . .
May we finish it
We have already captured it
The lands of our enemies
We capture them

Finally, and again as a sort of sermon, the *slufay* relates ideology to action by imbuing events with purpose and meaning. This is especially apparent in their representation of their own process of expansion, as the example in Text 21 illustrates. Here the speaker triumphantly proclaims as fact what is in reality wishful thinking; but they have been moving gradually northward, and, should they eventually capture Dulen, it will be done as a fulfillment of the desires that have been publicly stated in a legitimate forum.

The *slufay* is also a prayer since it declares the state of the land and the wishes of the peoples, placing these formally before the spirits of the air, *lo'a,* and of the earth, *netlangw,* and asks that evil be made good and the goodness be allowed to continue. It is an attempt to regulate their well-being through an appeal to the cosmos. They hold that if they are all of one accord, the spirits will be compelled to bless them with goodness. They believe, and state in the prologue to the *slufay,* that even if some people are evil, their unity and overall goodness must be rewarded by good fortune, fertility, and rains. In this case, the performance itself is the realization and symbol of their unity. It establishes a sacred "we" in the response of the audience to the speakers phrases and the blessing of the assembly by sprinkling them with beer. It is this symbol of unity that the *slufay* most frequently talks about. It is in this sense, especially, that the *slufay* is metacommunicative—a communication about other acts and other elements of communication (Sanches and Blount, 1975).

Just as a metalinguistic vocabulary (i.e., words that have as their referents other words or speech acts) allows us to talk about talking and to refine and clarify our meanings and intentions, the *slufay* allows the Iraqw to talk about ritual, cursing, meetings, and other communicative activities with the same goal of refining and clarifying meanings.

The metacommunicative form of discourse, therefore, is a creative form of discourse. Metacommunicative acts appear to operate "recursively" on cultural content to generate an infinite number of cultural forms. The *slufay,* as we have seen, is one way in which the content of culture may be discussed. Communication *about* content is allowed in a formal, legitimate setting. Without the elaborate framing and restrictions, it seems that the fragile representations of reality are in danger of being cut too deeply. By endowing events and social changes with cultural meanings, and by serving in many contexts as a symbol of legitimacy, the *slufay* has played a part in the adaptive cultural response to social change. It has allowed a creative look at the culture, and allows for a creative response to change without endangering the communality of belief that bonds people together in a common culture.

Chapter 7

Talking about the Past: Time in the Iraqw World View

Oral Texts as Historical and Cultural Data

Talking about the past involves orders of thought that are different from those employed in talking and thinking about space. However, it appears that talking and thinking about the past depend on the capacity to talk and to think about the relations of space, since speech about the past in Iraqw, and perhaps in many other languages, draws on the resources of the language for talking about spatial relations to formulate expressions that convey their view of the past from the perspective of the present. Frequently these expressions are spatial metaphors that liken the relations of events in time to the relations of points and areas in space. This is perhaps a human universal, but the relations that do exist between the way a culture talks about space and the way a culture talks about time have not been adequately explored. First of all, talking about the past requires a grouping of events into related sets of events, and a separation of classes of events that have already taken place from events that are currently taking place or that are about to take place. The first activity of thought required to enable speech about the past to exist, then, is the act of classification of events. Such a classification of events is implicit in the system of time deixis or "tense" in the language, but in order to talk about the past, it would seem that some means of referring to the idea of past events as an object is also required. In the English phrase "the past," we have a sign that designates a set of events, and ideas about these events, that has already taken place at a time prior to the present.

There are, however, many different sorts of "the past," such as the historical past, the nation's past, or my family's past, which designate not merely a set of events that are significantly related in some way, but also a way of thinking about those events that give them meaning. In this chapter, I shall discuss the ways in which the Iraqw "thinker about the past" defines his subject matter, the way in which he classifies the events that compose "the past," and insofar as it is possible, to discuss the ways in which he thinks about these events and by which these events become meaningful. I shall rely on many different types of oral performances recorded in the field, and presented in the texts as transcriptions and translations.

I will show that the Iraqw way of thinking about the past is different from our own "historical" ways of thinking about it; and I will maintain that any attempt to force the Iraqw's "facts" about the past into a western, historical way of thinking about the facts, is not merely a translation of one language's speech about the past into another language's terms, but is a distortion of the way in which the Iraqw conceive of and communicate about the past. There is first of all a question concerning the very nature of the so-called facts. The ethnohistorian's idea of what actually exists, of reality and truth, differ from the Iraqw talker-about-the-past's idea of these things, insofar as they are talked about in the narrative of the past that he offers. In the following discussion, we begin to investigate the truth value *for the Iraqw* of some of the narratives that they commonly recite. There is also the question concerning the ordering of "facts" in the narrative itself. The order in which narrative episodes are presented by the Iraqw is different from the order in which they would be presented in a history artificially drawn from them by the ethnohistorian. In this chapter we also attempt to investigate some of the principles of order in narrative. We find that these principles of order in narrative are in fact deep cultural assumptions that underlie other forms of cultural behavior and performance.

This is not to say, however, that ethnohistory is not possible, or that it is not a valid undertaking, but only to signal a departure. I am attempting to show that there is another way of dealing with the same material that tries to "translate" some of the underlying cultural assumptions and structures of thought that inhere in the material itself. A different approach may be taken to yield a history, strictly speaking, but it should be noted that this is a different approach, with a different aim, producing a different product.

Part of the difference between the approach taken here and one taken by other ethnohistorians lies in the range and nature of material that is considered in the analysis. Usually the ethnohistorian, in search of the history of a nonliterate people, proceeds by asking informants for narratives about a particular time, for example, or about the events surrounding a well-remembered drought, or the initiation of an age grade.

The fieldworker who takes this course collects from many informants narratives that can be related to events such as droughts or initiation ceremonies, that can themselves be ordered into a time sequence. The seriation of these key events then serves the ethnohistorian with a chronological framework into which he or she can fit other data, and according to which he or she can compare the narratives collected. If the people with whom the ethnohistorian is working proceed on similar assumptions about the way events are to be related to one another, then this methodology does no violence to their thought about the past, but simply serves to collate and reorder many narratives into a larger one that may in turn be related to a larger conception of a national history, or to other sequences of events that may have influenced another separate sequence of events (for example, the slave trade on the succession of Nyamwezi chiefs).

If, however, the events that are talked about in the narratives collected by the ethnohistorian are not ordered according to a local, traditional chronology, then the traditional western "history" that *can* be written does violence to that other systematic organization in the thought and performance of the member of the culture with whom the ethnohistorian works. If the native logic in speech about the past is to be discovered and described, the ethnographer must not, first of all, prejudice the inquiry by requesting from the informant, and using as data, only those narratives that answer his or her questions for information about specific events at specific times. Instead, the ethnohistorian must collect a corpus of material of all sorts of oral performance, formal and informal, without hint of the purpose for which he or she is collecting it and then proceed to sift through it to discover the contexts that elicit speech about the past, and to analyze the logic that links one event to another event in the speech of the subjects. This course is the one I tried to follow in the collection of materials in the field, and which consequently changes the aims and outcomes of the analysis.

The *alqado* are perhaps the most revealing texts, and the most accessible to the outsider with a limited knowledge of the language. Virtually any narration relating to events in the past, or to traditional and customary ways of doing things (*getlangw,* 'tradition') may be called *alqado.* Since they are told primarily to instruct or to relate information about Iraqw cultural knowledge, they do not contain as many obscure references as do *da'angw,* 'drinking songs,' for instance.

Texts 22 and 23 are lengthy excerpts from *alqado.* The first is a narrative about a group of people (the kindred) whose descendents today live in Irqwar Da'aw. The action takes place before their migration to Irqwar Da'aw from a previous homeland in the south.

I have presented the first narrative (Text 22) in its "raw" form, as nearly as possible to the way in which it was told to me and a research

TEXT 22
Alqado: A Cursing of the Land

Alqado of Hhay Bo'ok (narrative about the past)

1. The name was *Hhay Bo'ok,* and their lineage was *Hhay Tsuhhay,*
2. when *Hhay Tsuhhay* lived at Bashe.
3. The day they were at Bashe,
4. they stayed there for a long time, they had plenty of milk in their milk containers.
5. The youths did not know their fathers.
6. The youths passed here and there and went about their business.
7. One day, they went off to live [they moved away] taking the cattle.
8. The youths were full of pride.
9. One father [elder] said,
10. "They have gone."
11. "They are staying near an anthill [or termite mound]"
12. and a small boy, a small boy on that day
13. one such as you [indicating Christopher (Ch:), a research assistant about 18 years old]
14. at about that time, was told [by the elder]
15. "Boy! return to me my cattle."
16. The boy said, "No."
17. Then an elder said [prophesied]
18. "the welfare of the people of *Hhay Bo'ok*
19. "it is not known to us
20. "there is something that will do away with their happiness."
21. Then another said, "How shall we master them?" [the youths who took the cattle]
22. "The thing that will master them is hunger."
23. Nine years of hunger, they were cursed with it.
24. At that time something was said at the termite mound.
25. May that place be devoured.
26. [Ch: Something?]
27. A thing which is not known.
28. [Ch: A thing which is not known?]
29. Yes, it is not known [what was said].
30. Then this little boy
31. did he not hear this thing? Yes!
32. Those youths already passed in this manner [died]
33. So the boy went home,
34. given life by lo'a,
35. the boy went home.
36. When he came home he cried very hard.
37. He cried very hard and did not eat
38. Even if his grandmother gave him food,
39. he did not eat it, he just cried.

40. [Ch: Who was this boy?]
41. He was the one who stayed with the elders.
42. Then the grandmother said,
43. "Why do you not eat? Why do you cry so hard?"
44. Why don't you ask about the matter?
45. The day was about the second
46. So the father asked him,
47. He said, "My boy, what is it? Why do you cry?"
48. He said to the father,
49. "Why should I eat, when there is no life to live?"
50. "That is the reason."
51. The elders talked.
52. The boy said, "At that time in the past some youths refused
53. to return the cattle,
54. so there is a thing,
55. an anthill which has been spoken [cursed], the place is ruined."
56. "One elder said, 9 years of hunger."
57. He said, "You eat, I understand now,"
58. Then the boy ate, and eating,
59. he lived, he lived with lo'a [God].
60. The sun shone brightly.
61. They lived and the sun beat down.
62. They lived and the sun shone,
63. until they were finished.
64. Now the year was finished.
65. The cattle were weak.
66. Then he said to the boys,
67. he said to them, "Go into the forest."
68. "See if the valleys are wet."
69. "How are the valleys?"
70. Then the boys went away
71. into the forest.
72. [Ch: Who were they?]
73. The ones of that old man, the one whose child cried.
74. So they went to look at the valleys in the forest.
75. They said, "Father, that swamp in the valley,
76. there are things that have not dried.
77. The grass is yet green."
78. The father said, "That's fine."
79. The boys said, "Yes."
80. They castrated the goats.
81. There was no entire male among the goats,
82. They did the same with the sheep,
83. the bulls they did likewise.
84. He said, "so let's go to the forest."

85. But some people were left in that place.
86. The place was Bashe.
87. Some people were left behind.
88. Now, some were left behind.
89. they stayed, they, animals, bees
90. animals, bees, animals, bees,
91. the cattle revived,
92. bees, cattle
93. They wanted for bulls to be born,
94. because of the famine, so that it would not hurt them.
95. The 9-year famine left.
96. It went far away, far away.
97. And so they lived, they lived,
98. The seventh year, they said,
99. "Let's go, let's see clearly
100. our old home."
101. They went to see it.
102. There was not a single person there,
103. not even a single animal,
104. not a tree.
105. And the earth had fried, not even a blade of grass.
106. [Ch: because of the sun?]
107. Yes, they only saw a bird in the heavens.
108. The father said, "Wait a bit,
109. when the eighth year comes.
110. "In the middle of that year," he said,
111. "Go there, then, and take that bull
112. to the termite mound, together with that honey.
113. Take the bull to that place and kill it
114. in the termite mound and put it inside.
115. Make an offering of the honey.
116. Our curse will be made good [lifted],
117. the evil-spoken returned."
118. So the youths went there,
119. and they slaughtered their bull there.
120. They finished sacrificing the bull and the honey also.
121. As they returned home, the rain
122. met them on the path home.
123. The evil-spoken was cleansed away.
124. They met with rain on the path.
125. It rained very hard.
126. And they returned; "Now go again to see."
127. And they went.
128. They saw that grass had sprouted.
129. They returned to where they had come from.

TEXT 22 (continued)

130. They went south.
131. They walked and walked and walked,
132. to Bashe. It is there where the bones are,
133. around the bridge at Bashe, the south side,
134. where there are the bones of the people killed by the famine,
135. there together with their cattle.
136. [Ch: Are the bones still there?]
137. Even today they are there.
138. [Even now?]
139. Yes, even now.
140. Even today if we were to go there we would find them.
141. There. If you pass that bridge,
142. you have already passed the place of ashes
143. and of bones.
144. [The people were completely finished by the famine?]
145. They were all finished. Now, who would
146. want to go there. Famine is no game.
147. [Yes, nothing to eat. . . .]
148. There was only the sun!
149. [There was no rain?]
150. The only thing was the sun.
151. They died right there.
152. They died as they slept.
153. And the cattle died likewise.
154. There was not one remaining.
155. [And then?]
156. Those who were in the forest returned.
157. Now they had increased; there were other lineages; they had grown;
158. they walked about here and there;
159. They went south to Guse.
160. Now they left Guse, the place of *Hhay Bo'ok*
161. And they were full of pride.
162. [*Hhay Bo'ok* were young men?]
163. *Hhay Bo'ok*? *Hhay Bo'ok* is an Iraqw name.
164. Those of *Hhay Tsuhhay* their "clan" was *Hhay Bo'ok*.
165. How many are the clans of Iraqw now?
166. They are many.
167. The clans of Iraqw let's say . . .
168. As we were saying . . .
169. The people who came from the south long ago had three clans.
170. *Hhay Bo'ok* is *Hhay Tsuhhay*
171. *Hhay Tipu Bonday*, among whom was the one whose . . .
172. who moved the lake to the east;
173. *Hhay Tipu Bonday*.
174. *Hhay Duway* were people of the south with them.

175. All of them moved.
176. The clans drew together.
177. The place is Guse.
178. Guse is called Ma'angwatay.
179. They stayed; they lived there; they grew proud;
180. They began to quarrel with the elders.
181. [They quarreled with the elders?]
182. Yes, they danced in the forest.
183. Even today the place is there.
184. They danced in the forest,
185. Then they fought with the elders; some were killed.
186. Haymu hid himself.
187. The girls came back from gathering firewood.
188. "This fortune of *Hhay Bo'ok,* what will cure it?"

Source: Ami Slaqwe, Hhay Sali (Kainam) with Christopher Ginwe, research assistant;
translation from Iraqw transcripts.

TEXT 23
Alqado: The Story of Moya

1. At first the people came from Ma'angwatay, but I don't know
2. any stories about that. But there are many stories [*alqado*] about
3. Ma'angwatay that some old men know. But after that the people lived in
4. the forest *Noow.* They were hungry there and had no cattle. Then they saw
5. the valley that is called Mama Isara [Irqwar Da'aw], but it was covered
6. by a large lake. They came out of the forest to a dry part and the people
7. came to the medicine man [*qwaslarmo*] to ask if anything could be done,
8. The medicine man told them to find a boy who was left-handed. He would be
9. found in the country of the Fiomi [Wa-Gorowa, who live to the southeast of
10. the Iraqw]. So the people went to the country of the Fiomi and they found
11. a left-handed boy. And when they found him, they
12. knew that he was the right one that the medicine man had told them they would
13. find. His name was Moya. They took Moya back to the medicine man. The medicine
14. man told them that he needed a long walking stick and a hoe which was

164

TEXT 23 (continued)

15. worn out from too much use. They brought him these things. First, he made
16. a fire by twirling the walking stick between his palms like a fire stick.
17. Then he put on firewood until he had a big fire. He put the hoe into the fire
18. and heated it until it was red hot and then he handed it to the boy,
19. Moya. Moya took the hoe as it was handed to him and he was not burned.
20. Then the medicine man knew he was the right one. He gave the boy the stick.
21. He blessed the stick by spitting on it. Then he gave the
22. boy the hoe. He told Moya to advance to the edge of the lake and
23. strike the water with the stick. This he did and the water divided
24. before him. The medicine man told him to walk between the water until
25. he came to the water again. He struck the water again and it parted.
26. He continued walking into the lake. Then the medicine man told him to strike
27. the water again. He struck the water again and it rose up on either side of
28. him. And there in front of him stood a great tree called *ti'itar.* The
29. medicine man told Moya to cast the hoe into the water. This he did.
30. Then, he was told to pierce the tree with the stick. He threw the stick
31. at the tree and it pierced the tree. Then suddenly the water rushed
32. back in upon him, swallowing him up with the tree. For a moment the
33. waters swirled about them and then they all rose up together and rushed over
34. the cliff, falling into the Rift Valley below the plateau. They went to
35. make what is now [Lake Manyara]. But the Iraqw call it Moya, because
36. it is not just a lake, it is the boy Moya.

Source: Recorded in Swahili from a number of Iraqw informants, *Kwermusl.*

---

assistant. The story was elicited at my request that he tell me *alqado.* I did not specify the topic. The second Text (Text 23) that I have presented for consideration follows this one in a temporal sequence, since it involves the first entry of the Iraqw into Irqwar Da'aw from the south by way of the *Noow* Forest. This example is somewhat "cooked," being a composite of a couple of different narratives of the same episode. The variation between tellings of this story is very slight, however, and the consolidation of these variants into a single story does not interfere with the aims of the analysis. The story in this form, when read back to a number of Iraqw (which I did in Swahili) was judged by them to be complete and correct. Texts 24 and 25 are stories, *ti'ita,* that would be told in the home. These

TEXT 24
Ti'ita: The Elephant and the Rabbit

1. *Baloka'in ama dawe gana bara qaymori eer*
   Once upon a time an old mother met an elephant in her field.
2. *iwa qaytsiit taxes dawe âmu gwa âak*
   While she watched, the elephant ate up all of her pumpkins.
3. *alu ina a', ina o' ador ni laq*
   Then she cried, and she said, "What am I to do?"
4. *alu kwa'ângw guna aan ina o'*
   Then she saw a rabbit and she said to him,
5. *Kwa'ângw kwa âmu kwa faak*
   "Rabbit! My pumpkins are finished!"
6. *Kwa'ângw iri o' aning adorin a xuu, kiing lakit*
   and the rabbit said," I know what'll fix him. You wait."
7. *ama ngir bay hani âmir wak daqni dawor daawe aning a xuu'*
   And as he told the woman, "Give me one pumpkin now, I know the elephant's medicine.
8. *ama iri hanis âmir wak. Kwa'ângw amiros gari oh*
   The old woman gave him one pumpkin. Rabbit took his pumpkin.
9. *âmiros giri ay. Lo'itler iri bara qaymori tlay ne tsatayos*
   He ate his pumpkin. The next day he went to this field with his knife.
10. *iwa hardah bara qaymoro ami giri gwa foxiis*
    When he came into the field, he cut a hole in one of the pumpkins,
11. *iri dah bara gur'u'dah ne firimbirose bara guru âmi*
    And he climbed into the pumpkin with his flute.
12. *dawe iwa hardat amu guna gu' gu'*
    When the elephants came to the field, they gobbled up all of the pumpkins.
13. *iwa ax iri tler iri amosing tlahh'mu'er*
    When they were satisfied, they went to rest.
14. *alo kwa'ângw firimbi giri bara guru dangwa ufahh*
    Then the rabbit began to play his flute inside the belly of the elephant.
15. *dawe iri akmiit sleme tin lak geger asma dee*
    The elephants jumped up so fast they hurt themselves in their fear.
16. *kar dawe bira sihhit, kwa'ângw filimbi gan male slahh*
    And if the elephants stopped to rest a moment, the rabbit blew his flute again.
17. *dawe gar iwa qas tiingo tin lak hari a eer sleme*
    The elephants all ran until they were exhausted,
    alo kiima hatle'e, dawe iri o' ax magowara'
    then later on the elephants said, "Hey, let's not run so hard."
18. *kiima tame firimbi gari male slahh dawe iwa tlahh*
    The third time the rabbit blew his flute, the elephants all gathered together.
19. *alo kiima hatle'e, dawe iri o' an magowara'*
    Then the next time, the elephants said, "Let's not run so hard."

166

TEXT 24 (continued)

20. *ax gitlare gari a tsahhaan asma alo tiingw taw tintaw faak*
    Let's try to discover what this thing is that is causing us to exhaust ourselves.
21. *ne sleme tin taw slehh' emisangw*
    We are hurting ourselves for nothing."
22. *alo tiri sehhit slemero tiri burumburie*
    Then they stood and all gathered together for a meeting
23. *kar kwa'ângw firimbi ngi male slahhi bara guru daangw a ale*
    And the rabbit blew his flute again from inside the belly of that elephant.
24. *tana male dam kwa'ângw filimbi gana male slahh*
    They waited and the rabbit blew his flute again.
25. *tari o' ariyo' kar ga bare bara guru dangwi*
    They said, "Why, this thing is coming from the belly of this elephant."
26. *ino'in ngi xuiaka ga lati kwa'ângw guna âmu al gu'ir*
    They did not know that the elephant had swallowed the rabbit together with the pumpkin.
27. *alo daangwdada âmi ga kwa'ângw al gu'*
    Then that elephant swallowed the pumpkin and the rabbit
28. *kuna bay xaygan aten kuung a gura fehhisaan*
    And they told him, "Well, we will have to split open your stomach.
29. *gasir bara gurwok a araan asma alo slahh'aymayer yarir tin taw faak*
    We must see what it is inside you, otherwise we shall all die of exhaustion.
30. *kar alo daangw dada ami ga kwa'ângw al gu' iri ya'an*
    Then the elephant who had eaten the pumpkin with the rabbit agreed.
31. *kuri gura fehhis alo gar ta bara gur i daangwi ay a kwa'ângw*
    Then they cut open their friend and found the rabbit inside.
    (The story continues through many other similar episodes.)

Source: Told by Mama Ginwe, Mangoya.

---

provide especially good data on the way in which narrative is ordered in meaningful sequences. Finally, Text 26 is an example of a song, *da'angw,* that would be sung at a beer party or dance.

Characteristics of the Texts

Now, it is certainly possible to use these texts to interpolate a history in the Western sense that would order events in terms of temporal sequences. Contingencies and causal relationships between them could indeed be inferred. But this is not our immediate aim since, for the Iraqw talker-about-the-past, these causal and temporal relationships are not the

TEXT 25
Ti'ita: The Existence of Death

The people had just satisfied themselves with a big feast. They began to argue about death. Some were saying, "Does a man really die?" Others said, "That's a lie; there is no death." They all agreed to make certain about this matter for themselves.

One of them had a serious illness. They carried him to an open place and gathered round him, holding their spears, shields, and sticks in order to frustrate anything which would take the spirit [*fuqurangw*] *from this* sick person. Among them was a very short person. As they were talking and telling each other, "Move over there," or "Others go to close that space completely," or "Leave not one opening," the invalid's spirit was lost [he died]. They were astonished. They turned on the short one and reproached him severely. "It is you who left a space open. You did not close it adequately because you felt bitterness at being so short. You let in that thing which took the spirit of our sick one. Today we'll teach you a lesson woodcutter style." They beat him soundly with sticks until they had driven him to the farthest horizon. They returned to take the corpse and bury it. They made certain that day that death truly exists.

Source: A story from Hhay Sule, taken from *Mapokeo ya Wa-Iraqw* by Mzee Ramadhani, a Swahili-speaking school teacher (see Bibliography).

TEXT 26
Da'angw: Karatu

1. *O Bura Maala*
   Oh, Bura Ma'ala
2. *hee gera har mmm ha*
   is the man who led us,
3. *a hee gera har mmm ha*
   is the man who came before us.
4. *Ganako Awtu a dahangw gera mm ha*
   Ganako Awtu is his first beer gourd [his chief lieutenant].
5. *doren gwa surkus ay karatur yarir*
   We moved our house to Karatu.
6. *karatu yarir a karatur gantsar*
   Grand Karatu is green Karatu.
7. *karatu yarir a uway gembut mmm* [a]
   Karatu the grand now inclines towards the west.
8. *hiya he o iyu gwa ot mmm*
   hiya he, oh, you have already captured the north.

168

9. *iyu ugwa ot iyu gwa ot mmm*
   The north you have captured; the north is taken.
10. *ina hara warahh amor yama Mbulumbulu mmm* [b]
    You passed through the ground of Mbulumbulu.
11. *hiya he inko fanur kiîmiis mmm*
    hiya he, the north lands of Fanu are returned to us
12. *yama masay, masay gantsarmmmm*
    On the blessed land, the green medicine,
13. *ne yana dabaqeet mmm*
    and in the land called Dabaqeet.
14. *ha duwangqeet ugwa uway surukasaan mmm*
    Ha, the Masai warriors have been driven westwards,
15. *ha he aten tari tlahhasaan*
    and so we justly take pride,
16. *mmm tari tlahhasaan ar yama karatu mmm*
    and we rejoice on the ground of Karatu.
17. *karatu gantsar Bura ga tsaat* [c]
    The green land of Karatu is cut [divided] by Bura
18. *an Bura Ma'ala Bura Ma'ala*
    He is Bura Maala, Bura maala,
19. *dahh'o hema? a Ganako Awtu mmm*
    whose beer gourd, it is Ganako Awtu.
20. *ha hemi humala humali mmm*
    ha hemi humala humali mmm
21. *uway qaytsitaqay, uway gaytsitaqay*
    Now turn your gaze to the west. Turn your gaze to the west.
22. *ha hemi O uway qay taag mmm*
    ha hemi, Oh to the west, march!
23. *Bara uway qay taag giye guu kiimis* [d]
    Although he went to the west, he was caused to return by the sleeping
    sickness.
24. *humaqa giye tiiqiit* [d]
    That illness goes on hurting.
25. *iri baray eet tanday baray eetaan mmm* [d]
    And he fell to the ground; we fell to the ground;
26. *ha hemi ar yama garangw mm* [d]
    ha hemi, the ground with the rats,
27. *yama tlawta yarir* [d]
    the ground with a big lake.
28. *ha hemi uway qaytaan mmm*
    ha hemi, we go westwards.
29. *tari baray eetaan yama Mangola*
    And we follow him down to Mangola,
30. *ha hemi yama Mangola* [e]
    ha hemi, the land of Mangola

TEXT 26 (continued)

31. *Mangola kawa slawaan, tata tarar ori mmm* [e]
When they reached Mangola, they confronted the Mangati.
32. *tay uway qaytaan mmm*
We look to the west,
33. *alok aqo ma ti'imitaan ay giyer mara*
and then we go out toward Giye Mara.
34. *Sakwelir Bura Maala mahhat ay danda*
The ostriches of Bura Maala have the shade on their backs.
35. *O bare xuumisaan*
Oh, if we were to look into the matter,
36. *bare xuumisaan, bura una baw*
If we were to look into something, then Bura would inform us.

Source: Tluway Masay, Karatu.

[a] Although the land does slope toward the west, the meaning here is most likely that this is the direction in which the settlers could continue to expand. Ngorongoro massif is to the north of Karatu. When they first arrived in this area it was held by the Masai. Since then it has become a national park. To the east, below the Rift Valley escarpment, the land is again inhabited by the Masai and is in any case too dry for Iraqw to practice agriculture successfully. Expansion has been prevented, then, to the east and the north, leaving the west toward the shores of Lake Eyasi more available.

[b] Mbulumbulu is a fertile area overlooking the Masai steppe on the edge of the escarpment. It was first settled by Bura Ma'ala, but he and his companions were driven back to Karatu by fierce raids by the Masai. Later it was successfully settled by Iraqw under the leadership of Qambesh Bura, the son of Bura Ma'ala.

[c] It was the duty of the *kahamusmo* to divide the land among the settlers who followed him.

[d] Disease was a major problem among the Iraqw settlers who left the highlands of Irqwar Da'aw to settle areas such as Karatu. Here the singer refers to sleeping sickness, bubonic plague, which is endemic, and malaria (Line 27, lake).

[e] Mangola is the northern area of the Lake Eyasi depression. It is inhabited by the Mangatti, people of the Tatoga group, who have been largely absorbed by the Iraqw.

important ones. In reviewing a larger corpus of oral performances, one first of all finds no points of reference that can be tied to a chronological framework (such as the succession of chiefs, or the names of sequences of age grades). Second, the events of the past are usually imbued with a magical character or magical cause. In particular, curses, other forms of verbal performances, and ritual are the primary content of narratives. This is important to the Iraqw, and here we attempt to discover some of the reasons that this is so. Third, there is only a very limited notion of change over time, of progress, or of degeneration. Instead, there is a marked insistence on what we might call "conservation" of qualities, place, movement, and objects. That is to say, although things change in relation to one another, they remain more or less the same: Change is relative, not absolute, and although the terms of existence may be reordered in the turn of events, those terms are neither obliterated nor created out of the flux. Finally, place and relations of space (existence in a place, motion between places, neighborhoods) are given a prominence that is held by relations of time in Western histories.

To summarize, the chief characteristics of Iraqw narratives are (*a*) the lack of chronology; (*b*) the importance of oral performance and ritual; (*c*) the conservation of quality, place, and objects; and (*d*) the prominence of spatial relationships of events systematically related to one another in a topological way. Here we attempt to explore each of these aspects more fully.

Chronology and Sequence

In a formal, mathematical sense, topology is a geometry of space in which measurement of length, distance, angles, is not allowed. Measurement entails a standard of length or angle, and an act of comparison by which this standard is applied to the whole space. Distances may be stated precisely with reference to the chosen standard, although the length of the standard itself may be arbitrary. Measurement of space, or of time, requires the existence of a standard and the act of comparison. The Iraqw do have a standard of measurement. One may talk of years (*kuru*), months (*slahhangw*, literally, 'moons',), days (*delo*), or hours (*loa*, literally, 'suns', as in *loarmagá*, "What sun is it?" or "What time is it?"). They do not, however, use these standards of measurement comparatively to produce a general concept of uniform time, a chronology, that is, against which all events may be compared. Years, months, days, and hours are partitions of the flow of time, and in the way we use the term here, are topological. The creation of a uniform (e.g., Euclidean) space or a uniform time standard (e.g., a chronology) requires a logical act that the Iraqw do not perform. Again, the *experience* of time is manifestly the same, but the use of the *concept* is different. Among other peoples, a genealogy of chiefs, or a succession of generation sets are examples of elementary chronology. Bourdieu (1977:105) has commented on this aspect of a temporal topology:

> Just as genealogy substitutes a space of unequivocal homogeneous re-
> lationships established once and for all, for a spatially and temporally
> discontinuous set of islands of kinship, ranked and organized to suit

the needs of the moment and brought into practical existence gradually and intermittently, and just as a map replaces the discontinuous, patchy space of practical paths by the homogeneous, continuous space of geometry, so a calendar substitutes a linear, homogeneous, continuous time for practical time, which is made up of incommensurable islands of duration. . . . By distributing guide marks (ceremonies and tasks) along a continuous line, one turns them into dividing marks united in a relation of simple succession, thereby creating *ex nihilo* the question of the intervals and correspondences between points which are no longer topologically but metrically equivalent.

Like Bourdieu, I am making the distinction here between the topological character of practical, sequential time and the linear, metric character of chronology. In each case, there is a concept of a unit of time—a discrete partition of temporality—such as the reign of a chief or the longevity of a generation. There is also the implicit logical act of comparison between one reign and another, one generation and the next, which posits an equivalence of units and uniform ordering of units that derives from experience in the real world; namely, chiefs beget chiefs, generations beget succeeding generations. Here we draw the distinction between the partition of time and the act of ordering these units into a uniform sequence (but not sequence itself) that can serve as a general system of temporal reference.

For the moment, it will be necessary to bypass the question of why no central genealogy or other means of absolute time reference exists in Iraqw narrative.[1] Given that it does not, however, it might well be asked how is it possible for narrative about the past to exist at all? First of all, we must note the distinction between sequence and chronology. *Sequence* is a physical and biological given. It is perceived in the natural rhythms of the body and of the physical world. *Chronology,* on the other hand, is a cultural, imposed order. A notion of sequence is clearly present in the texts we have to consider. The youths steal the cattle, *then* the elders curse them, *then* the land is parched, *then* some of them go into the forest, *then* they return to find the bones of their former neighbors, and so on. The first story recorded here is temporally prior to the second one (Text 23) since it occurs before the people fled into the forest, and in the second, the events occur after the people have come out of the forest and settled the land. These events, however, occurred only "at some time in the past," a phrase that implies sequence, but not chronology.

The time of the event—how long ago it occurred—is not stated in the narrative, nor can such information be elicited. A question of the

1. Reasons for the lack of genealogy are discussed in Chapter 9, pages 232–234. The lack of an origin myth is considered later in this chapter, pages 179–181.

form, "When did it happen?" is difficult to phrase in Iraqw. Unlike the question forms, "Why did X happen?" "How did X happen?" or "What is X?," there is no simple form that corresponds to "When did it happen?" One must ask, in order to elicit a statement about time in the past, a question of the form "At what time . . .?" (*"Goma Amila?"* or *"Xayla a mila?"*). The order of thought underlying the questions "At what time?" and "When"? are not the same. This is evident first of all from the fact that the interrogative form "When"? parallel to the interrogative forms "Why"?, "What"?, and "How"? does not exist.

The form of the question "When"? in Iraqw corresponds in form to the question "Where"? There is a set of simple grammatical particles that distinguish between persons in the speech situation and third persons, in asking questions that relate to the cause, object, or manner of an action. Consider the following phrases:

'What did he tell you?' (object question) *Inos kuung mingi babay?*
'Why did he tell you?' (cause question) *Inos kuung mihar babay?*
'Why the hell did he tell you?' (cause question, emphatic) *Inos kuung misingi babay?*
'How did he tell you?' (manner question) *Inos kuung mingir babay?*

There are no exactly similar forms of asking "*Where* did he tell you?" or "*When* did he tell you?" since there are no interrogative particles for these questions. Instead, one must use the nominal form meaning 'time-of' or 'period (of time) of', *qoma,* to ask the question *"Qomar inos kuung u babay a mila?,"* which literally means 'period-of-time-of he you he-to-you tells is what?' This is formally similar to the question *"Dir inos kuung u babay a dima?,"* literally, 'Place he you he-to-you tells is place-what'? or 'Where did he tell you'? These formal differences between asking questions of place and time and questions asking about the object, cause, or manner of an action indicate that the ways of talking about space and time are similar, while the ways of talking about objects of actions, cause, and manner are different. While this does not imply that the fundamental experience of time and space are confused by the Iraqw, it does mean that the practical means of dealing with these experiences are structurally the same. In a segmental society such as the Iraqw, time is segmented. This is what Ian Cunnison (1951) meant, when in discussion of "history on the Luapula," he concluded that no "universal" history existed among the Bemba, only memories of events associated with particular places.

In particular, the means of inquiring about the time of an event places certain restrictions on the answer; that is, the linguistic forms available in the language embody certain presuppositions about the nature of time. The words that we may gloss simply as "time words" imply discrete partitions of moments or "durations" that are quite distinct from other intervals or durations. Just as the locative particle *di-* in Iraqw implies a definite place in contradistinction to an area or a sweep of space, so do the time words *qoma, xayla, siwa,* and *kiima* imply discrete and definite periods of time or duration, in contradistinction to an undifferentiated flow of time.

Furthermore, these words convey something about the character of the moment to which they refer, and to its place in a sequence. Both *qoma* and *xayla* appear to designate a discrete moment of time; *qoma* nearly always refers to a time in the past, while *xayla* nearly always refers to a time near, or during the present and in the future. *Siwa* designates a duration or period of time. One may say, for instance, *siwa matlatlero,* 'morning time'. *Kiima* designates a period of time in a sequence, what we might gloss as 'a turn,' as in *kiima tsar* 'second turn' or 'second time'. It designates a discrete moment of time within a sequence of other such moments of time. All of these words presuppose a discrete topological structure on the abstract (and to the Iraqw, irrelevant) notion of time as a continuous flow. Of course, we must do this to talk of time at all, but what is different for the Iraqw is that there is no "axis" of time, a measuring stick with which to compare one moment to another.

There are in Iraqw a number of words that indicate the temporal neighborhood of an event in a narrative. There are a number of "once-upon-a-time" openings for stories. *Bal geera* (literally, 'first days'), *baloka'in* (literally, 'days-specific-those-type'), and *siwakaro* (literally, 'duration-that-[specific]') are stock opening phrases that fix the time in the past or in timelessness (much as the English phrase "once upon a time [there were three bears]" fixes the time of the story). Usually the *alqado* begin with phrases such as *qomar ang,* 'in those (past) times' or *bal ang,* 'in those (past) days'. In addition they may also employ the forms used for storytelling as well. Once the narrative has begun, however, there are two sorts of time indexes that order events within the story itself. The words *daqni, daxta,* and *taxes,* and occasionally a particle, *-qo,* which is affixed to the normal selector, all indicate roughly "at that time" or "meanwhile." Sentences that describe coordinate events or actions that occurred at more or less the same time are begun with these words, or the particle *-qo* is inserted. These indexes have the function of indicating membership in a common temporal neighborhood of a number of events or actions. By contrast the words *alu* and *aluda* indicate an action that succeeds the previous mentioned event in time. These words and other words like them, for example *lo'itler,* 'on the following day', allows the storyteller to order in sequence the events in a story. The use of these

---

Excerpt from Text 24, Lines 1–7

1. *Baloka'in ama dawe gana bara qaymori eer*
   Once upon a time an old mother met an elephant in her field.
2. *iwa qaytsiit taxes dawe âmu gwa âak*
   While she watched, the elephant ate up all of her pumpkins.
3. *alu ina a', ina o' ador ni laq*
   Then she cried, and she said, "What am I to do?"
4. *alu kwa'ângw guna aan ina o'*
   Then she saw the rabbit and she said to him,
5. *Kwa'ângw kwa âmu kwa faak*
   "Rabbit! My pumpkins are finished!"
6. *Kwa'ângw iri o' aning adorin a xuu', kiing lakiit.*
   And the rabbit said, "I know what'll fix him. You wait."
7. *ama ngir bay hani âmir wak daqni dawor daawe aning a xuu'*
   And as he told the woman, "give me one pumpkin now, I know the elephant's medicine."

---

temporal-neighborhood indexes is illustrated well by Text 24. The first seven lines are excerpted.

In Line 1 of the excerpt, the phrase *baloka'in* sets the temporal neighborhood. Once this has been done, the tense-marked indexes are not employed. Only the simplest forms are used, and sequence or coincidence of events is indicated through the use of the indexes that we have mentioned or by use of the relative-of-time and narrative forms. In Line 2 of Text 24, the relative-of-time index *iwa* is used together with the temporal neighborhood index *taxes*. These usages indicate that the action occurring in Line 2 is coincident with that of Line 1. In Line 3, *alu* indicates that the action described here follows the previous action in the sequence of the story. The same usage is observed in Line 4.

In Line 6 we see an example of the use of the narrative form *iri*. This index is used only in narrative speech; that is, in storytelling and in the recitation of *alqado*. It also is a sequence index, like *alu*, but unlike *alu*, whose meaning is general, the narrative form implies a special relationship between the speech act and the action it describes. Its use requires that the sequence of speech acts be isomorphic with the sequence of events that it refers to. In other words the use of the narrative forms entails that for every statement in which is occurs, there is a statement that precedes it and a statement that follows it, *and* that for every statement there is an event to which it refers and an event both preceding and following it. Finally, in Line 7, we see an instance of the use of another index of temporal neighborhood, *daqni,* roughly equivalent in meaning and usage to the narrative use of the English *now,* as in "now it came to pass (that . . .)."

To summarize briefly, the analysis up to this point has shown that although the language is clearly able to discuss the sequence of events, its resources for talking about time in the abstract are somewhat limited. There are no words in Iraqw by which the English word *time* in its abstract sense can be adequately translated. Instead there are words that denote discrete moments and periods of time, and words that index relations of temporal sequence. To express longer periods of time, of continuous duration, the Iraqw raconteur most often resorts to repetition of phrases to symbolize a long and uninterrupted duration. Lines 58–64 of Text 22 use repetition in this way.

For the telling of a particular story about a particular event or sequence of events, these resources are adequate. But there exists no central sequence according to which all events that are talked about in all narratives may be related one to the other and placed into a comprehensive temporal sequence. This, of course, would be essential were a Western-type history to be prepared from the Iraqw data. Similarly, there is no metricization of time. Although there are words for year (*kuru*) and month (*slahhangw*), I was never able to elicit from any Iraqw person who had not had some formal education any inclination to place an event in the past in terms of *countable* numbers of years in the past. It usually seemed to have appeared to my informants a rather irrelevant task, and one that would be difficult, if not impossible, to accomplish had they

---

Excerpt from Text 22, Lines 58–64

58. *Kar garma iri âyiin kar gam*
    Then the boy ate, and eating,
59. *tari hoot, tari lo'a hoot tari hoot*
    he lived, he lived with lo'a [God].
60. *tse'ama na gwa'aat*
    The sun shone brightly
61. *ta hoot tse'ama ne gwa'aat*
    They lived and the sun beat down.
62. *ta hoot tse'ama na gwa'aat*
    They lived and the sun shone,
63. *daxta tay kuqa a faak*
    until they were finished.
64. *kuru kway faak.*
    Now the year was finished.

wanted to. We see then that the idea of temporal neighborhoods of events are important to the organization of Iraqw narrative, but a chronology is not. In consequence of this, it would be a distortion of the Iraqw concept of their past to write a "history," properly speaking. To do this, we must depend on other resources, about which I shall later speak.

The Function of Ritual in Narratives

The moral of many of the Iraqw texts is that ritual and speech acts, when performed by legitimate actors or spokesmen, are efficacious. Indeed, the texts may be seen as anecdotal "evidence" of the effectiveness of instrumental symbolic behavior in achieving social order.

The "plot" of Text 22 revolves around two things: the conflict between the youths (*masomba*) and the elders (*barise*), and secondly the use of magic and cursing. The dichotomy between age and youth, although not as highly institutionalized as among some other East African societies, is nevertheless fundamental to the political order. The *use* of ritual, magic, and cursing by the elders helps to maintain this age-dichotomous social order. *Talking* about the use of ritual, magic, and cursing, however, is a means of representing the social order to themselves. It is a sort of social theory of the effectiveness of instrumental ritual and magic.

The "action" of Text 22 begins when the youths become prideful and scornful of the elders. They take their cattle and move away, staying near an anthill which, supposedly unbeknown to them, is soon to be their undoing. When they refuse to return, one of the elders prophesies that some harm will befall all of them. Prophecy, in the context of *alqado,* occurs again and again. Like the Greek tragedy, the tragedy of the people at Bashe is foretold and inevitable (Lines 17–26 and following).

Prophecy itself is spoken of as "seeing." The prophet himself is called *arusmo,* an agentive noun derived from the verb *ar,* 'to see'. The prophet, in reality and in the narrative that recounts the event, begins his prophecy with *"gar ni ar a,"* " 'the matter which I see is . . . ' " and follows this with a statement of what event he foresees. Prophecy as a verbal performance links the present with the future, by implication, since what is seen must exist *in potentia* at the moment of the act of prophecy. Its fulfillment is the inescapable denouement of the episode.

The retelling of an instance of phophecy that occurred in the past, therefore, must link events together in an unbroken sequence that appears thereby to be given in the nature of things. The elders' curse brings down famine upon all of them, elders and youth alike. The story theme strongly reinforces the belief in the commonality of their welfare, and in the continuation of the social status quo. What the Iraqw learns from "the past," and what the Iraqw talker-about-the-past attempts to convey, is not that one may learn from mistakes, nor that mankind is degenerating from a formerly greater position, but that what happened may happen again.

The role of the anthill is not obvious from the story. The curse, *lo'o*, is delivered either standing upon an anthill or standing in a stream bed. The curse is 'thrown' (*huw*) while the person is wrapped in his inverted cloak. I was not able to discover what the verbal formula is for the obvious reason that it could not be said; hence, the vagueness about what was said in Lines 24–29.

The anthill or termite mound on which a curse might be delivered is of the type seen towering out of the surrounding bush and scrub everywhere in the African savanna lands. Its central tunnel penetrates deeply into the earth, disappearing into blackness. Likewise, the stream bed cuts through the earth. The anthill and the stream bed break the surface of the earth, creating a sort of "conduit" between the domain of the spirits of the air and sun and the spirits of the earth and water (*netlangw*). Because of this, these features are used—appropriated as symbols by the culture—in the cursing ritual which enlists spiritual aid in punishing the youth for their transgressions (i.e., 'sins', or *irange;* see Chapter 6) against the elders.

In Text 22, after the people of *Hhay Bo'ok* have escaped to the forest for the first time, they shelter there for 7 years. When they return to see where they used to live, they find it parched. Upon nearing completion of the period of the curse, they make a sacrifice at the anthill to end it. Following this, the people grow strong again, the youth become prideful and begin to quarrel again with the elders (Line 150). The cycle of conflict engendered by the two age groups begins again. This time it leads them into the forest from which they emerge to find Irqwar Da'aw covered with water.

Text 23, in which the magic employed by Haymu Tipe is described, is among the most important of Iraqw *alqado*. This story is, in effect, the deed to the land. By securing the land from the water it is recovered from uselessness and made into useful, inhabited land. The water and the tree that appears in the middle of the water are both, in many other contexts as well, symbols of the outside, the bush, the uninhabited beyond. The story thus describes a symbolic transformation wrought through the use of magic that creates useful land out of useland land. In this way it is similar to the *masay* ceremonies used today to either redefine and resanctify inhabited land, or to claim it from the bush. It would certainly be safe to interpret the Moya story as a symbolic rendering of what in all likelihood was a ritual event similar to the ones performed today. For the Iraqw, however, it is through the repetition of these symbols of the danger from the outside that the story derives its rhetorical force and interest. The story becomes an example of how well ritual of this type has worked in the past. Its existence in the oral literature of the Iraqw provides part of the justification for the instrumental use of symbols in other contemporary contexts.

Change over Time

The Iraqw share with certain non-Western peoples a very limited notion of change over time. This is not, I suspect, because they do not perceive change in their circumstances or in the society. In informal conversation change is much discussed, whether brought about by schools, government policy, the weather, or the exodus of Asian shopkeepers. In formal discourse, however, balance and repetition are emphasized.

The limited notion of change is coordinate with the function of the *alqado*. In order for the *alqado* to serve as evidence of the effectiveness of instrumental ritual, there must be a feeling that the terms of existence do not change very much. There is other evidence that this is true for the Iraqw. In the Moya story (Text 23), it will be noted that the lake, the boy, and the tree do not disappear; they are simply moved. It will be noted, too, that the narrator of Text 22 asserts that the bones of the cattle and the people at Bashe and Guse (Ma'angwatay) still exist there where they fell. The spirits who cause misfortune do not come and go, nor change very much; they are either more accessible, as for example on a termite mound or in a stream bed, or less accessible, as when there is no breach of the social order and where boundaries are strong.

The contrast between the informal recognition of change and the formal denial of any overall, long-term change that does not simply repeat itself, reveals a contradiction between the formal cultural ideology and individual experience. Death, for example, is an irreversible change that cannot be denied or undone. The story (*ti'ita*) presented in Text 25 deals with death. In it a group of youths attempt to prevent death by surrounding a dying man with their shields so his 'soul' (*fuqurangw*) cannot escape. In doing this they are creating an analogue of the ritual designed to protect the *aya* or the house. The man dies, of course, and while they are forced therefore to admit the existence of death, they nevertheless blame it on a short person who left a hole in the line. The story deals with an

apparent contradiction in the Iraqw ideology, namely that if the rituals
that delineate the boundaries and purify or curse whole areas are effective
in preventing the evil influences of the outside from entering, then why
can't they prevent death by preventing the soul from leaving the body?
The story of Text 25 seems to present a skeptical view of the effectiveness
of ritual, but like most such stories that deal with essentially insoluble
problems of human existence, it is ambiguous. The question of the true
effectiveness of the ritual is neither proved nor disproved because one individual fails to perform his part adequately. But even a skeptical view
would be impossible were it not for the fact that the original statement
of Text 25—that death can be prevented by means of boundary ritual—
is plausible to an Iraqw audience. The meaning of the story, and its appeal, derive from the fact that it deals with this apparent contradiction:
That death cannot be prevented even though it is generally held that
boundary rituals are effective in frustrating the influence of evil. The absolute change that takes place upon death cannot be dealt with by human
means. Unlike many other African societies, the Iraqw pay little attention
to the spirits of the dead. The continuity of living with the world of the
spirits that is so much a part of the life and ritual of almost all Bantu-
speaking peoples is much less emphasized among the Iraqw.

In contrast to the amount of ritual that is directed to the land, which
for all practical purposes is objectively unchanging, there is very little
ritual observance of death. Funerals are not important foci of ceremonial
observance. The dead are dealt with quickly. Young children who die are
rarely buried. Their bodies are left in the bush where they are consumed
by the hyena. I am told that in the past, all persons with the exception of
important ritual specialists were also disposed of in this manner. Ritual
specialists were buried in graves marked with heaps of earth and beer
offerings were made to their spirits (*gii*). The spirits of ordinary people
were deemed less worthy of offering inasmuch as their spirits would be
least likely to have the power to affect the living from wherever they dwelt
after death. Today, I am told that the dead are simply and quietly buried
near the doorway of the house that they occupied in life. I did not, however, witness any death observance myself, and saw no graves.

I was unable, as well, to elicit any clear statement about the meaning and explanation of death, or about the ultimate fate of the spirit after
death. In general, the spirit of the living person, called *fuqurangw*, is believed to leave the body (*tua*, 'corpse' or *slaqwa*, 'living body') and to go
into the air. Its ultimate destination was unclear to me. Some claimed the
spirit went into the bush (*slaa'*), others claimed that it went into the air
(*fura'a*), while others told me it went into the earth (*yamuwo* or *yami;*
literally 'down'). It is clear, however, that the spirits of the dead may

come back to trouble the living. In this troublesome form, they are called *gii,* and they are placated by sacrifices of meat left outside where they can be devoured by hyena during the night. In death, too, there is no absolute change, no progress or degeneration that is symbolized by death, but instead a reordering of relationships between things that continue to exist in different forms.

This underlying assumption of discontinuity between the life and death and of the limited change would also not be in harmony with an idea of a creation. In fact, I was unable to discover any form of creation myth. For the Iraqw, it seems, since the terms of existence are given today, they always have been and will be. In the development of Western social (or religious) ideology, time and its passage have always been central concepts. As a consequence, the Creation and Judgment have been for most people, for most of the history of the Judeo–Christian world, the end points of a finite flow of time. For the Iraqw, by contrast, there are no end points in time; their world is defined much more with respect to space, which is concrete, than with respect to time.

Similarly, there are no stories that deal with the end of the world. There is little fascination with a future that can be foretold by seers of the present. There are no stories that deal with what we might call the "destiny" of man. Their goals, expressed in stories, *alqado,* and *slufay* are concrete: to continue their expansion into new lands and to preserve the territory they already occupy.

The lack of creation myths, the lack of a teleological mythology, and the lack of a great deal of ceremony to mark the passing of the social person on his death, are all consistent with the assumption that there is no real change in things in the world, but merely a reordering. This concept is also consistent with the lack of reliance on a system of absolute time reckoning as a means of ordering thought about the events of the past. We have seen also that the legitimation of authority depends on the effectiveness of the ritual and magical means under their control. Authority is not legitimated, as in many other societies, by virtue of a continuous genealogical linkage to a hero or famous ancestor of the mythical past. The narrative that deals with the past presents it more or less as evidence that the present means of accomplishing political ends through ritual are the proper and legitimate means. The use of time and the past as a means of legitimation of authority is therefore quite different among the Iraqw. The lack of chronology, the magical character, and the limited notion of change that we observe in the oral traditions of the Iraqw are integrally and logically related. Consequently, it is safe to say that there is no "history" among the Iraqw, if by "history" we mean the critical examination of narrative tradition about the past.

The Topology of Time

On the other hand, there is an ordering of narrative about the past that is not based on time. It is based on the relations of space. The beginning lines of Text 22 place the events in space, not in time. Here the narrator tells us that the name of the section (see Chapter 1) was *Hhay bo'ok,* and, secondly, the people who lived there were of the kindred called *Hhay Tsuhhay.* They lived in the *aya* called Bashe. Bashe is a well-known place today, located to the south of Irqwar Da'aw. In fact, the name itself appears to mean "south," or at least to be derived from the word *'south',* *basa.* (This is linguistically plausible since the /*s*/ and /*sh*/ sounds in Iraqw are allophones of the same phoneme. The /*sh*/ in *Bashe* has simply been regularized by its use on maps and road signs.) This beginning is very similar to the opening lines of another *alqado* given as Text 29 in Chapter 8 ("The End of Women's Initiation"), which says, *Mu ang i bara basa,* 'those people were in the south'. In fact, most *alqado* dealing with an event in the past open with a reference to the place in which the event occurred.

In this same vein, it is obvious that the rest of Text 22 is concerned with movements from place to place and with the ritual and physical condition of the land. The physical condition of the land, furthermore, is a result of its ritual condition, and ritual itself is built up out of spatial manipulations and definitions of areas and points.

Events are associated with points and places in space that are known and can be pointed to or visited. This gives a clearer idea of the important distinction between time and sequence. Sequence is a spatial phenomenon as well as a temporal one.

The sequences that occur in the *alqado* and other oral literature of the Iraqw are spatial sequences. These sequences are given by the nature of motion itself, which is an ordered set of changes in space. It is this sort of sequence, rather than an abstract temporal sequence, that gives order to the narrative of the past.

This fact has certain implications for the type of order we see in these narratives. Since events are associated with places and since places themselves never change with respect to one another, it is to be expected that the Iraqw would posit no direction or absoluteness with respect to change. Narration of events of the past serves the needs of the present, and is structured by the same modes of thought. We have already seen the extent to which the orders of space are the orders of social relations. The same applies to relations between events of the past since they exist only in the minds of the present.

The central importance of place and changes of place is seen in all forms of Iraqw oral literature. Text 26 illustrates this fact more clearly than my own words. It is a dance song collected in Karatu at the northern limits of Iraqw migration. It is part of the story of Bura Ma'ala, the *kahamusmo* who led the first Iraqw settlers to this area in the 1930s. The song consists merely of repetitions of places encountered by the settlers and their leaders.

Conclusion

It is clear that the Iraqw use the relations of space to order their thought and narratives about the past. The experience of sequence in language and in motion is also important. The sequence that arises from the act of moving from one place to another serves to order thought and narrative about the past. While sequence is important, it is not a metric sequence since the intervals between events and the duration of events is not stated. Where metric expressions are used, as for example in Lines 23, 56, 98, and 109 of Text 22, they refer to ritually significant numbers (here, the number 9) and not to actual durations. Thus, the sequence of events is topological since the order of events is given, but the interval is not fixed. There is, furthermore, no "master sequence" by which all narratives can be placed in relation to one another. Instead, disparate narratives place events in relation to place, and places in relation to one another. Since the mental images of space in the thought of most Iraqw are not exact themselves, but instead characterizeable in terms of topological relationships, we must characterize their thought about the past as "topological" as well.

Consider, for purposes of clarification, the English phrase, "It happened during the reign of George III in A.D. 1776." This phrase, which locates an event in time, combines three logically distinct systems of temporal orientation. "During the reign of George III" is a topological designation that specifies the "neighborhood" in time of an event. It does not locate it with respect to the present (assuming we do not know how George III fits into the separate reference sequence that we call the royal succession to the throne of England), nor with respect to other events except as they occurred during this same reign (the temporal neighborhood), or outside of his reign. The expression "A.D.," however, places the event with respect to a zero point on an axis with two arms called "A.D." (after the birth of Christ) and "B.C." (before the birth of Christ). Both A.D. and B.C. are defined with respect to an event that is central to the ritual and world view of Western society. This sort of temporal orientation is an exact analogue of the projective axes of spatial orientation, the

cardinal directions east and west, or north and south. It still does not exactly locate the event in time, but it gives us a fixed axis of reference.
The number "1776" gives us a more or less exact designation of the time
of the event. It is a metric expression and depends on the concept of a
year for its meaning, a year defined astronomically with respect to the
motion of the earth about the sun. Time is "measured" by the act of comparison with this astronomical standard. Three different systems of
thought about time, with their ultimate roots in thought about space, are
thus combined in the expression. If we had information that George III
was a King of England who succeeded his grandfather George II and was
followed on the throne by his son George IV, then we have another means
of fixing the time of the event with respect to this central genealogy and
history of succession of English kings and queens. A system of succeeding
reigns such as the royal succession of the English throne provides an
ordering of sets of time during which events occurred. We speak of the
Victorian period or the Elizabethan era in talking about some events of
the past, and this allows us to think more clearly about the sequence and
relationships of events. I have drawn this example out in some length as
a means of talking about the Iraqw ordering of events. The *only* statement that they consistently make about the temporal location of an event
corresponds to the phrase: "It happened during the reign of George III,"
which we have characterized as a "temporal neighborhood."

Perhaps the most telling fact of all, however, is the lack of any myths
of origin. There is no zero point against which to set a regularized chronology. But this lack is more significant in the realm of politics and
political structure since it means that there is no legitimate order given
from the beginning of time, as it were. Processes and means are legitimated by the oral tradition, not structures and ends. It is this that has
served the Iraqw well by permitting flexibility and adaptability in changing circumstances.

Chapter 8

History

On the Limitations and Possibilities of History

In this chapter I undertake to write a rather limited history of the Iraqw of Irqwar Da'aw. For practical reasons the research was limited to Irqwar Da'aw, a small part of the area in which the Iraqw now live.

In addition to this limitation of area, I also was unable to make use of the extensive colonial archives that are housed in Dar es Salaam, also because of practical limitations of time, money, and transportation. For these reasons, the impact of colonial government and policy has not been seriously dealt with and remains to be considered.

Here the Iraqw texts—*alqado, slufay, da'angw*—are approached as historical documents, which are now considered together with colonial records and other ethnological, linguistic, and geographic information, instead of in relation to each other. If we had to rely on the texts themselves we could not write history, but the critical examination of these texts in the light of other independent information, and according to the canons of historical method, can, as Vansina (1961:187) claims, approximate the "ultimate historical truth."

In this chapter and Chapter 9, I discuss the nature of the evidence on which the historical inquiry depends. In these sections I pose the central historical questions with which I attempt to deal: the development and definition of ethnic boundaries, the role of language, the central importance of spatial categories. I also indicate the way in which ethnic variety, linguistic information, and spatial distribution provide valuable historical information that helps to corroborate and interpret the oral tradition.

The Iraqw, like others, remember the past only selectively, and having remembered tellings and retellings of events that have preceded the present, they transform them in ways that give the telling of these stories a significance that goes beyond the mere content of the stories. The act of telling the stories, the conditions of appropriateness under which certain stories are told and others not, the character and role of the narrator, and the patterns of prosody and style in the narrative itself are all patterns or structures that we can isolate from the simple content of the narrative itself and which go beyond the significance of the "history" that may be communicated in the words themselves. These structural features of the narrative communicate social information in different ways. In Chapters 6 and 7, we have examined some of these patterns and the messages they apparently convey, along with their functions as social instruments in a system of social control. The structure of the narrative seems always to take precedence over any historical content that might also be conveyed. Nevertheless, I attempt to describe some aspects at least of the process by which the contemporary Iraqw culture has come to be, and to show that—and in what manner—the process continues today.

The patterns of meaning and signification that we call "culture" are constituted as "encompassing totalities." The concept of a neighborhood, *papahhay,* or the concept of the kindred, *tlahhay,* encompass the reality of the social individuals (or things) that they define, but they do not have a direct relationship to the individual elements that compose them. The same is true of the topological distinctions of insideness or outsideness with which we have already dealt. They encompass and define, but they do not enumerate. History, by contrast, concerns itself with an "enumerated totality" in which facts, and the events, individuals, and interpretations that relate them are detailed in a way that shows how these are conditioned by events that have preceded them in time.

This, of course, is not the whole of history, but it is its backbone. The enumerated totality of historical content is what we *cannot* achieve in a history of the Iraqw—at least not completely. The discussion of cultural process that follows, is, because of the nature of its source material, a history without a backbone. The structure of the argument is an encompassing totality in many ways akin to the cultural structures it uses for its data, and which therefore necessarily condition my attempts to understand cultural structures of the Iraqw. The meaningfulness of what I describe is in part due to its incompleteness—an incompleteness derived from the structuring of the text itself.

P. Bourdieu (1977:20) discusses this aspect of the cultural structuring of events in Western-type histories, and in the "oral traditions" of nonliterate societies. The schemes of organization that we use in talking about the past are, in Bourdieu's terms, of the "second order"; that is, they are theories of theories of "relationships within which individuals or a group define the real space of practical relationships." For Bourdieu, since the native theory of the cultural constitution of relationships is nothing more than the product of the same generative cultural schemes that produce the relationships in the first place, "history" is really only the rationalization of events that must be accounted for and "explained" in terms of practical ends and habits. This is similar to the position I have taken here when I show, for example, that the practical activity of the *masay* ritual is revalued in a particular historical instance to provide *protection* and demarcation of boundaries rather than (or in addition to) rain or good crops. The same practical activity (circumambulation, suffocation, etc.), given different values, has been so used in other societies in Tanzania (e.g., the Warangi, see Fosbrooke, 1958; or the Swahili at Kilwa, see Lienhardt, 1966). The same point is developed with respect to the *marmo* ritual. Bourdieu acknowledges, as do I, a debt to Franz Boas, whose theoretical position of historical particularism was similar (Bourdieu, 1977:200, note 22, who references Boas' *Anthropology and Modern Life*, 1962:164).

This rationalization of customary behavior (*getlangw*) and the revaluation of specific acts introduces lacunae in the historical record. The corpus of oral tradition demands a cultural interpretation and even this will be necessarily incomplete.

Specifically, the Iraqw account of events in the past lacks a chronology, a fact that necessarily handicaps any attempted history of the people and their culture. Therefore, the historian must construct a logical but rough chronology on which to build an account of the facts. For this possible observer's bias one need not apologize, but it must be noted, since *it is not* a part of the way the Iraqw themselves construct a view of the past.

In this chapter I limit chronological discussion to the barest minimum that will make sense of the material. While this leaves many questions unanswered, and while it is doubtlessly frustrating to the historian, it does remain faithful to the nature of the oral information on which this discussion is based. I begin the discussion of history with an account of the origins of the Iraqw people. For this, I use information on the geographical distribution of the languages that are genetically related to Iraqw, together with the collected oral traditions. Historical depth is, however, severely limited.

The substantive discussion of the Iraqw past must begin around 1800 in a place called Ma'angwatay. This is the farthest that Iraqw memory and traditions (and those of other, surrounding peoples) will carry us in our attempt to recover the past. There is some archaeological evidence from the site of Engaruka that has been linked with the Iraqw by a number of investigators (Sutton, 1966), but this does not carry us very far either. In any case, the history of migrations is not of primary interest.

Following upon the discussion of the origin of the Iraqw people, the traditions relating to the first settlers of the isolated valleys of Irqwar Da'aw are examined. In explaining this event and the subsequent expansion out of this area by the descendants of some of these original settlers, we are faced with two alternatives: Either the event is to be seen as the result of demographic and economic process (population growth, strain on resources), or as the result of other cultural and social processes. J. Vansina, for one, would strip away what he sees to be the cultural overburden to mine the underlying economic reality. The fact of population pressure would "explain" the historical event. In contrast to this approach, I attempt to reintroduce the cultural representation of the event in order to show that, in addition to the fact of population movement, we can also recover the social–structural and cultural motives that gave the event its particular form at that historical instant. The sterility of most migrational histories derives from their underlying assumption that there exists something that is *simply* migration. Here I insist that, while we may speak of "migration" as a general class of observable social phenomena, a description of this "fact" alone tells us nothing of sociological or cultural interest. Although human biology determines that we must wear clothes to keep warm, it does not determine that men wear slacks and women wear skirts, or that one must wear a hat to the opera. Similarly, population pressure does not determine what form a migration or territorial expansion will take. The cultural and social structures in place at a given time will determine the particulars of the response. Indeed, population pressure itself does not even determine, in general terms, that there will be migration as its consequence. C. Geertz (1963) has shown that the cultural and sociological conditions that pertained in Java in the last century led to an "agricultural involution" in which labor investment was vastly intensified within a limited area. Migration did *not* result. Part of the problem we seek to define and to answer is, therefore, why did migration and territorial expansion occur at all, and how was it rationalized, justified, and represented among the Iraqw who actually participated in it? In other words, I wish to include in this history the data as well as the problems of the cultural representation of historical events.

In part this involves an anachronistic extrapolation of contemporary sociological observation into the past. There is, however, limited but independent evidence from German and English accounts that, in combination with the interpreted Iraqw texts allows us to corroborate independently statements that would otherwise be mere anachronism (at least for this century during which independent accounts have been written). Again, linguistic and geographical evidence aids in the inquiry.

In the rest of the chapter, I investigate the way in which the particular social and cultural structures came about. The migrations of people into Irqwar Da'aw provided a collection of cultural ideas that were integrated into a new cultural unity under the influence of ritual specialists. The institution of ritual specialists is widespread in northern Tanzania; they are called *ntemi* (or some variant) among the Bantu-speaking peoples, and *olaibon* among the Masai. The *qwaslare* of the Iraqw are similar in many respects to these ritual specialists in other societies, in that they prescribe for a wide range of clients a ritual practice that serves a multiplicity of needs (rain, protection, fertility, etc.). In the Iraqw instance I try to show the particular way in which these ritual specialists were central, active participants in the creation of an ethnic identity and a cultural ideology and practice. They drew, of course, from elements of a regional culture, but they assembled these elements in a unique way according to the historical conditions of their times. I try as well to show the political aspects of this cultural synthesis in a historical frame.

The spatial ideology, for one thing, was probably largely the result of the ritual innovation and practice of these specialists. In Chapter 9 I detail the structural imperatives that made a spatial ideology of social organization appropriate and necessary. I try also to show that the terms and practices out of which it was composed were present in the regional culture from which Irqwar Da'aw drew its population. Finally, the combination of population pressure, the practice of exile, and the presence of the colonial government led to a highly successful movement of expansion. As the final step in my analysis of Iraqw culture, I show how the form that this movement took was determined by the history of cultural development in Irqwar Da'aw that preceded it.

Language and History

Although the Iraqw share many features of culture and society with other groups around them, they are unique in their language. Nevertheless, this linguistic singularity has almost no relevance to the historical question. Even those scholars who would argue that the Iraqw language is related to the Cushitic languages of Ethiopia admit that the Iraqw language and those related to it in the so-called southern Cushitic groups of languages must have separated from the other Cushites at a very early time. H. C. Fleming (1969), who supports the Cushitic hypothesis, states that:

> Not only do such Southern Cushitic languages such as Iraqw, Mbugu, and Sanye differ from each other a great deal, but, as a whole, they are significantly remote from East Cushitic and Central Cushitic languages as to be genetically controversial. Lexicostatistically, retention figures between Southern Cushitic and Eastern Cushitic, Central Cushitic or North Cushitic languages run from 6 to 13%, which are percentages comparable to the lowest found in Austronesian by Dyen [1962] and much lower than anything in Indo-European. . . . Comparable figures from Indo–European, Austronesian and the rest of Hamito–Semitic suggest that Southern Cushitic languages have been in Tanzania well over 5000 years. (p. 31)

Clearly such ancient contact with other Cushitic cultures, if in fact such contact existed, is not an adequate basis for historical arguments about cultural and social similarities between the Iraqw and Ethiopian Cushites. About the only thing we can conclude from findings such as Fleming's is that they have been there for a long time—a dubious conclusion if it cannot be supported by other independent evidence. To argue that the uniqueness of Iraqw language guarantees a unique culture, or that the presence of the Iraqw language implies the presence of a distinct racial identity would be foolish. We cannot rely on the classification of a language to give us information about the history or identity of a culture.

The problem of language is also indeterminate in another way: Although the Iraqw identity as a people depends, in part, on the fact that they speak a unique language, I am unable to account for its universal adoption by all of the immigrants who came into Irqwar Da'aw from other regions. Elsewhere in Tanzania, one or another of the Bantu languages have dominated and absorbed all other linguistic groups. In the Pare Hills, to the east of Irqwar Da'aw and across the Masai Steppe, the language of the Mbugu peoples (which is apparently related to Iraqw) is even now in the process of being assimilated by the Bantu language spoken by the Shambaa and Pare peoples (Feierman, 1974; Copland, 1933; Goodman, 1971). There is considerable evidence that this process of assimilation has almost always favored Bantu or Nilotic speakers across all of East Africa. I am able to offer only a weak hypothesis as to why this has not happened in Irqwar Da'aw: Just as we have seen that certain genres of Iraqw oral narrative are appropriate only to certain places, so it seems, the Iraqw language itself is judged to be appropriate to Irqwar Da'aw. Although I recognize that this would appear to be an analogical retrodiction offered as pale hypothesis, it is consistent with other aspects of Iraqw culture. Like the question of the origin of Iraqw language, or the question of the degree of cultural influence "contributed" by the original small group of Iraqw speakers, the question of why the *Iraqw* language was preferentially adopted must remain unanswered at present.

Space and History

Perhaps the most difficult problem in this study concerns the relationship between the spatial structure of Iraqw society and culture and the temporal process by which this came into being, for not only are we immediately engaged in the philosophical and ethnological problem of the nature of space, but also in the long-standing sociological debate (in its broadest sense) over the issue of structural versus historical description and explanation. In this chapter I develop the argument that the cultural order of the Iraqw as we observe it today (and also within this century, which is to say within the recorded period) is the product of historical circumstances; but the structure so constituted is also, at any moment in the process, the producer of a continuing history. Structure and history thus account for each other. In this analysis, we have to account for the emphasis on space and boundary ritual as a product of the history of the Iraqw. Recourse to arguments that would derive these cultural features from hypothetical migrations of Iraqw-speaking peoples who "brought with them" such practices would be weak at best. Although Iraqw-speaking peoples clearly did migrate there, bringing with them their own culture, the evidence suggests that these were a very small group of people and that their cultural influence was very small indeed, at least in the period between the settlement of Irqwar Da'aw and the present. The question of whether there were large Cushitic populations in the area that were later absorbed by Bantu and Nilotes in their gradual immigrations into the area, and who contributed elements of their cultures to a greater synthesis, can perhaps never be fully answered. Instead, the stronger historical argument is that the culture of the Iraqw is the result of a long period of borrowings and interaction with other groups. We are interested, therefore, in exploring the process of cultural synthesis.

Why did boundaries and spaces, in particular, focus so much attention in Iraqw ritual and self-concept? There are two hypotheses that I would put forward to account for this.

By their own testimony they have been under attack or the threat of violence since their settlement of Irqwar Da'aw. It is clear that since military action failed for lack of strength or organization, they fell to depend on the efficacy of ritual and ruse to protect them. Abner Cohen (1976) in a recent analysis of symbols and politics feels that "under certain structural circumstances some groups cannot organize themselves formally as political organizations, but resort instead to informal modes of organization that depend on the manipulations of symbols in order to articulate organizational functions which otherwise would be denied them." The "structural circumstances" that have denied the Iraqw the opportunity to organize themselves formally and to protect themselves militarily have been first the Masai and Barabaig warriors, and after them, the German and British colonial powers. In this case, they have resorted to the manipulation of ritual symbols to assert their identity and their claim to the land. The spatial concepts that we see integrated into a coherent whole among the Iraqw, concepts that they are able to use in mobilizing the manpower for expropriation of more territory and for the protection of what they have, also exist in less coherent form among their neighbors. The synthetic cultural achievement of the Iraqw has been their articulation of these symbols and concepts into an effective means of organization. The historical aim of this chapter is to show how change in ritual and symbol has come about.

Secondly, we may take a social–structural approach. Irqwar Da'aw absorbed large numbers of peoples of diverse ethnic origin who accepted the leadership and supernatural protection of the *qwaslare,* or rainmakers. Settlement in small groups and a continuing exchange of children and exiles among the Iraqw and their neighbors vitiated the force of genealogical sentiments as the primary bond of social structure. Among the Bantu-speaking neighbors of the Iraqw, groups are defined first of all by genealogical relations of the members, secondarily by the space they occupy. Among those people who immigrated from all over to settle in Irqwar Da'aw, these genealogical relationships did not exist, or were extremely tenuous. Since in all of the areas surrounding the Iraqw there is some notion of a ritual neighborhood or precinct, we might reasonably assume that the immigrants to Irqwar Da'aw brought these ideas with them at some time in the past. But, whereas before the idea of neighborhood or ritual precinct was overshadowed by the dominant, regulating structure of kinship—or, in some cases, such as the Nyamwezi, to a nascent hierarchy based on patrimonial redistribution of the tax (*hongo*) on trade—the situation in Irqwar Da'aw made a spatial mode of definition of group membership and practice of ritual–politics both more appropriate and more practical. The actual creation of specific cultural forms that served organization functions, however, appears to have been accomplished by the ritual experts, the *qwaslare* and *kahamuse,* who, in more than one case, used their proficiency in creating acceptable ritual forms to acquire their reputations as ritual experts. According to my reading of the historical process, then, the creative and integrative effort of certain ritually proficient individuals served the personal ends of those responsible as well as the political ends of those people who were clients of the ritual expert, in other words, the people of the section or of the *aya* that a particular expert served. Although these individuals were apparently rarely able to amass goods or capital, or to acquire coercive power, they did achieve a legitimacy as cultural arbiters, and gave to Iraqw culture the degree of coherence and regularity that it does possess. Even so, it is not strongly coherent or regular, and traditions vary in form from place to place and command varying degrees of loyalty from person to person or from context to context within the Iraqw cultural domain. The sociological aim of this chapter, then, is to show how a limited structure of politically significant roles (*qwaslare, kahamuse, barise,* and *masomba*) has functioned to provide a degree of cultural and social order, and how this function has changed over time.

In the discussion that follows, I begin by sketching a chronological framework within which history can be meaningfully discussed. The native viewpoint, taken in the preceding chapter, is thus abandoned for the observer's "objective" history. I raise the question of "origins" of the Iraqw-speaking peoples, but although I am able to make some suggestions about this, the question must remain essentially unanswered. The discussion of origins, however, provides the background for presenting the evidence for multiple origins of most of the people who today consider themselves to be Iraqw.

A Chronological Framework

I will begin the chronology of Iraqw history with the approximate period of 1770–1800. The remembered genealogies of elders and *kahamuse* never reach more than 10 generations into the past. If we were to assign an appproximate average of 20 years to each generation (i.e., the time between the succession to role of *kahamusmo* upon the death of his father to his own death), this arithmetic would take us back no farther than 200 years from the present. This figure corresponds with R. F. Gray's estimate of the length of settlement by the Wambugwe in the valley below the escarpment (Gray, 1963; also Wada, 1975:49).

A period of 200 years would give enough time to achieve the cultural integration that is observable today, but would also be limited enough to make the lack of historical depth and the apparently ad hoc nature of much of their cultural and social practice seem plausible and necessary. Demographically, too, the period of 200 years of settlement in the limited area of Irqwar Da'aw is reasonable. The German explorer Oscar Baumann found the Iraqw limited to the upland valleys of Irqwar Da'aw in 1893 (Baumann, 1895). He traveled in the area between 1892 and 1893, passing directly through Irqwar Da'aw (*Kirumusi* on his map is *Kwermusl* in the orthography adopted in this work). At this time, they had not yet begun to overflow the boundaries of this area into the larger plateau. Later travelers and writers, including C.W. Werther in 1896 and Fritz Jaeger in 1906, continued to place the Iraqw only in Irqwar Da'aw. The rest of the plateau was pastureland grazed by the various subtribes (*eimojik*) of the pastoral Tatoga. Wilson (1952:43), an ethnographer of the Tatoga in Mbulu district, commented

> When the early German explorer Fritz Jaeger visited the area at the turn of the century, they [the Tatoga] must have made a lasting impression on him, by their numbers and their physical characteristics. He seems to have spent considerable time among them and took the trouble to describe them in some detail and also to record many photographs. He called them the Wambulu and he scarcely mentioned the Iraqw who have overrun the area. Early German maps refer to this district as the Tatoga Plateau. Today, however, it is almost completely inhabited by the rapidly increasing Iraqw.

But immediately after Jaeger's account of the district, or perhaps during the first decade of the century, the Iraqw did begin their first concerted attempts to migrate out of Irqwar Da'aw and to establish themselves in the surrounding territories. F. J. Bagshawe, an English district officer of Mbulu district, wrote in the early 1920s that the Iraqw had begun to migrate down the escarpment and to establish themselves in the areas below them and immediately contiguous with Irqwar Da'aw. The Germans built their administrative center at Mbulu in 1910, and it is this event which, according to Bagshawe (1926:64), caused some of the Iraqw to leave Irqwar Da'aw and to move away from the German settlement and administrative "Boma."

> Since the Boma at Mbulu was built, there has been a constant and troublesome migration of Erokh [Iraqw] from the top of the escarpment to the country of the Tatoga below. The Germans made a great effort to stop this migration, posting guards on the paths down the mountains, and finally settling a company of troops at Dareda, which was removed only on the outbreak of war [i.e., World War I]. Efforts to induce these Erokh to return proved fruitless. In 1918 their houses were burnt and they were all marched to Erokh [Irqwar Da'aw] under supervision. . . . but within six months all were back again and their number had increased. It has now been decided to leave them to become permanent residents of Kondoa.

While Bagshawe, together with most of his contemporaries, always looked for the exogenous cause of events, whether it be Hamitic superiority or, as in this case, pressure from the German administration, it would seem from Bagshawe's own remarks that the reason for the Iraqw migration, especially since it was so determined, could only have been the result of internal developments. At the time of their migration to the lands below the escarpment, the Iraqw had had almost no contact with the Germans. Although the Germans had been in control of the central part of the plateau since 1899, and had acted strongly against resistance by Tatoga, hanging several "Wambulu" (Tatoga) chiefs in 1906, they had yet to successfully make inroads in Irqwar Da'aw itself (Gwassa, 1969:112; and *District Book*). The Iraqw today clearly remember their successful defense of Irqwar Da'aw. They insist that while the Germans did control the area around the Boma in Mbulu town, they did not effectively control any of the Iraqw *aya* of Irqwar Da'aw. They credit, as we might expect, the effectiveness of their *masay* ritual's protection (*pa'asamo*) in keeping the German administrators at bay. Therefore, it seems unlikely that the Iraqw were forced by the Germans into the plains below the escarpment.

In the same passage, Bagshawe notes that the Iraqw with whom he dealt as an administrator of the district between 1915 and 1920 no longer attempted any armed resistance, but were "experts in semipassive resistance." It is my impression that most of the Iraqw elders who remember the early colonial times in their district would accept this characterization of them as experts in passive resistance.

Contained in Bagshawe's comments, then, are two characteristics of Iraqw history in this century: a slow but persistent migration from Irqwar Da'aw motivated by forces internal to Iraqw society, and a passive resistance to outside threat whether from colonial administration or Masai raiders. We must note as well that the barrier to expansion posed by both Masai and Tatoga peoples was considerably weakened by the German presence. The German administration of the district attempted to bring all of these populations under its control, by force if necessary. Unlike the British of a later period, they did not encourage Iraqw expansion between 1906 and 1916. They dealt with Iraqw efforts to expand as forcefully and as negatively as they did with Tatoga or Masai "unauthorized" migrations.

Thus, we have two historical markers to orient the discussion in time. An approximate date of 1770–1800, during which Iraqw-speaking peoples in small numbers apparently first migrated into Irqwar Da'aw, marks the beginning of relatively reliable historical knowledge of the area.

Of course, the extent of memory about residence in Irqwar Da'aw does not establish with any certainty the actual length of residence in the area. The date may be considerably in error. It represents the latest time that they could have arrived. From 1800 to 1900, the Iraqw were confined to Irqwar Da'aw and continued to absorb migrants from all directions and all ethnic groups. Between 1900 and 1910, numbers of Iraqw began to move out of Irqwar Da'aw into the surrounding areas, a process that continued through this century to the present (Winter and Molyneaux, 1963). These dates divide this period of Iraqw history into two periods: first, a period of in-migration and consolidation of an ethnic identity with distinct cultural and social forms; second, a period of expansion and expropriation of land from their neighbors. This broad and rough framework will serve to focus our discussion.

Origins

By their own accounts, the Iraqw today claim to have come from an earlier homeland located to the south of the present Irqwar Da'aw. The name of this place was Ma'angwatay, and they remember it in their stories as a place very rich in grass for their cattle, rain for the crops, and so, food for the people. Here they claim to have grown fat and to have swelled their numbers considerably. They shared this place, Ma'angwatay, with another people whom they called *tara*. Today, *tara* (or *tarmo* in the singular) refers to the group of people known in the ethnographic literature as Tatoga or "Mangati." The Iraqw frequently use the term *mangati* interchangeably with *tara* in referring to these peoples, and it appears from much evidence that the ethnic label *mangati* and the early homeland of the Iraqw, known as Ma'angwatay, are possibly related.

Iraqw traditions tell us nothing about the nature of Ma'angwatay other than that it was a rich land from which they were driven in a fight with their erstwhile neighbors, the *tara* or *mangati*. It is clear, however, that the close interaction that exists today between the Iraqw and the Tatoga goes back to this earlier homeland of Ma'angwatay. Many of the institutions of the Iraqw today can be traced to Tatoga institutions. A large part of the Iraqw-speaking population is today undoubtedly of Tatoga origin. In fact, the original Iraqw-speaking group was very small. Only three clans (*tlahhay*) trace their origins today back to this small band of Iraqw speakers who came from Ma'angwatay into Irqwar Da'aw.

Tatoga traditions, on the other hand, give us a little more information on who may have been living in Ma'angwatay. The Iraqw word probably refers to the gently sloping plains around Mount Hanang, immediately below the Rift Valley Escarpment and adjacent to the highland forests that grow along the high edge of the Mbulu Plateau. This area is labelled *Mangati* on Oscar Baumann's map of 1894. He himself passed through here during his travels of 1892–1893 and obtained this name for the area in conversations with Tatoga tribesmen. On later German and British maps, this same area is called the Mangati Plain or the Barabaig Steppe (e.g., Jaeger, 1911). Furthermore, this area is located where the Iraqw tradition would suggest we should find such a place since, upon leaving Ma'angwatay, the Iraqw climbed either a mountain or a cliff and went into hiding in a forest.

It is worth noting, however, that most Iraqw resisted the idea that Mangati and Ma'angwatay were in all probability the same place. This resistance, I suspect, comes from a widespread confusion about the use of the word *mangati* in Tanzania today.

C. H. N. Jackson (1942:8), a district official of Singida district, who wrote on the Mangati in the 1942 issue of *Tanganyika Notes and Records,* claims

> [The Tatoga] call themselves Barabaig, but are more familiarly known as *mangati.* This, I am told, is a word derived from the Masai word mangat, meaning enemy, a worthy title to be bestowed by such a war-like people. . . . Like the Masai, they are Hamitic speaking.

Jackson does not say who told him this, but G. Wilson (1953), writing in the same journal a decade later, tells us that, while it had been "long assumed that the word same from the Masai *ol-mangatinda* as recorded by H. N. M. Harvey in the *Tanganyika Police Review,* No. 1, page 19," in fact, this word was a legitimate name for themselves that probably had no connection other than a fortuitous resemblance of sound with the Masai word meaning 'enemy'. Wilson states that "the subtribe lived in the Ngorongoro and Katesh area and it is quite possible that they had contact with the Masai there." Today, however, the subtribe at Itigi state that *Mangati* is the name given erroneously to the Barabaig by the European" (Wilson, 1953:40). This, of course, would account for Jackson's misuse of the term quoted above. Nevertheless, the folk etymology of the name that derived it from the Masai word has a very wide currency today since it was taught in Tanzanian schools and used by administrators for decades. It had the further appeal of being an accurate description of these people from the viewpoint of European administrators and certain of the other African peoples who neighbored them, for they were cattle raiders and frequently killed adult members of other ethnic groups who trespassed on their territory. They acquired the reputation of being "ritual murderers." Because of these widespread misconceptions, the independent Tanzanian government ruled that the term *Mangati* should not be used in public discussion, governmental proceedings, or in public media. It is probably for this reason that the Iraqw today resisted my suggestion that *Ma'angwatay* and *Mangati* were the same word in different forms. Among the Tatoga themselves, the word *mangat'k* (*mangatiga* in the singular) is the proper name of one subtribe or subgroup (*eimojik*) of the Tatoga who live near Itigi, a town considerably farther to the south than the Mangati on the old German maps.

The people whom the Iraqw call *tara* call themselves "Tatoga." This is the generic term for numerous subgroups who all speak similar languages and who all derive ultimately from the "Proto-Nandi-Kalenjin," who lived on the slopes of Mount Elgon in western Kenya (Ehret, 1970). (Wilson [1952; 1953] cites Tatoga tradition in support of this.) The whole group of people who call themselves "Tatoga" and who recognize a linguistic and cultural similarity among themselves do not act in any way as a group. Instead, they are divided into named and localized subtribes and these are distributed over quite a large area of northern Tanzania and southwest Kenya. These subtribes are today called Iseimajek, Rutageink (located in Musoma district), Sirikwajek (a few members in 1952 living among the Nandi), Buradik, Bajut (Maswa, Nzega, Singida, and Mbulu districts), Bajut, Dororajek (Mangola area of Mbulu district), Daragwajek, Reimojik, Mangat'k, Gumbiek, Bianjit (Itigi area), Gisamajek (Dongobesh, Bashonet, Karatu areas in Mbulu district), Salagwajek (Shinyanga), and the Barabaig (Katesh in Hanang district and Dongobesh in Mbulu district) (Wilson, 1952).

Among these, the Bajut, the Dororajek, and the Gisamajenk in Mbulu district have been assimilated almost completely by the Iraqw (Tomikawa, 1970, 1979; Wada, 1975). Nearly all of the Tatoga in contact with the Iraqw are bilingual to some degree in Iraqw and their own language. Only the Barabaig have maintained a strong and unassimilated identity in the face of Iraqw encroachment. But even they feel the pressure of changing circumstances most acutely. In 1975 a group of Barabaig young men attacked an Iramba settlement on the borders of their pasturelands near Dongobesh, ostensibly with the aim of stealing cattle. Rumor in the district had it, however, that they were more intent on driving the agriculturalists from their pasture than on stealing cattle. The government reacted quickly to the attack and eventually forced all of the Barabaig into settled villages where they were required to apply their efforts to the plow and the hoe. Much larger numbers have, however, turned to agriculture before this event under the pressure of Iraqw population movements and Iraqw ideas and language. This large-scale assimilation of

Tatoga-speakers should not surprise us, however, when we consider that the Iraqw and Tatoga must have been in close association for over 300 years at the very least.

Tatoga traditions claim that the first of them entered what is now Tanzania in the vicinity of Ngorongoro Crater highlands. They came from the slopes of Mount Elgon. G. Wilson (1953) tells us:

> The Ghumbiek and Mangat'k are the people of Ghumbangaing, an early Tatoga ancestor who it is claimed was the first to enter what is now Tanganyika in the neighborhood of *Fuadi,* the Tatoga name for Ngorongoro. There they were called Sirikwajek [i.e., the Sirikwa of Mount Elgon]. . . . The first groups which arrived at Hanang Mountain and grazed into what is called the Barabaig Steppes . . . were the Mangat'k and Binajit. The latter means land or territory. They must have arrived and been well settled before Ruida . . . arrived there about 250 years ago. Ruida found the Hanang area already occupied by Tatoga groups of the Bianjit, Daragwajek, Mangat'k and Ghumbiek who were living among an agricultural people, the *Gobreik,* the Tatoga name for the Gorowa. (p. 42)

We may safely conclude then that in the period before the move to Irqwar Da'aw from Ma'angwatay, the Iraqw (and the closely related Gorowa) lived together with the Tatoga-speaking Mangat'k, Bianjit, Ghumbiek, and Daragwajek subtribes (*eimojik*) on the valley-bottom plains surrounding Mount Hanang. Using linguistic evidence (Ehret, 1970) and the evidence of oral traditions (Wilson, 1952; 1953) it can be clearly shown that the Tatoga-speaking peoples in the area migrated from the north and west; that is, from Mount Elgon to Mount Hanang by way of the Ngorongoro highlands. Perhaps these Tatoga immigrants found the Iraqw-speaking peoples in the Mangati plains around Hanang when they arrived. Neither Tatoga nor Iraqw tradition enlightens us on this point.

In fact, we are unable to make any good guesses about where the original Iraqw-speaking peoples may have come from. Mzee Ramadhani (n.d.), a Swahili school teacher who taught for many years in Mbulu, wrote a short tract on the Iraqw, basing his account on collected traditions and on some conjecture. Much of what he writes in his "Mapokeo ya Historia ya Iraq (Mbulu) kati ya Miaka 1700–1900" (n.d.) ('Received Traditions of the Iraqw History between 1700–1900') is valuable, but his statement about the origins of the Iraqw provoke some doubt.

> The exact origin of the Iraqw is not well known, but they are Hamito-Nomads [his term] who are mixed with Bantu. There are many stories which are told concerning their origin in Iraq [Mesopotamia], Asia,

from whence they crossed Egypt, and others crossed a great body of
water in canoes [*miringamo*]. They arrived in a land with a range of
high mountains. Others went through Ethiopia up to Somalia, and
others went even farther, arriving at Lake Victoria. Others crossed the
Blue Nile and they came up to the land of Ma'angwatay which is in
the District of Kondoa Irangi, Central Region, Tanganyika.

Stories such as these mentioned by Ramadhani in the passage above
do, indeed, have wide currency. The mention of such places as Iraq (the
mid-eastern country), Egypt, Ethiopia, and the Blue Nile are almost certainly inspired by contact with Europeans and European education, but
the mention of the canoe and the crossing of a wide body of water are not.
It is these two features that are interesting and that are occasionally repeated yet today by some Iraqw elders, although they disclaim any knowledge of what significance these traditions might have and do not attest
to their veracity. The type of canoe that Ramadhani mentioned—and for
which he gave the Iraqw name, *miringamo*—is still carved from a single
log by the Iraqw today even though they live high in the mountains and
do not use boats on any of the lakes in the area. The *miringamo*, which in
form and construction looks something like the dug-out canoes or *dau* of
the Swahili coast, or the canoes on Lake Victoria, are used among the
Iraqw for brewing beer.

Bagshawe (1923:Part IV, p. 60), writing about "the aboriginal
races of Kondoa Irangi," brought the Iraqw from Lake Victoria.

> Seven or eight generations ago they lived in the neighborhood of Lake
> Nyanza [Victoria], whence they migrated southward to their present
> locations. This migration was the result of their defeat in a long war
> with their neighbors—then as now—the Tatoga. . . . Their final
> destinations were·not reached for several generations, and the migra-
> tion was attended with considerable hardship. The Erokh [Iraqw] ap-
> pear to have settled first in their present location and to have made a
> peace with the Tatoga, which has persisted ever since. The Goroa
> appear to have settled somewhere in or near Turu [Singida] in a
> country which they call Ma'angwe. Next they moved to below the
> escarpment, occupying the present Tatoga country. . . . These mi-
> grations were all the result of pressure from the Tatoga, then infinitely
> more numerous and powerful than now, who were themselves migrat-
> ing southwards, not so much as the result of war, as in search for
> pasture for their cattle. That the tribe under consideration came of
> Lake Nyanza is clear. They have a distinct tradition that they once
> lived near a big lake, which they still know as Yaiquanza.

Bagshawe's certainty notwithstanding, his story would have depended on whom he talked with. The Iraqw who live near the town of
Mbulu in the *aya* known as Gehandu are certainly immigrants from the

Iramba or from Sukuma to the west. The Iramba and Isanzu, further-more, have clear traditions bringing them from the Lake, and the linguis-tic evidence supports this (Greenberg, 1966). If Bagshawe had spoken with any of these people they certainly would have told him stories about origins near Lake Victoria. For peoples who formerly spoke Tatoga or Bantu languages, an origin near Victoria is clearly attested by similar place names and similar languages both in Mbulu district and near the Lake, especially around Speke Gulf in the southeast corner. Widespread and coordinate traditions corroborate this story of origin for large numbers of Iraqw, but there is no evidence that any group of people *then speaking* Iraqw came from near Victoria or from anywhere in the west. The lin-guistic evidence points the other direction, towards the coast of the Indian Ocean.

Although the supposed link between Iraqw and the Cushitic lan-guages cannot be supported with very much certainty, it is clear that Iraqw is genetically related to a series of languages that are distributed between Mbulu district in Tanzania eastward toward the coast of Kenya. There is a corresponding gradient of decreasing lexical overlap in the re-corded vocabularies of these languages as we move from the coast toward the Iraqw. Dahalo or Sanye, located on the coast of Kenya north of Mom-basa, is most distantly related to Iraqw (Fleming, 1969:17; Tucker, 1967; Ehret, 1974), but there is enough good evidence that links it with Iraqw to lead us to the possible conclusion that Iraqw speakers once lived on the coast and migrated inland. This would fit with the vaguely remem-bered stories of life on a vast body of water. As we move westward, the speakers of Ma'a of Mbugu are encountered in the Pare Hills. These people have been almost entirely assimilated by the Bantu-speaking Shambaa, but enough lexical material of an older language remains to link them rather clearly with Iraqw (Copland, 1933; Ehret, 1974:7; Fleming, 1969:17; Goodman, 1971; Murdock, 1959; Greenberg, 1966). Between the Pare Hills and the Mbulu Plateau there is, or was, a small group of hunters and gatherers living in the Masai Steppe. These people, the Asa or Ara-manik, spoke a language even more closely related to the Iraqw language than the other two to the east, but less closely related to it than those last few languages known as Ngomvia (or Qwadza), Alagwa, Burungi, and Gorowa, which are grouped in the area near the present location of the Iraqw. This last set of languages are much more closely related to Iraqw than the other two, just as they are more closely located in space to the Iraqw lands. Fleming (1969) posits a common ancestral language which he labels "Proto-South Cushitic" as the ultimate source of all of these lan-guages. He diagrams the degree of relationship between these languages as shown in Figure 8.1.

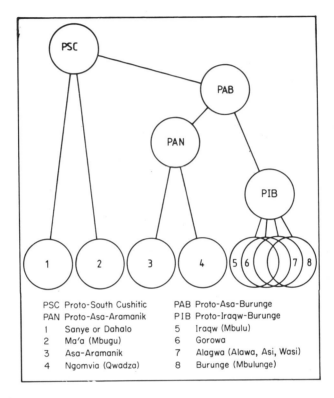

FIGURE 8.1. *Lexical comparison of Iraqw with some related languages. The languages and their interrelationships are represented here. The languages are geographically distributed along an east-west line, from the northern coastal areas of Tanzania to the Mbulu plateau.*

This linguistic distribution suggests a connection with the coast at some time in the past, but it would be extremely risky to try to put a date on this possible ancestral homeland, and even more so to use such conjecture in place of history. Nevertheless, it is probably the best guess that can be put forward at present about the ultimate origins of the people who brought the ancestor of the Iraqw language into the area where we now find them.

Other scholars would disagree with me. Ehret asserts that the "Proto-South Cushites," as he labels the hypothetical linguistic ancestors of the Iraqw speakers, were once widely distributed over East Africa as far as southern Tanzania, the lakes in the west, and east to the coast (Ehret, 1974, especially the maps on pages 19–23). J. Sutton (1966, 1969) would trace the Iraqw speakers back to "certain presumed Cushites" (1969:49) who inhabited Kenya and northern Tanzania as early as the first millenium B.C. He links the Iraqw with the ruins of Engaruka, a large village complex built with stone that lies to the north of present Irqwar Da'aw along the Rift Valley. G. Murdock (1959:197) links the Iraqw with the Kenya Capsian cultures, or with a hypothetical population of "Neolithic Cushites" who are supposed to have inhabited Kenya well before the first millenium B.C. Ehret (1974:7) states that the "third millenium B.C. would not be an impossible dating for the Proto-South-Cushitic era," for which he suggests a location in central Kenya. The reader will appreciate, I am sure, the complete indeterminacy of this debate!

Other neighbors of the Iraqw have come from all other directions. The Masai, as has been very clearly shown, came from the north relatively recently, probably reaching the northern Tanzania steppes from 200 to 300 years ago. Robert Gray (1955; 1963:145) has shown that the Mbugwe people moved to their present location from the south, moving through the lands now occupied by the Gogo. Such movement probably continued well into this century when colonial regulations put a stop to migration. The Wambugwe and the Warangi are closely related in langauge and culture (Gray, 1955) and both have traditions that would indicate earlier residence to the south and east. The Iramba, too, came from the south from 200 to 300 years ago, settling in a plateau area to the west of the Mbulu Plateau (Kidamala and Danielson, 1961). From here, groups of people continued to move to the east, assimilating the Iraqw, the Ihanzu, and the Iambi. Most of the Ihanzu derive from Ukerwe, a large island near the southeast coast of Lake Victoria. According to their traditions, they came to their present location across the Serengeti Plain relatively recently (perhaps four or five generations ago) and today live in the villages they originally built when they came from the shores of the Lake (Adam, 1963:14). Their largest and earliest clans, called Anyansuli and Anyampanda in their language, have contributed population to the Iraqw as well as certain important political ideas. Among the Iraqw these clans of Ihanzu origin are known as Hhay Sule and Hhay Manda. The Manda clan especially, is important to the history of the Iraqw in the first period that we have distinguished from approximately 1800 to 1900.

The point is that population has come into the area in question from all different directions and from places quite distant. This is an important fact because it has contributed a great stock of cultural traditions that have been passed on and transformed in the formation of the Iraqw ethnic identity and cultural unity. Thus, we see in Iraqw culture the transformed elements of cultures and ideas that are clearly recognizable in all of the other cultures that surround them in Tanzania and Kenya.

Although I did not conduct intensive research on the origin of Iraqw clans or the residents of the various *aya,* it was my general impression in talking with elders from all over Irqwar Da'aw that the large majority of them have traditions of coming from other ethnic groups, moving to the highlands of Irqwar Da'aw during times of drought or other hardship in their homelands, and adopting the Iraqw language and mode of agriculture upon their arrival. In his research in the early 1950s, E. Winter (1955) came to the same conclusion: That "the vast majority of the Iraqw clans trace their origin to men of other tribes, Mbugwe, Iramba, Tatoga, Masai, etc." Of all the clan names that I encountered only two were clearly descendants of those who originally spoke Iraqw when they entered Irqwar Da'aw. These are Hhay Irqa and Hhay Tipu Bonday, the descendants of the first ritual specialist who reclaimed the land of Irqwar Da'aw from the mythical waters that covered it. Ramadhani (n.d.) lists the origins of several clans in his history of the Iraqw:

Wamang'ati [Tatoga]:
Hay-Modaha, Hay Tsuhay, Hay Naman

Warangi:
Hay Tsakhara, Hay Karama, Hay Gurti, Hay Panga, Hay Farae

Wamasai:
Hay Matia, Hay Ane, Hay Male, etc.

Wanyesanzu [Ihanzu]:
Hay Manda [Manda Hay Bayo]

Wambugwe:
Hay Lawi, Hay Boay, Hay Lolo, etc.

Gorowa:
Hay Amu, Hay Masay

Washashi [from Musoma district near Lake Victoria]:
Hay Sule, and Hay Masay

There are many more named *tlahhay,* and the majority of these would appear to derive mainly from Tatoga, Gorowa, and Wambugwe stock, some of them as recently as two or three generations ago. I never encountered any clan group who claimed to have spoken Iraqw upon their arrival in Irqwar Da'aw except for the two already mentioned.

The First Settlers of Irqwar Da'aw

The first Iraqw-speaking groups came to Irqwar Da'aw after they were driven from Ma'angwatay in a war with the Tatoga among whom they lived. It is said that they followed a ritual expert by the name of

Haymu Tipe, who is credited with a number of magical acts. It would appear that the war with the Tatoga, and therefore the move from Ma'angwatay up the escarpment wall and into the high valleys above the plain, was motivated by pressure on the resources of Ma'angwatay which were then being shared. The young Iraqw men spoiled for a fight, but when it came down to it, they were defeated and forced to flee. The story of this event is often recited in various forms, one of which is presented in Text 27.

The "event" described in this passage, whether or not it actually

---

TEXT 27
Alqado: Haymu Tipe

Those people were in the south. It is said they were in Ma'angwatay. The people in Ma'angwatay lived well. People were many; much milk; food was plentiful. Then one day people said, "Our young men now in this place—our youths are many." Now, in this place there was no fighting to do. No person came there. There is no fighting. We first want some fighting. They liked war. They said, "Say, the child of the elder *qwaslarmo* [ritual expert] . . . let's hide him. Perhaps he will do some thing for us." . . . We were hurt very much in Ma'angwatay. The elder was Haymu.

The child of Haymu was hidden. When the child was taken, the youths danced. The youths danced. The elder said, "Young men! My child! [where is he?]." The young men said, "Elder, if you want your child, then get this for us, get for us [a war—the narrator indicates his meaning by gestures and warlike poses]." Now, the youths, their blood does not go forth—they only sit around and eat. They are healthy. "Speak for us—don't just go on about your child" [the youths said]. He [Haymu] said, "Aha, young men, really. . . ." And they said [threateningly], "Yes, really, old man. Now you will see your child again if you get us into a good position."

The elder went away, far away—to a far-away place. He took meat for the journey of many days. He went to the land of the *tara* [Tatoga]—to *Balang da Lalu* [a lake] in the south—exactly where I don't know. He searched for the *tara* because the youths were so contrary. Then that day when he came to the land of the *tara* they said, "We will kill you. Why is this man in *tara* land?" And he said, "I am an Iraqw." And they said. "We will kill you. Why did you come?" And he said, "Before you kill me, I will say my piece." And he said, "My youths in that place refuse me. They want some fun. Are you with me? Do you understand?" And they said, "These youths, what are they like?" He said, "They are very numerous. They cry out." That is what the elder said. The people came for war up to this place. And so the people came.

People came for war. The young men were not enough. They ran into the forest. They shouted. The young people were finished [killed]. And he

TEXT 27 (continued)

[Haymu] said, "Those people, if you want to get them, then cut the *tiita* tree." I don't know the leaves of this *tiita* tree [i.e., the medicine of the leaves], but I know [the medicine of] the branches. The *tiita* tree was cut. Each one of them took a leaf until it was finished. And he [Haymu] said, "I think you will get them now." Then, when they went home he said, "Young men, now get me my child." They said, "Elder, the people and that thing [the war] you did not get. So what of the child?" [mocking the elder, Haymu]. And they gave the child to the elder.

The elder and his child went into the forest. Although people were coming—on one side people were killed, on another side they danced. They said, "Come over to our place. Let's not hurry. Ours will come." Later, the whole area was killed.

The people who remained followed after Haymu into his cave in the forest. And as they went they said the *slufay*. This *slufay* which we say so that we increase, and that we get along together. The thing that we want is that our people become like those in the south [i.e., of the past]. Even now, as we were there even now we grow. The ones who survived grew up again. The clan of Haymu was here. Each of his houses used his name. As it was there, so it is here.

Now whether he was a *qwaslarmo* or whether he prepared medicine, the reason they followed him, I don't know.

happened in history, is a paradigm of the Iraqw political and historical process, as well as being a valuable illustration of a number of important aspects of Iraqw culture. It is paradigmatic at two levels: in its performance (in this case, at a beer party by the son of the *qwaslarmo* Naman), the structure of political oppositions between elder and youth, inside and outside, "own people" and "others," which are described by the narrative itself, are enacted; and, in the content of the narrative we see the playing out of a political conflict that brings about radical social changes that are nevertheless made predictable by our knowledge of the opposing interests represented in the story by the elder Haymu, the youth, and the Tatoga warriors. To the Iraqw listener, this same structure of interested parties makes the outcome inevitable and necessary, and this gives the narrative its paradigmatic character as well as its rhetorical impact. For as we have already indicated, the narrative event has virtually the same validity as the lived experience. The telling of the story, the act itself, communicates much more than the mere "history" of the flight from Ma'angwatay and retreat to the forest. Indeed, if it were only this, it seems unlikely that it should have been remembered and repeated at all.

First, certain features of the context in which this story was told me must be explained in order to discern some of the finer points of information contained in this example. I collected this particular version of the story of Haymu's flight from Ma'angwatay from the son and heir of one of the most important *qwaslare* of Irqwar Da'aw. Godiye, the son, told me this story with great glee upon seeing that his father, Naman, disapproved of his loquacity. By the time he launched into this narrative, however, tongues had been well loosened by generous quantities of sorghum beer. The fact that many other persons were present, many of them clients or potential clients of the *qwaslarmo* Naman, and eventually of his son Godiye who would succeed him, clearly affected the telling of the narrative and its content. The telling of the story in the appropriate forum of the public beer party, by the son of an important ritual specialist, contributed to the significance of the act of narration as an event in itself.

Note, first of all, the narrator's disclaimers that he only knows the medicine to be derived from the branches of the *tiita* tree, but not the medicines to be derived from the leaves. In fact, he would not have the right to claim knowledge of these medicines until after his father's death when he succeeded him in the role of ritual expert. He hastened to add this disclaimer when he glanced over at his father and saw the old man's displeasure at his presumptuousness. His behavior already disturbed his father since he had launched into the story without permission when it should have been the old man's right to tell the story. This interaction resulting from the telling of the story reflects the structure of the first episode of the narrative itself: the effrontery of boisterous youth toward an elder of rank and position.

In the "historical" narrative, the conflict is motivated by this same opposition. The young men of Ma'angwatay are strong and they are eager to display their prowess. They force the elder Haymu to bring them enemies to fight by kidnapping his child, who may be ransomed only on the condition that he bring them enemies to fight. In this version, told by a young man, the vigor of the young men is stressed, and the helpless compliance of the elder is the outcome. In other versions, told by elders, it is the baseless pride of the youths who provoke Haymu into punishing them by bringing the Tatoga warriors down upon them.

The variants of the narrative that are encountered today again reflect the same conflict of interest between the youth and elders that caused the warfare in the narrative. The structure of the context, the variation among different versions of the story, and the action of the story itself all reflect the underlying political opposition of elders and youth. In this way, cultural and social structure decreases historical veracity, but we may conclude, albeit without certainty, that the same set of forces that acted in the twentieth century to force Iraqw youth into the peripheral areas, acted in the beginning of the nineteenth century to send the remnants of the defeated Iraqw into the hills in search of refuge.

Also germane to the question of the interaction of context and content is the final disclaimer of the narrator in this passage. The original Naman, founder of the lineage of the current *qwaslarmo* Naman and his son who told the story, was a Tatoga ritual expert who entered Irqwar Da'aw probably a generation or so after Haymu Tipe had led his followers there. Haymu Tipe was the first ritual expert of Irqwar Da'aw, but the ancestral Naman was able to better his descendants' positions with his magics and medicines. (Naman, the one alive today, says that it was his ancestor's skill at driving off insects that were plaguing the crops of the people that gave him ritual superiority over the successor to Haymu's power.) This first Naman, a Tatoga, thus won ritual hegemony, but his successors still compete with other *qwaslare* for clients, some of whom claim descent from the original Haymu. Thus, the narrator professes ignorance of the reasons why people followed Haymu, whose medicine had been shown to be inferior to that of the founder of his own lineage, to which office he would one day succeed.

The narrative also illustrates a number of points concerning the political culture of the Iraqw. In complying with the youths' demands, Haymu leads the Tatoga to attack them. By so doing he is utilizing what we have called the violence of the outside. I use the term *violence* (of the outside) in preference to *power* or *danger* in order to convey the qualities of injuriousness, infringement, turbulence, and distortion or destruction with which the idea of the "outside" is imbued. Bringing the Tatoga into the Iraqw lands to attack the prideful youth there is merely the reverse of exiling the prideful youth into the lands of the Tatoga. The narrator emphasizes the violence with which they credit the Tatoga: They tell Haymu, who is a stranger in their land, that they will kill him forthwith. At first glance, the story appears to be about the danger to the Iraqw people posed by the warlike Tatoga, and we might expect its effect to be that of emphasizing the Iraqw ethnic identity and solidarity in contrast to the Tatoga. Perhaps it also does this in part. But more importantly it helps to give coercive force to the sanction of exile wielded by elders over youth. The episode is therefore more clearly "about" a structural dichotomy in Iraqw society that is manifested in the political event, than it is about ethnic identity or solidarity.

Similarly, the equation of ethnic difference with spatial distance is interesting in this regard. It is extremely unlikely that the Tatoga lived very far away from the Iraqw; indeed, elsewhere in this same narrative the speaker claims that they lived amongst one another. Nevertheless, Haymu is said to go to "a far-away place" in order to make contact with Tatoga, who in fact were their close neighbors. The distance is a symbolic one, then, which is quite predictable from the knowledge we already have of the spatial representation of ethnic difference in Iraqw culture.

Another facet of Iraqw political culture is revealed in the narrator's mention of the *slufay*. The reader will note that it is the survivors, the legitimate claimants of the land, who recite the *slufay* on their flight. In the use of the *slufay,* as in other aspects of ritual, performative competence may legitimate other rights and powers. This is especially evident in the story of Moya in which Haymu legitimates his claim to the land.

As a foreshadowing of this, however, one more point is worth noticing. Haymu's child is used as a pawn in the struggle for power. Children, in fact, are frequently the pawns and tokens in various sorts of exchanges. Children are given away if they are polluted, they are exchanged for adoption, they are traded for food in famine time, and as in this story and in the story of Moya (Text 23), they are used as political tokens.

The story of Moya is also very widely known and recited in Irqwar Da'aw. It is a sort of charter to the land. In this story, Haymu and his followers arrive in Irqwar Da'aw. But unfortunately, the land is covered with water and guarded by a vast *tiita* tree.

The immediately accessible "historical" information that may be derived from this story is that Haymu Tipe, in all probability, led a band of people through the *Noow* Forest that today lies south of Irqwar Da'aw into the high valleys they now occupy. The rest of the story is meticulously concerned with ritual acts of the *qwaslarmo,* Haymu, since in the minds of the Iraqw it was by these acts that he obtained the land. The story of Moya is the Iraqw "charter" to the land of Irqwar Da'aw. As we have seen, the space in which people live is, for the Iraqw, ritually created in the *masay* ceremony. In this story of the founding of Irqwar Da'aw, although the specific ritual acts are different, the principle is the same: Useful land is created out of useless space. In this case, that useless space is symbolized by the lake and the tree that covered the land. In the case of the *masay* ceremony performed today, "useless space" is the bush that surrounds the community. The ritual acts that are performed by Haymu are meticulously described since it is by means of performance of the ritual that useful (cultural and social) space is created, and by which a people's claim is legitimated.

It is not primarily the "historical" value of this story that is of interest to the Iraqw. It is clear, however, that Haymu was accompanied by a relatively small group of people who spoke Iraqw, and that these people were the first to settle here. There are no traditions of any other people living in Irqwar Da'aw before the arrival of Haymu's band. Nevertheless, the claim to the land, it is stressed, does not arise from their historical precedence of settlement. If this were so, one would expect that the original Iraqw-speaking settlers would attempt to assert a supposed historical precedence in political affairs. This is not even at issue today. I never encountered mention of historical priority as a factor in political events either today or in the past. Instead, ritual competence yields pre-eminence. Since it is always the ritual control of rain, insects, land, or crops that is in question, we see that symbolic control over the flow of resources and the productivity of the land are the political basis of legitimacy rather than a principle of historical precedent.

Whether or not Haymu actually moved the waters is unimportant since it is the symbolic creation of useful land that is at issue. In the following century, more or less, political power was traded around and competed for by a number of ritual specialists. Haymu lost out relatively soon to a Tatoga ritual specialist, who came from the west, by the name of Naman. Naman achieved his paramountcy by his superior medicine; that is, by the greater appeal of the ritual, instrumental acts that he was able to prescribe. That he came from the outside undoubtedly gave him greater appeal in the eyes of the Iraqw, for this idea of the "power of the outside" seems to have been one of the enduring concepts in the culture of the whole region. The boy Moya, for example, was brought from the outside, just as the Tatoga warriors were brought from the outside in the previous story. The ideas of the power or violence of the outside, its opposition to the secure, culturally defined inside, and the ritual acts that are designed to "close" and "seal" in order to "protect," together with other elaborations of these distinctions, were probably developed more and more clearly in the period following the settlement of Irqwar Da'aw that preceded their expansion into the rest of the plateau. I think we can see this period as a formative one during which many people in small groups came into the land of Irqwar Da'aw and began to come under the influence of the various *qwaslare.*

Before we turn to the shifts of power among these ritual and political figures, however, it will increase our understanding of these events if we examine some of the cultural influences that seem to have come into Irqwar Da'aw with different groups of people during this period. Since political power rested on competence and innovation in ritual, it would appear that the process of creating a common culture among diverse peoples was aided considerably by the competitive creativity in ritual that was certainly fostered among the leading ritual specialist. Each one of them attracted a following according to the services he purported to offer. Since it was primarily the duty of the *qwaslare* to "prescribe" the nature of ritual acts for clients to perform, a ritual expert's ideas would have spread quickly among his clients, and beyond into the larger community. No person seems to have been bound to any one *qwaslarmo.* If one *qwaslarmo's* medicine did not work to bring rain, people would resort to going to another one (see Text 16; Tomikawa, 1979; Wada, 1975). Frequently, a *qwaslarmo's* appeal would extend beyond his own ethnic group. The Iraqw say that if the *qwaslarmo* could not bring rain, they would go to a Tatoga or an Mbugwe ritual specialist for medicines that would. This, too, contributed to the development of a distinctive culture among the Iraqw by introducing new ideas that were combined with those already being practiced in Irqwar Da'aw.

The Politics of Cultural Synthesis in Irqwar Da'aw

It is generally true of the whole region surrounding Irqwar Da'aw that cultural knowledge, especially the knowledge pertaining to the conduct of rituals, the tellings of myths and stories, and the proper performance of all types of ceremonies are the legitimate properties of relatively small groups of people, usually of the elder males, but also of elder females. This cultural knowledge is transmitted only in certain legitimate contexts. These limitations of cultural knowledge make of it a sort of symbolic capital that then figures into a political economy of ritual concept and ritual practice. As we have seen, among the Iraqw, the several forms of this cultural capital are regulated much as if they were objects of value in an economy of symbolic tokens. They may be used in certain places and for specified ends. The *slufay, alqado, da'angw,* and *ti'ita, lo'o* ('curse'), *marmo,* and *masay* are all types of symbolic knowledge that, while they also encode information about the past or about the way life should be lived, are preeminently political tools and symbolic types—things that are used in the conduct of political life. This being so, the synthesis of cultures that took place in Irqwar Da'aw was a process controlled by the interests of the ritual experts, as much political as it was cultural. Today, the elders and ritual specialists continually create and revise the rituals they perform for the protection of the country or for rain. In the past, it is reasonable to assume that they must have acted similarly. Since in this case it is not the content of the oral literature or ritual that legitimates constituted authority, but the performance itself, there have been no forces operating to maintain an oral tradition or ritual practice in a constant form. But neither was change simply a symbolic mimesis: It was motivated in the historical event by political contingencies.

The oral traditions of this period claim that the position of the ritual specialist, *qwaslarmo,* was lost or gained by different persons of entirely different ethnic origins. Each time, so the tradition goes, the ritual paramountcy was seized because of superior "medicine," *ma'a'e*; that is, by

means of formulation of, and performative competence in, a new or re-
vised ritual practice that succeeded in acquiring for its formulator a certain clientele. While it is no doubt that the ritual expert who took power
from another did appear to have a superior magic in the eyes of the
farmers and herdsmen who were his new clients, it is equally clear that
what he truly succeeded in doing was to create a new and appealing
synthesis of ritual ideas and practices appropriate for a given moment,
either to bring rain, to rid the land of a plague of cut-worm, or to enclose
the land to protect against Masai raids. The man who proclaimed the
ritual practice that won the most clients could translate his ritual and
symbolic "capital" into goods in the form of maize or honey, but it seems
that no ritual expert acquired outright political dominance nor control
over coercive force. There was, nevertheless, a premium placed on the
creation of a ritual practice, usually in the form of gifts that could be as
substantial as an ox or sheep (see Figure 8.2). Generally speaking, this
ritual system was created as a sort of *bricolage* from an assembly of ritual
elements made available by migration and drawn from a widespread
regional culture. During the period between the coming of the *qwaslarmo*
Haymu with his followers up to the beginning of the German colonial
rule in 1906, cultural creativity and synthesis was strongly favored
against cultural conservatism. The political history of this period is, consequently, the history of ritual practice and cultural concept (cf. Hallowell, 1955:202). A few brief examples illustrate this clearly.

    The elements of this bricolage are encountered all over northern
Tanzania, and clearly existed in the past. For example, in the early
1880s, the early traveler Joseph Thompson reported on a ritual performed
for him by the Chagga at Shira on the slopes of Kilimanjaro. The ritual
involved strips of skin cut from a sacrificed goat that had been pierced
on one end so as to slip them over the finger. Thompson described this
rite as a means used by the chief of the area "to make friends or brothers
with me" (Thompson, 1885:101). This description caught the attention
of Van Gennep who cited it as an example of "incorporation of strangers"
(Van Gennep, 1960:31). Thompson (1885:101–102) reported that

> A goat was brought and, taking it by one ear, I was required to state
> where I was going, to declare that I meant no evil and . . . to
> promise that I would do no harm to the country. The other ear was
> then taken by the sultan's ambassador, and he made a promise on his
> part that no harm would be done to us. . . . The goat was then
> killed, and a strip of skin cut off the forehead, in which two slits were
> made. The [ambassador], taking hold of this, pushed it on my finger
> by the lower slit five times, finally pushing it over the joint. I had
> next to take the strip, still keeping it on my finger, and do the same

FIGURE 8.2. *The bond between the sacrificers and the land. The bestowal of skin strips in this way betokens a bond between members of a community among the Iraqw and elsewhere in Northern Tanzania.*

for [the ambassador] through the upper slit. This operation finished, the strips had to be cut in two, leaving the respective portions on our fingers; and the Sultan of Shira and I were sworn brothers.

The use of skin strips in the *masay* ceremony is very nearly alike. The ritual practice itself is, of course, the same, but the meaning conveyed by this act in the *masay* ceremony is appropriate to its context: Here it symbolizes the bond between the runners and the elders who push the strips onto the young men's fingers. At another level it signifies the identity of the sacrifice and the land's protective boundaries that it represents (see Figure 4.2). In both the Chagga case of nearly a century ago and the modern Iraqw case, the ritual is explicitly associated with the moral bonds between people living on (or traveling across) the land, and is concerned to minimize the "harm to the country."

Precisely the same ritual use of the raw skin strips as that described by Thompson was made by my Iraqw hosts during the performance of the *masay* ritual that I witnessed, in order to incorporate me into the group that had undertaken to perform the ritual. An extra strip of skin was cut from the animal, slit at one end and pressed over my finger by the sacrificer and the elder who was master of ceremonies for that day. Everyone present insisted that I leave it on for the rest of the day. I protested weakly because it was bloody and clammy. It was then tied back around my wrist so that it would be out of the way. On the path home that night everyone who greeted me expressed delight that I was wearing the *hhamangw gurta*. Although there had been some reluctance to let me attend the ritual at first, once this brief ceremony had been performed, I was allowed to interact and participate as freely as I liked.

These examples indicate that this particular ritual element has a wide historical and spatial provenience in northern Tanzania. It further illustrates the flexibility of meaning, within a limited range, that can be expressed in its performance. It is clear that the Iraqw ritual specialists have selected this aspect of a regional culture to achieve their own religious and political ends.

Rituals similar to the Iraqw rituals have been attested for most of the groups surrounding them. V. Adam (1963) described the demarcation of ritual areas in similar terms among the Ihanzu, and Peter Rigby (1968) and A. Hartnoll (1942) have noted the attention paid to direction and boundary during sacrifices for rain among the Gogo. H. Fosbrooke (1958) reported on a ceremony among the Warangi and Wasi of Kondoa district that is similar in many respects to the *masay* ceremony. This ceremony was performed explicitly for the protection of the land, and for rain, and involved slicing the skin of the sacrificial animal into strips and collecting the chyme. Strips and chyme were distributed around the boundary by runners in a manner exactly like that of the Iraqw. Although similar to the Iraqw practice, none of the rituals described for other peoples is exactly alike, as each is tailored by ritual specialists to respond to different conditions and answer different needs. Most important, however, is the fact that different ethnic groups use the same ritual symbols, albeit in different combinations and contexts. Different groups, therefore, attribute efficacy to each others ritual practice, and this allows for its use in incorporating each others' members as migration, expansion, and resettlement demand. It also means that the ritual practice is non-esoteric, generally meaningful within the region, and therefore usable in the political contest of claims and counterclaims to arable land and pasture.

Political Succession of
Ritual Specialists

I was unable to obtain any information on the tenure of Haymu as *qwaslarmo* who led the original Iraqw speakers into the land, other than that he was the one responsible for reclaiming it from the water and trees that guarded it. Evidently, he was not succeeded in ritual paramountcy by his own descendants. According to Iraqw traditions, ritual paramountcy was assumed by an immigrant named Ido Karama from the Bantu-speaking Warangi. He established the *tlahhay* Hhay Karama which is still an important name in Irqwar Da'aw. There are few traditions about him except that he had a more powerful medicine than that of Haymu Tipe, whom he replaced. His possession of a stronger medicine is explained by Iraqw elders today as having derived from the fact that he was from the outside, that he had "walked in the bush," and that therefore such powers would necessarily have come to him.

Again, apparently during the lifetime of Ido, or perhaps upon his death, the ritual paramountcy passed to another man of Tatoga (Dara-majeg subtribe) origin by the name of Naman. Naman had magic that was particularly good for agriculture. Indeed, it appears that he may have introduced a number of refinements in the performance of the *masay* ceremony of boundary closing and of purification of the land. He immediately attracted most of Ido Karama's clients from him to himself.

The next change of ritual paramountcy was by all accounts engineered by Naman (the first) who "captured" a ritual expert of the Ihanzu and brought him to live with him in his own settlement (*tango*). This new *qwaslarmo* was called Yandu and founded the lineage which thereafter continued to have ritual sway in Irqwar Da'aw. Naman and his descendants nevertheless continued to have a somewhat smaller ritual clientele during the several generations up to 1967 when the last great medicine specialist of the Yandu line died.

Interestingly, Ihanzu and Iraqw traditions agree very closely on the origins of Yandu who founded the clan known as Hhay Manda in Iraqw. According to Ihanzu traditions the first Ihanzu people arrived in the area where they live today from the island of Ukerewe in Lake Victoria. It is generally agreed that there were two important clans—the Anyansuli and the Anyampanda (Adam, 1963:14). The two leaders of these people from Ukerewe were known as Ikomba and Kingwele. There was a dispute between them over the possession of the rain stones—the ritual implements by which they controlled the rain. As a result, Kingwele was forced to flee where, according to Ihanzu tradition, he died in the basin of Lake Eyasi either in a flood or in quicksand.

Now, according to the Iraqw tradition reported by Ramadhani (n.d.), the man known as Yandu was only called that by the family and clients of Naman who welcomed him to Iraqw land. In fact, so it is said, his name was Kingwele, and he was of Ihanzu origin. When he came to Irqwar Da'aw, he declared "I am from Yanjuda." Yanjuda is the Tatoga name for the place where the Ihanzu now live. When the Iraqw heard this, they called him "Yanjuda" which later became shortened to "Yandu." In any case, Yandu seems pretty clearly to be the same person mentioned in Ihanzu traditions, and it appears that he came from there into the domain of the Iraqw together with his wife who was then pregnant and ready to give birth.

According to the traditions of the clan Hhay Naman (descendants of the Tatoga ritual specialist Naman who succeeded Ido), the coming of Yandu was foretold. Godiye's account, ingenuous and dissembling, is given in Text 28.

In this and other versions, the man and his wife are taken to the household of Naman who grants them land and wealth. The woman gives birth on the path where they are overtaken by the Iraqw who have come to escort them to the house of Naman. The child's name was Hado, and this spot is remembered as *Lohir Hado,* the path of Hado. The government offices in the *aya Muray* were later built on this same spot.

Yandu is said to have taken over many of the activities and powers of Naman; and the line of ritual experts that he established through his son Hado, called Hhay Manda, has held ritual paramountcy to the present time.

The name Manda is problematic. The Iraqw call the Bantu-speaking people to the west of them the west Manda (*Manda uwa*) and those to the east of them, namely the Mbugwe, east Manda. Both Ihanbu to the west and the Mbugwe are today ruled in ritual matters by members of the clan Anyampanda (Ihanzu) or Manda (Mbugwe). It appears that these clans of ritual specialists may all derive from the Anyampanda clan from the island of Ukerewe.

We see then that the early political history of Irqwar Da'aw was characterized by a succession of ritual specialists all coming from the outside. Only the first Haymu of the clan Hhay Tipe was originally Iraqw-speaking. He apparently arrived with enough people to settle Irqwar

TEXT 28
Coming of Yandu

Now, I don't know if divining still goes on in our house . . . [pause, a glance at the elder Naman, and a chuckle from the crowd]. There *was* a thing that told him things in the night [a deliberate irony]. If someone was ill that thing tells . . . [reference here to the divining gourd of stones that is believed to cause prophetic dreams]. And he said some day a man will come to live in this place. And he said he will live in my place. And he said in that place a woman with her child. And he foretold that if the child cries in pain, he will divine the cause and it will be well. A man in our place dreams [i.e., the house of Naman; here, the original Naman]. His speaking [prophecy] goes forth. It means a certain man will give us good fortune. A man comes from the west. That man will come from *Manda uwa*. He is called Yandu. Our man said he will have a donkey and a wife. That man is first [greatest]. That man brings down goodness on people. Another day the people were herding near the mountain's threshold between the aya and the threshold [*duxutamo*][1] of the mountain *Noow*. That certain person approaches; he and a woman is following. A pregnant woman. A man and his donkey. The pregnant woman and the man have doubts [fears]. They say, "We will be killed. Let's hurry to Mbugwe." But they do not reach that place, because this is the man who is to bring us good fortune. Later they stopped to cook. There, herders [Iraqw] see them. And the herders run until the house of our elder [Naman]. They say that that thing which you dreamt the other day has come to pass. A man and a woman following. That man is cooking. That man and the woman whom he has, they are cooking near the stream in the forest *Noow*. And they ran there. Our elder threw the stones [in order to divine] and said, "Indeed, it is he. Do not leave him."

Source: Godiye Naman, *Muray.*

[1] *Duxutamo* normally refers to the threshold of the house. Here the narrator uses the word to refer to the boundary of the *aya,* normally called *digmu.* The symbolic equivalence of the house and *aya* that this suggests has been noted in Chapter 1.

Da'aw sparsely and to establish the language. The next ritual specialist was originally a Bantu speaker from the southeast of Irqwar Da'aw, the next a Tatoga speaker from the south of Irqwar Da'aw, and finally a Bantu-speaking immigrant from Ukerewe by way of Ihanzu. At least Naman and Ido appear to have come with significant numbers of others who either came with them or who moved to be near them later.

By the time of Naman, it seems that succession to ritual paramountcy by a person from the outside was a well-established pattern.

Whether Naman thought to secure his own power by capturing and so co-opting the power of an outsider, or whether he intended to pass paramountcy to this outsider in the first place, it is difficult to say. It is nevertheless evident that the outsider with a new set of rituals or perhaps a new regional synthesis was highly valued by the people who used their rituals in their attempts to reap larger harvest or have larger herds.

Marmo: An Example of the Rise and Fall of a Ritual

During the period between the establishment of Yandu by Naman and the arrival of the first Europeans, it appears that Iraqw culture was in the process of forming itself, developing a set of distinctive rituals and oral traditions, which, if taken piece by piece, have many parallels with those of their neighbors, but which appear distinctively and recognizably Iraqw when considered together as the product of a particular set of historical circumstances.

Among the most interesting is the women's rite known to the Iraqw as *marmo*. The practice of this rite and many of the details seem to be shared with peoples over quite a wide area of Tanzania, but is especially important among the Ihanzu, the Wanyaturu, the Warangi, and the Sandawe, and to a lesser extent among the Gogo (Rigby, 1967). It is also widespread—or was widespread although largely abandoned today— among the so-called matrilineal peoples of eastern Tanzania, the Luguru, the Kutu, Kaguru, and others (Brain, 1976; Beidelman, 1967:20 ff.).

In general the geographical provenience of this rite in different forms seems to extend from the Iraqw, as the northwesternmost representative, southward to the Gogo, and thence toward the coast. Among the "matrilineal" peoples, this rite involves the seclusion of girls for periods from a few weeks to a year during which they receive instruction in sexual lore and the duties of a wife. They are circumcised upon their emergence and marry soon afterward. The names of this rite, the period of seclusion, labiodectomy, and emergence, and the terminology that has been reported for these vary a great deal from area to area within the group of matrilineal peoples, and also among the patrilineal Gogo who border the Kaguru, both of whom speak closely related languages (Beidelman, 1967:x).

Men were excluded from these rituals. Some authors (Beidelman, 1971; Brain, 1976) feel that these rituals expressed male dominance and suppressed a supposed tendency to rebel among women, especially in the matrilineal societies. Among the Gogo, however, the rites seemed to have a different significance, emphasizing solidarity among women and among the members of a ritual neighborhood. These puberty rites for girls, among the Gogo at least, were not structurally important to the lineage, but were functionally related to the structure of the local community in terms of relations between linked lineages within a ritual neighborhood (Rigby, 1967).

North of the Gogo, among the Warangi and the Wanyaturu, a similar set of girls' initiation rites was practiced. It was called *imaa,* a word that means 'power' or 'strength' or 'upright bearing'. Like the similar rites among the Gogo and the matrilineal peoples, *imaa* involved a long period of seclusion during which the girls were instructed, circumcised (underwent labiodectomy), and a coming-out ceremony when the newly marriageable girls were presented to the community. H. K. Schneider (1970) reports that among the Wanyaturu the rite asserts the solidarity of women in the face of male dominance. According to him, Wanyaturu women "insist that the *imaa* rite is not anti-male, it merely controls male dominance for the sake of peace [p. 137]." He notes, however, that, to the men, the rites are viewed as an expression of hostility and resistance to men.

Elements of this rite, then, seem to have spread from among the Bantu-speaking groups in the region (the Warangi and the Wanyaturu)— who seem to have had the rite in its most elaborate form and from whom most of the vocabulary is borrowed—to the non-Bantu Sandawe, as well as to the Ihanzu (who came from the northwest). Among the Sandawe, the rite is practiced in some form among those Sandawe who have had most contact with the Warangi (Ten Raa, 1970:143). The rite is called *mirimo* among them, which appears to derive from the Turu word *murimu,* 'ritual secrets of women' (Schneider, 1970:139). Among the Sandawe the rite involves seclusion and is a rite of initiation into the exclusively female ritual society.

Finally, the elements of the rite seem to have been adopted by the Iraqw, although in a slightly different form. Like the *imaa* rite of Wanyaturu women, the Iraqw *marmo* emphasizes the solidarity of women, and like the practice of the rite among the Sandawe, it is the initiation rite into the exclusively female ritual society. There are many secrets associated with it that no woman who has been initiated into it would ever divulge. Although the rite is supposed to be no longer practiced today, women who had been initiated into it before the rite was banned are vehement in their refusal to discuss the matter. Among all of the peoples we have so far mentioned, although the rite seems to have different functions among different peoples, it is limited in geographical extent, and always involves a period of seclusion from a period of weeks to years.

The Iraqw word *marmo* may derive from the Warangi word *murimu,* 'secrets', or it may derive from the Wanyaturu word *imaa. Marmo* is analyzable into three morphemes: /*ma-*/ possibly deriving from *imaa;* an obligatory linking particle /*-r-*/ that occurs after a vowel and before a consonant in the formation of compounds; plus, /*-mo*/, a frequently occurring singular formative suffix.

The cultural elements and the terminology that accompanied this rite seem to have been widely known and distributed at some time in the past, but the significance of it among the Iraqw is subtly altered. The seclusion is likened to the rite of *masay* which encloses the *aya* in a protective border. It is believed to be necessary not so much as a period of instruction, but as a means of protecting young girls from the influence of external harm (*homa,* see Text 17). Like the Gogo rite reported by Rigby (1967), the Iraqw rite occurs within and for the ritual area (in the Iraqw case, the *aya*), but unlike the Gogo rite, the Iraqw was primarily aimed at creating a solidary group among the women initiates. The creation of a socially solidary group by a symbolic act of enclosure—like the creation of the solidary grouping of the residents of the *aya*—seems to have been the primary aim and significance of the ritual.

The rite was under the control of the ritual specialists (*qwaslare*) of *Hhay Manda.* The coming-out ceremony could not be begun except upon the permission of the *qwaslarmo* who obtained his cue from divination. The *qwaslarmo* was customarily paid a rather high fee (I was not able to discover how much, except that it had come to be exorbitant by the 1920s). This set of cultural elements, although clearly borrowed from others as part of a larger, regional set of cultural elements, was integrated into Iraqw culture. It acquired new meanings and political ties that were congruent with the structure of Iraqw culture and society.

In other words, the historical development of Iraqw culture owes much to the interested and practical assembly of ritual "elements" (practices or rites) by persons who derived status from their successful assembly of certain ritual and symbolic forms, and who consequently legitimated through their created rituals the rest of the social undertaking. This idea was perhaps first formally stated by Franz Boas in a paper on a similar topic, namely, "The Social Organization of Secret Societies of the Kwakiutl Indians," in which he discussed the Kwakiutl tendency to create new ritual traditions, "the material for which was necessarily taken from existing ideas (of the tribe) or from ideas of neighboring tribes" (Boas, 1897:633–634, quoted by G. Stocking, 1974:6). In a more modern

---

TEXT 29
The End of Women's Initiation

Nade Bea (the most powerful ritual specialist of the Manda) was charging
an unfair fee to the people before giving his permission and medicine for
the ceremony [*marmo*]. . . . They came to take Michael Ahho's daughter
to the *marmo*. It was her time to go in. He refused to pay the fee. He told
the British. He took all of the girls out of *marmo* [with help from the colonial
akidas, or soldiers] and brought them before the people. They were all
kenduso [i.e., girls who have not completed the ceremoney of *marmo*. Traditionally they were less desirable in marriage] and had lesser status
among women. He decreed that there would be a very high fine for returning to *marmo*. And so the custom was stopped.

Source: Marmo Isara, interviewed in Babati, Hanang district.

---

form, we have, of course, C. Levi-Strauss' idea of the *bricoleur,* the ex-
amplar of the symbol-smith *sauvage.*

But the rite was apparently abolished in 1930 as the result of a
political struggle between the representatives of *Hhay Manda* and the
colonially appointed chief by the name of Michael Ahho. Ahho had been
appointed chief (*wawutmo*) of the Mbulu district in 1926 after a conflict
with one of the Manda had been resolved in Ahho's favor by the British
district officer. Ahho was a Christian and a reformer, and he apparently
felt some strong hostility toward the Manda ritual experts whose power
had been acknowledged formally by the British colonial government. Directly as a result of this conflict between himself and the Manda, Ahho abolished the women's rites by decree in a fashion that again reflects the exploitation of external force or power for the settlement of internal disputes.
Text 29 is, in the words of Marmo Isara, a member of the Manda lineage
who preceded Ahho in the office of *wawutmo* (he was relieved of the
office by the colonial administration for "misbehavior and drunkenness").

It is, however, by no means clear that *marmo* was immediately
brought to an end. It came as a complete surprise to the British that
marmo was being practiced when Ahho brought it to their attention, and
it may well have continued in secret after Ahho's decree. Indeed, the
ritual organization of women is still apparent in dances and at beer parties
and the secrets of the rites are so jealously guarded from uninitiated girls
and from men that one suspects that it is still practiced among at least
some women.

The incident described by Marmo Isara is important to our understanding of Iraqw history in several ways. First of all it shows the way this rite was politically appropriated by the Manda lineage of ritual specialists. It was primarily a political assertion of solidarity by women; but it was also an affirmation of ritual clientship to the *qwaslarmo,* who controlled the elements of nature, the fertility of soil and animals, and the dangerous influences of the outside including Masai and colonial administrators. In bringing the rite to the attention of the British, then, Ahho essentially usurped the ritual specialist's right to control external powers. It is characteristic of Iraqw political practice that Ahho, in making his play for power, recruited the power of the British from outside instead of attempting to challenge the ritual specialist Nade Bea from within the Iraqw political structure. In fact, there was no effective means of challenge from inside since the meeting, *kwaslema,* locally restricted as it was, could mount no effective sanction against the ritual specialist himself.

In this brief account of the rise and fall of *marmo* rites, we see in outline some of the structural imperatives of Iraqw culture operating in history. Specifically, the *marmo* ritual and the ritual statuses that it engendered appear to have fulfilled political and organizational functions among women in Iraqw society. Parallel structures for men came from different cultural sources. But among both men and women, organizational functions are fulfilled by forms which, on the surface, are concerned with the ritual condition of the land and of the person.

The Rise of Male Political Organization

Fundamentally, male society is organized into two opposing age-moieties consisting of 'youth' (*masomba*) and 'elders' (*barise*). The elders were responsible for the ritual condition of the land within the boundaries of the *aya* that they helped to maintain. In fact the *barise* controlled all of the material resources of the *aya*—either directly in the case of allocation of land, or indirectly, in the case of allocation of rain—which they believed they controlled through the ritual specialist whose ritual prescriptions were carried out in the *aya*. Youths, on the other hand, since they directly controlled no resources in the *aya* were in a vulnerable position. If they were judged capable and obedient by the *barise,* and if they did nothing that could be construed as harmful to the ritual state of the land, a youth may expect to receive an adequate portion of land within the *aya* to farm, and he would be loaned sufficient animals to begin a herd. If he did not please the elders, or if he violated the community standards in one way or the other, intentionally or unintentionally, a youth could be exiled or otherwise encouraged to leave the *aya*. Even those youth in good favor had little to keep them home. They had only a small stake in the status quo of the constituted *aya,* and had that only so long as they remained in good grace with the elders.

For a long period in a young man's life, then, he was effectively free to range as widely as he dared, constrained mainly by the threat of Tatoga and Masai warriors, who dominated the plateau up to the establishment of German control in the area in 1906. Speaking of a time 30 years ago, E. Winter (n.d.:13) noted that:

> The individual has always felt himself able to move freely through-out the extent of the tribal territory. . . . As the Iraqw have ex-panded from the confinements of their original homeland in the Kainam area [i.e., Irqwar Da'aw] new counties [presumably, he means the *aya*] have come into being. There has been no feeling however that new states have been set up, but merely that the tribe as a whole has expanded and that new terrritorial units have had to be created in order to deal with the problems created by expansion.

It is this mobility that most accurately characterizes the youth, *masomba,* as a group. In general, however, wherever youth traveled, they traveled together in groups that consisted of neighbors and coresidents of one sec-tion or of an alliance of sections that made up an *aya.* The mobile groups of youth were the key elements in the expansion of the Iraqw when the constraints of warfare were removed by the colonial presence.

We shall return to this aspect of Iraqw history in Chapter 9, but we must note that the institution of mobile youth seems to derive from, or be closely related to, a similar phenomenon among the people to the west of the Iraqw, notably the Sukuma.

Among the Sukuma, each "village"—a territorially defined unit—has an informal organization of youth called *basumba.* The *basumba* group was exclusively composed of young males who had little stake in the political establishment. As among the Iraqw, the Sukuma *basumba* group was recruited from a limited neighborhood (Cory, 1954, 1951).

Among the Sukuma, it appears that these *basumba* act as economic free agents. They were able to travel long distances during the dry season when there was no cultivation to be done, and so were able to develop a long-distance commerce with the coast. R. A. Austen (1968:140), argu-ing against the view put forward by R. Oliver and G. Matthew (1963) that the long-distance trade activities of the Sukuma and Nyamwezi were dependent upon the political organization of the ritual specialists known as *ntemi,* claims that it was the village youth organizations, or *basumba,* who were responsible for organizing trade parties with the coast. In his essay on trade and chiefship among the Sukuma, R. A. Austen (1968) argues against the view put forward by Oliver and Matthew (1963) that long-distance trade activities of the Sukuma and Nyamwezi were dependent upon the political organization of the ritual specialists known as *ntemi*. According to Austen, with whom I agree, the *ntemi* ritual specialists merely amassed the trade groods that were made available to them by the trade initiated by the groups of youth who were free to travel long distances. As among the Iraqw, the appropriation and regulation of land by groups of elders generated large numbers of "free" young people who were in a position to initiate sweeping social changes. According to Austen's perceptive analysis, the development of trade and the development of the statelike chiefships under the *ntemi* were essentially unrelated phenomena (except to the extent that the *ntemi* were able to expropriate trade goods through taxation). The state developed under the *ntemi* along lines that paralleled the development of the state in the interlacustrine areas, while trade developed as a result of the social position of youth, organized in groups as *basumba,* who undertook to make such long journeys during the dry season. Among the Iraqw, the *masomba,* acting with relative freedom, had a similar great effect, although different in detail. Instead of organized expeditions to the coast, the wanderings of Iraqw youth, who were frequently not economically or politically comfortable in their own native location, took them to the periphery of the *aya* and beyond. Driven from behind by the multiple sanctions against pollutions (*meta*) or sins (*irange*), and drawn to the prospect of more land elsewhere, the Iraqw youth began the process of expansion very early.

Chapter 9

Territorial Expansion

Ethnos and History

Among the most important features of the general history of the region in which the Iraqw live is the differentiation of ethnic groups and the distribution of cultural traits among them. The ethnic contrasts and conflicts are as important to the history of this region as are the contrasts and conflicts among the various economic and political roles, statuses, and strata (or classes) of complex modern societies. Perhaps the most significant fault of the structural–functional school of African ethnography that has dominated the sociological description of these societies is the insistence on treating apparent linguistic and cultural groupings as self-contained "tribes," for which an economy, political structure, history, and so on, could be detailed without reference to the other "tribes" that surrounded them. The error of this way has been pointed out by scholars who have argued that this doctrine obscured the nature of participation among different ethnic groups. The view of these critics is that African society had been portrayed (falsely) as wholly fragmented and without regional levels of integration before the Colonial era. This criticism is correct, insofar as it concerns the political history of African states and chiefdoms that existed prior to colonial efforts at creating large-scale integrated client states and colonies in Africa. If carried too far, however, the view of these critics threatens to obscure the very real ethnic contrasts and conflicts that existed, and to discourage the study of how these came about and were maintained. For the Iraqw case, a focus on ethnic *differentiation* and ethnic *identity* is essential to an understanding of their history. The differentiation of ethnic units in the area is comprehended

225

in the spatial terms that are used to describe these differences. Clearly, spatial distance itself may engender social and cultural separation and isolation where communication is difficult or limited in other ways (such as by warfare or religious taboos). This limitation of contact among the different ethnic units of the Mbulu area is observably *not* the case. Social differentiation is not the result of spatial distance or location. Rather, spatial distance and location are exploited as cultural markers of differences that exist for other political, economic, and ritual reasons.

The central problem, then, is the definition of ethnic groups with respect to boundaries in space and time. In this case it is necessary to introduce several new concepts in order to comprehend the nature of boundaries in the Iraqw area. The matter is complex because time and space are frequently used to symbolize one another.

Consider, first, examples where time is symbolized in space, that is, a series of events or an event represented in a spatial "schema" or pattern. We see a striking example of this in E. Evans-Pritchard's (1940) description of the Nuer lineages, segments and tribes, the products of a history of segmentation but distributed over the land in a pattern that represents—to the Nuer themselves and to us—the time depth that separates them. Those who live in closest proximity are related, or believe themselves to be related, by a recent common ancestor; those who live farther apart trace their relationship to ancestors further removed in time, and so on. This representation of time in space is clearer in the symbolic capitals of Shang China (Wheatley, 1969) or in Cuzco, the capital of the Incas (Zuidema, 1964), or in the Kibuga, the capital of the kingdom of Buganda (Thornton, 1974) where beliefs relating to a mythological history are arrayed in space to represent their temporal relationships. In our own culture, when we arrange a series of artifacts in chronological order, or draw a time-line, we are doing the same thing on a smaller scale.

Similarly, space may be conceptualized temporally. When we travel through the countryside, space is arranged in a time sequence from the start to the end of the trip. This may be exploited in "charter myths" that explain the distribution of clans in terms of migration; for example, "In the beginning, we all started together. The A stopped in their place and became the A's (the name of a clan) the B stopped and became the B's, the C stopped and became the C's, etc." The pattern appears all over the world. A good example from East Africa is the Meru of Kenya, whose stories of origins are described by I. Bernardi (1959) and discussed by Rodney Needham (1960, *The Left Hand of the Mugwe*). We are familiar with the European habit, very pronounced in the Victorian period, of describing a distant place as if it were removed in time. Travelers wrote from Arabia, or Africa, that they were in the presence of their very ancestors!

But with respect to culture, and to specific cultures in particular, there is a much more fundamental relationship between space and time. We speak of the historical development of a society, or an institution, meaning that a society changes over time. These changes are dependant on a multitude of physical, cultural, and social factors. The account of this change is what we may properly call "history." But we may also conceive of what I would like to call a *spatial development of society and culture*. We know that societies change as well "over space." Especially in Africa where we witness very striking changes over relatively short distances, and where migration and movement are very important sociological factors, the analogy becomes extremely useful. The relationship between these two concepts is not metaphorical or artificial. A culture of the past—an immediate ancestor of a contemporary culture—is nonetheless a different culture. The membership is different, the technological base may be different, the language may be different; yet it bears a certain relationship and a continuity of ideology with the culture that succeeded it. Similarly, a culture separated in space—an immediate neighbor of other cultures that surround it—is clearly a different culture, in exactly the same ways that one separated in time but antecedent to a contemporary culture is different from that contemporary culture.

Yet in both cases, especially in East Africa, there are no clearly definable discontinuities of culture. One culture becomes another as one "moves" in time or in space. Here we see that migration, exogamous marriage, and group fission resulting in residential mobility are the spatial analogues of descent, filiation, and demographic change through time. The ethnic homogeneity or heterogeneity of an area is analogous to continuity or discontinuity of ethnic identity over time, and cultural diversity in a region is the analogue of historical change.

Having drawn this analogy between the "historical development" of a society and the "spatial development" of a society, we are led into a consideration of the definition of and identification of boundaries in time and space. The boundaries that concern us are cultural boundaries defined as the cultures own conception of its identity and extent, its membership and characteristic symbols or diacritics that distinguish one "ethnic group" from others that preceded it in time or adjoin it in space. When the question is posed in this way, we see that ethnicity in northern Tanzania in general, and for the Iraqw in particular is like Emile Durkheim's (1915) definition of religion: The crucial groupings, historically and sociologically, are the moral communities that share a ritual practice.

The Iraqw meeting or *kwasleema,* the acceptance and practice of *meti-mani* and exile, the performance of *masay,* and the belief in the efficacy of the *qwaslarmo* and his deputies in ritual protection and management of affliction, all recall Durkheim's definition of religion. According to him:

> A religion is a unified system of beliefs and practices relative to sacred things, that is to say, things set apart and forbidden—beliefs and practices which unite into one single moral community called a church all those who adhere to them. (p. 65)

To apply this to the Iraqw context we can substitute "Iraqw ethnicity" for *"religion"* and we have a fair approximation of what the Iraqw take as their collective self-concept. Paraphrasing slightly, Iraqw ethnicity is a unified system of beliefs and practices relative to sacred things—beliefs and practices that unite into one single moral community called an *aya* all those who adhere to them. This definition of a community relative to shared beliefs and practices must be distinguished from the objective outsider's view of units based on language or economic mode of subsistence. It is in terms of such "objectively defined" boundaries that many social scientists have been content to work, for these are the categories of censuses and government reports. For many purposes this is adequate, but here it is not. Fosbrooke, writing on the Irangi and Wasi of Kondoa, gives an example of the inadequacy of the "objective criterion" approach where territories are defined by a moral community that includes people from different language groups who may also practice different economies. In the ceremony he described (Fosbrooke, 1958), invocations were delivered in two languages, participants were drawn from both groups, sacrificial animals were contributed by both Wasi and Rangi individuals, and all houses were blessed in the ceremony. It was remarkable in this case that the community that ritually demarcated its land paid no attention to administrative boundaries that were based on supposed "natural" linguistic and economic criteria. The ethnographer (Fosbrooke, 1958:26) commented

> It is interesting to note that the boundaries of the land unit (that was ritually defined) in no way coincides with that imposed by the political boundaries (of the colonial administration); the unit lying in three separate headmen's areas. It was noted how the bound-beating party was not deterrred by the fact that the Native Authority Headquarters sprawled across the boundary. They went right through the compound of the court and through the clerk's courtyard.

It is also characteristic of this area that ethnic, spatial, and political identity are relative ideas. There is a considerable mobility, especially

among the men for all groups in the area. Rigby (1969:14–18) describes
the pattern well with regard to the Gogo (to the south of the Iraqw), but
the pattern seems to be generalizable.

> Gogo have a relative idea of the boundaries of the area they inhabit as
> a "cultural group" and of the identity of their neighbors, both Gogo
> and non-Gogo. Although they move residentially over quite extensive
> distances, and the individual men move even greater distances in the
> quest for grazing and water, the identity of the Gogo living at any
> distance from a fixed point is usually expressed in an extremely broad
> and relative classification or in terms of their non-Gogo neighbors.
> For instance, the "Nyambwa" who inhabit the Cinyambwa area of
> west-central Ugogo refer to their *immediate* neighbors to the east as
> "Nyawugogo," the 'owners of Ugogo', and to those Gogo who live in
> the central and eastern Ugogo as "Itumba." The inhabitants of central
> Ugogo, on the other hand, although they refer to themselves as
> "Nyawugogo" refer to all those to the west of them (including groups
> called "Nyawugogo" by Nyambwa) as "Nyambwa." All to the east are
> "Itumba." Those who live in eastern Ugogo may refer to themselves as
> "Nyawugogo" and those to the west as "Nyambwa" including those
> who live in central Ugogo; all those further west are dismissed as
> "Kimbu," the neighbors of the Gogo in the west-southwest.
>   The same relativity of broad classification is seen on the north/
> south axis. . . . However these terms are only collective ones used
> in reference to people living at some distance by lumping them to-
> gether. Actual identification in more specific circumstances is always
> by clan membership and sub-clan name, and the ritual area and
> neighborhood of present residence. . . . The terms must be seen to be
> totally relative to the spatial position of the speaker, as outlined above.

This relativity of definition is common to many peoples of northern
and central Tanzania. Ten Raa has described the same thing occurring
among the Sandawe (living between the Gogo and the Iraqw). The general name of one Bantu-speaking people, the Sukuma, simply means 'those
to the north', and is the Nyamwesi designation for them that was adopted
officially. We might characterize the pattern by saying that peoples do not
define themselves, they define each other. Well known is the case of the
Nuer and the Dinka, where "Nuer" is the Dinka name for a people who
call themselves "Nath," and "Dinka" is the Nuer name for those who
call them "Nuer."

But in spite of this relativity, people *do* define themselves as groups
with distinct customs and traditions. From an analytic point of view, we
may well ask when is a contemporary culture different from one that
preceded it in time, or that adjoins it in space, and more than likely we
will fail to discover perceptible boundaries. We conclude that a continuum
exists and that there are no objective cultural discontinuities that are

relevant. A good example of such a continuum is seen among the Sandawe (Ten Raa, 1970:128):

> The Sandawe are a very egalitarian people, there is very little special-ization, and social stratification is almost, but not quite, nonexistent. (But) in a small isolated and unspecialized people like this, it is possible to distinguish different cultural areas with various degrees of egalitarianism and different levels of cultural sophistication. . . . In fact these differences divide the country into two distinct areas, a dis-tinction which the Sandawe themselves also recognize even though at the same time they maintain that all Sandawe are all one people, forming a single tribe. The point is that the Sandawe of the center and the west consider themselves to be the couth, and those of the southeast and the outlying districts the uncouth. This difference is largely to be attributed to acculturation which according to the San-dawe themselves (and in particular to the majority who live in the center and the northwest) has come mainly from the north and the west.

We see that a polarity of couth–uncouth has been established in this society as a result of what Ten Raa has called "cultural assimilation" but what I would call the "spatial development" of a society. We see further-more that this polarization of *values,* or of evaluation, is correlated wtih north–west/south–east geographic polarity. It is evident from the rest of the article that what Ten Raa has called "social stratification" is not "stratification" at all, by any generally accepted definition of the term, but is instead *a spatial differentiation with a correlative polarity of values.* Status is evaluated according to a set of beliefs and symbols, but it is not social "strata" (economically or politically defined) that is evaluated, but social *areas.* Different concepts are needed to deal with the situations be-tween the Sandawe and the Iraqw. I would call this differentiation and evaluation of areas *social arealization,* an analogue of social stratification that we find so frequently in other societies.

It is most closely analogous to the system of caste in India. L. Du-mont has shown that the hierarchy of caste is relatable to a few evaluative principles, especially a polarity of purity and impurity, and that these notions are relative. A Brahman is impure with respect to the gods, and to the cow, but is pure with respect to all of the other castes "below" him. Castes are clearly demarcated in any given context and their ranks de-termine the types of transactions that can occur among them. The caste boundaries find their primary sanction in the notion of pollution. Pol-lution results from any transgression across these boundaries, and sexual contact with a person of another caste, forbidden transactions (e.g., in-volving *pakka* foods) across caste lines, death, and birth constitute such transgressions—and all of them are believed to be dangerous (Dumont, 1970; Marriott, 1968).

It is a mistake, I conclude, to assume that territorial boundaries in any society correspond to ecological or ethnic distributions. One is constantly aware that the European partition of Africa, which took place on the maps of planners in distant capitals of Europe, had no rational relationship to the "natural" ecological and ethnic groups of Africa. If we ignore the fact that even the "natural" boundaries between forest and savanna in Africa are ultimately likely to be the products of human activity, the obvious unnaturalness of the European-legislated borders leaves the impression, implicit in most writings on the subject, that there were such things as "natural boundaries" and groups to begin with. In the case of the Iraqw–Tatoga–Bantu–Hadza–Masai interaction in Mbulu district, there can be no question of "natural boundaries." Peoples speaking different languages have interacted continually, learning new languages, learning new techniques, forging new associations. Boundaries where they have existed as definable entities were deliberately created, as much for "religious" as for "political" reasons. In other words, whereas the European partition, by virtue of its historically transparent unnaturalness, created the impression that previously either natural boundaries or no boundaries existed, it was in fact the case that boundaries did exist and that they were as much the product of implicit maps as European boundaries (albeit on a smaller scale) and, therefore, no more natural than today's national boundaries.

The peoples with whom the Iraqw have contact all represent these ethnic differences to themselves in terms of spatial categories. The Gogo provide an example (Rigby, 1967) of a people who represent ethnic differences in terms of spatial ones. For the Sukuma and Nyamwezi peoples to the west of the Iraqw, the direction "north" and the name of the ethnic group that lives to the north is the same word, *sukuma* (Austen, 1968:136). For both the Sandawe and the Iraqw the spatial–ethnic coordinates are evaluated as good or bad (Ten Raa, 1970). The Inhanzu (Adam, 1963:63) are not evaluated but there exists the same coincidence of direction and ethnos. The Hadza also divide themselves into four hunting territories whose name are synonymous with the names of the directions. These ethnic differentiations are thus structured and refer to the order of space. The structural differentiation of society in this context occurs between ethnic groups, while in Western society an analogous structural differentiation occurs between classes within one state (Sahlins, 1976:212).

In both the case of the multiple ethnic groups of northern Tanzania and in the case of the subgroupings (classes) of the modern state, certain ideas are shared among all of them. Different groups frequently define their identity by means of the same set of cultural symbols, but arrange and articulate these symbols in different ways. The culture of one sub-group incorporates elements of many other subgroups, but these are trans-formed and revalued in regular and definable ways such that new identi-ties are created out of a shared set of symbols common to the region.

The Spatial Mode of Social Organization

If the principal organizational forms of the Iraqw are all "borrowed" from those who surround them, it would seem that the Iraqw langauge is all that remains of what must once have been a larger cultural complex accompanying the language. It is difficult to sort out what might originally have been Iraqw culture as distinct from Ihanzu, Iramba, Sukuma, or Tatoga, or any of the other groups who have contributed population to the present mixture of peoples speaking the Iraqw language. Virtually all forms of social organization have their close parallels outside the Iraqw culture. For example, the coevals called *qaro* in Iraqw are formally very similar to the same sort of formal association of coevals called *raat* among the Tatoga and may derive from this source (G. Wilson, 1953). Yet it is only among the Iraqw that we find the territorial basis of organization so clearly and formally developed.

For most of the peoples surrounding the Iraqw, one form or another of kinship organization, based on either matrilineal descent (Kaguru, for example) or patrilineal descent (Gogo, Mbulu, Iramba, and Tatoga) pro-vides the dominant structures of social organization. For the Gogo, Mbugwe, Iramba, and Tatoga the patrilineage principle is most clearly marked and most clearly adequate to organizational requirements among a group of related people usually located at the center or "core" of the ter-ritory. Rigby (1969:5), for example, writes that "the central feature of kinship ideology is patrilineal descent," but notes that this is true only of *central* areas:

> The cultural and sociological overlapping in border areas is probably common to most of the peoples of central Tanzania, who have no centralized political systems and who inhabit fairly sparsely populated areas. . . . The material presented in this book [such as his discus-sion of patrilineality] applies mainly to Gogo social institutions com-mon to the more central part of their cultural area [p. 12].

Within this area, relations of descent, filiation, and affiliation through marriages and bridewealth obligations are actualized in the organization of labor, trade, warfare, and so on. All of these societies, however, have peripheral areas where the organizing potential of kinship breaks down, usually because of more intensive patterns of migration and interethnic interaction that attenuate links based on descent and marriage. Rigby (1969:109–153) gives a valuable discussion of the attenuation of kinship and the reinforcement of links based on spatial proximity or neighborhood that are caused by spatial mobility. He notes that "the high residential mobility of Gogo homesteads and domestic units ensures that relationships based upon descent do not account for a high proportion of links between homestead owners within each neighborhood, or even in neighboring localities [p. 146]." Moreover, he adds that "it only requires a drought or famine to cause the complete disintegration of the old agnatic groups in terms of residence [p. 148]."

In these areas one's neighbors become one's closest allies. Among the Barabaig, for example, most peoples can fit themselves into the fictional patrilineage that derives from the ancient eponymous ancestors who first came from Mount Elgon. But in addition to this means of social organization, the spatially defined grouping has other less politically important functions. According to one ethnograper of the Tatoga (Wilson, 1953:42)

> Not all of the groups in Barabaig (a subtribe of the Tatoga) can be said to be lineages. The neighborhood or community group, the *gisjod,* is an important exception. This group is made up of those Barabaig who because they live in close proximity have certain common interests, such as grazing, watering, and maintenance of social control. In the heart of Barabaig, the members of a *gisjod* can usually trace relationships by kinship, but in the border areas this group is made up of individuals of other tribes as well as Barabaig.

In other words, in the border areas, the *gisjod,* as an organization based upon spatial proximity, begins to be dominant as the people who live near one another and who interact most intensively are no longer able to trace links of kinship among themselves.

Wilson (1953:36) is even more specific on this point when he discusses the situation of Barabaig who live among Iraqw and who are being assimilated with the Iraqw (or, alternatively, forced from their pastures by the Iraqw). He writes

> The impact, however, of the cultivating pastoral Iraqw has been felt in recent years. In some areas bordering on Iraqw country only one in ten homesteads were found to be Barabaig. Moreover, it can be readily seen that the Barabaig leave an area if it is tending to become cultivated. . . . A few Barabaig, due to their lack of cattle have been

forced to cultivate on the fringes of their tribal lands. These, however, tend to be lost to their clans and rapidly adopt the customs of those groups among whom they live. Here the clan ceases to function as the basic political unit, and now we find that the "village," or more accurately the community group, *gisjod,* has replaced the clan.

A similar pattern is observed among the Ihanzu. V. Adam (1962) reports that there has been a slow but steady migration from the Iramba Plateau area into the plains that separate the Ihanbu from the Iraqw and Tatoga. On the plateau, in the areas of longest settlement, the patrilineages provide the basis for social organization. In the plains areas, that is, in the areas of more recent settlement, Adam claims "that it seems wiser to look at residential kinship groups" as the primary, though fragmented, means of organization. Here the patrilineages that are important in the "core" area have become attenuated through the process of migrating to new areas where the spatially defined residential group takes over the organizational function. Since it is through these same plains that the early Ihanzu (and Iramba) immigrants must have come into Irqwar Da'aw, it is reasonable to assume that the organizational differences that are noted along this continuum are similar to those differences that distinguish the Ihanzu core area from the Iraqw core area. In other words, what is typical of the periphery of the Ihanzu area becomes the dominant mode of organization in the Iraqw core area. The emphasis placed on neighborhood and coresidence as central organizing principles among the Iraqw is, therefore, not unique to them. It represents an elaboration and formalization of an aspect of organization that is observed in areas that surround it, but where it is subordinate to kinship as the principal structure of social organization. For the Iraqw, the spatial mode is dominant, and kinship is represented by dispersed descent groups that appear to be almost vestigial.

Today the Iraqw culture and people are easily recognizable as a culturally and socially distinct group of people. In the past, during the period when peoples of many different origins were finding their way into Irqwar Da'aw, this area existed at the periphery of other ethnic groups. The Iraqw ethnic identity and culture apparently crystallized around a small group of Iraqw-speaking people out of a mixed solution of peoples who existed at the edges of other cultural domains. Iraqw culture developed, that is, in an ethnic interstice as a formalization of what was a peripheral, subordinate form of organization among these other groups.

Over time, perhaps partly as a result of their relative isolation in the high valleys of Irqwar Da'aw, the Iraqw continued to grow more numerous and they continued to develop a cultural tradition of their own. The ritual specialists and the ritual executors—the *kahamuse* ('speakers') and the elders—consolidated their control over the cultural material. Eventually they emerged into a position where they began to put pressure on their borders as population pressures and political tensions increased within the various *aya* of Irqwar Da'aw. With this development, two things happened which are in fact opposite sides of the same coin: The Iraqw agriculturalists began to threaten the lands and pastures of the peoples who neighbored them, and the Iraqw themselves suffered the raids and attacks of Tatoga and Masai who saw them as a threat and as a relatively easy target.

The rate at which this source of conflict developed, however, must have been slowed by the ecology of disease in this region, factors that also had an effect on the development of Iraqw ideology. Pneumonic plague and tuberculosis were both endemic in the cool, high plateau regions in which the Iraqw lived. These factors, together with the vagaries of weather that brought either drought or floods, must have limited population growth. They also increased the feeling of threat "from outside" which the Iraqw ritual specialists were asked most frequently to deal with. The response of these specialists was to select from among elements of regional culture rituals that promised protection from these threats with which ordinary physical means could not cope.

It is clear from the literature that symbolic acts of closure, of sealing off openings, and circumscribing areas with magical lines are common ways of achieving such protection in cultures all over northern Tanzania. A recent article (Moore, 1976) has brought out the use of closure symbolism in Chagga rites of male initiation. According to Moore's account, the Chagga male initiation rite was believed to seal up or enclose the male person, thereby protecting his strength. Everyone professed to believe that initiated men, especially warriors, did not defecate or urinate (men went to do these things in the bush in secret). Women, by contrast, were thought of as "open": They defecated, urinated, menstruated, and had children apparently without shame and without taboo. Here we see the practical operation of one aspect of a cultural ideology that is widespread in northern Tanzania, that *enclosure* yields *strength* (cf. the Iraqw women's initiation rite of *marmo,* and *mirimu* and *imaa* rites among the Sandawe and Turu) and protection (cf. the *masay* ritual).

Another manifestation of the spatial ideology of enclosure is seen in the creation of the sacred precinct. Again this is common among Tanzanian peoples. I give one example from the Ihanzu. Here, there is a rain shrine (*mpilimo*), a small structure near the house of the ritual expert (*atata*) whose magic is believed to control the rain. The *mpilimo* contains pots that contain rain-making medicines and herbs, sacred "rain stones" said to come from the island of Ukerewe in Lake Victoria and other ritual implementia. The area around the rain shrine is a ritually protected and sanctified precinct.

> Only the *atata* rainmakers may enter the hut. It is said that anyone else who enters would be given a heavy fine. I have never met any-one who is not a *mutata* who has entered, or even heard of anyone who knows a person who has done so. When a *mutata* goes in, he must of course wear black (the color sacred to rain). The area around the shrine is sacrosanct [Adam, 1962:5].

Just as the idea of enclosure has a generalized regional currency, so also does the notion of spatial coordinates and "motion outwards from a point" that achieves a purification of space have a wide distribution. The Gogo provide an example in this connection. Rigby (1969:158) tells us that the "Gogo ritual area (*yisi*) are thought of as having six spatial aspects (*malanga;* literally, 'windows'): north, south, east, west, and up and down. In many senses, all space (particularly in the context of ritual action) is thought of in this manner by the Gogo." A Hartnoll (1942) gives us a description of a ritual that he calls "praying for rain" among the Gogo in which these six spatial aspects are realized in a ritual practice.

> On the day of the ceremony, the slaughtered animal is led to the grave [of one of the *mtemi's*, 'ritual specialist's', ancestors]; children pour water over it for purification and the assembly, male and female adults and children all dance round the sacrificial animal singing "*Mulungu, Mulungu, tuliwano wako. Chink'he imvua.*" ('God, God, we are your children. Give us rain'.)
> The sacrificial animal is slaughtered usually by the *mtemi's* sis-ter's son, who cuts out the liver and the heart, divides them into six pieces. He throws one piece to his left, one to his right, one in front, one behind, one into the air above and the last below onto the ground.

In this ritual, performed to cause the rain to fall, we see a number of aspects that are formally similar to the Iraqw practice of the *masay* pro-tection ritual. Most importantly we see the same use being made of the sacrificial animal as a model of the land, rather than as a means of com-munication with the divine. Among the Gogo as among the Iraqw, it is enough to communicate with the spiritual world through speech. In this case, *mulungu,* god, is addressed prior to, and separately from, the slaughtering of the sacrificial animal. The orientation of the performer of the ritual to the cardinal directions, the zenith, and the nadir of his ritual area is, again, formally similar to the Iraqw orientation of the sacrificial animal, *gurta,* during the *masay* ritual. Finally, the cutting of six pieces from the body of the animal, and the throwing of these in six directions is analogous to the cutting of skin strips (*hhamangw*) on both the first and second days of the ritual and the running of these strips from the center to the periphery of the *aya* on the second day of the *masay* ritual.

I shall present one more evidential example of the generalized provenience of the aspects of Iraqw ritual practice and cultural ideology that relate to space. This example concerns the use of chyme, the slaughtered animal's stomach contents, in rituals whose aim is the purification of land or the bringing of rain (which often amount to the same thing). Bagshawe (1925:328) writes that among the Sandawe:

> A really big affair, if a whole family or clan feels it necessary to be present—they often do—must take place on the sacred hill of the clan, to which all must go, including women and children. On arrival the victim is laid on its back and is split open alive. Everyone present takes a handful of the liquid contents of the paunch, and, shouting prayers, scatters it over the graves on the top of the hill, as the case may be.

The use of chyme in this case is similar to the use made of it in the *masay* ritual or in the ritual for the purification of the house that was discussed in Chapter 1. In both this and the Gogo example, above, the participation of the whole community in the ritual event is comparable to the Iraqw *kwaslema*. In the last example, the ritual site, what Bagshawe called the "sacred hill of the clan," is comparable with the Iraqw *tlahhay*, a word that denotes both "site for ritual and public ceremony" and "clan" or "kindred."

Thus, the Iraqw focus on space in ritual is merely an elaboration or a variant synthesis of ideas that have a wider provenience than one ethnic group. That these ideas and ritual practices have risen to a central importance among the Iraqw is conditioned by the fact that they have seen themselves as an encircled and endangered people, threatened from the outside, even though they have peace on the inside. The importance of this spatial symbolism is both structural and historical. The presence of these ideas in a regional culture was the historical precondition for the development of Iraqw culture in its present form. But we must also consider the role of structural isomorphisms and logics that became cultural imperatives. The image of the *aya* as a surrounded land is congruent with the image of the *aya* as a land enclosed by medicines that protect, and with the image of land cut from—created out of—the bush. The *marmo* rite of enclosure, the practice of exile, the protection of the house and its orientation all partake of the same structural images of enclosure, orientation, proximity, and so on, which we have discussed. We must conclude that the unusual spatial character to the Iraqw social and cultural organization is structurally and historically "overdetermined" by a multiplicity of interrelated factors. These ideas and practices were brought together under certain historical conditions to produce and maintain a ritual and political community. In particular, the *masay* ritual represents the political use of ritual symbols and acts that in other contexts have a comparatively reduced range and function. The *aya*, in most respects a political territory, is constituted as a sacralized, ritually protected space that is structurally homologous to the Ihanzu rain shrine. What distinguished the Iraqw is that the sacred precinct was drawn to include all of the territory in which a community existed and conducted its affairs (compare Van Gennep, 1960:15).

Ritual and the Organization of Iraqw Territorial Expansion

We have already seen how the Iraqw practice of exile resulted in a region surrounding Irqwar Da'aw that was "incipiently Iraqw." In other words, the movement of Iraqw population out of the crowded Irqwar Da'aw into the pasturelands of Barabaig and Masai created a population that was partially "mixed." Iraqw adults who had been forced to leave Irqwar Da'aw apparently married Tatoga women fairly regularly. M. Tomikawa (1970) has collected Tatoga genealogies in the Mangola area (to the north of Lake Eyasi) that show considerable intermarriages among Tatoga and Iraqw as far back as the late 1800s. The same would be true, no doubt, even earlier if reliable genealogies could be collected for those times. Iraqw children who had been polluted by circumstances of their birth were either killed, or perhaps more frequently, given out for adoption by other ethnic groups. The Barabaig, and probably other Tatoga subtribes, could not adopt a young Tatoga child, but it was possible for a Barabaig man to adopt a child from another tribe for a wife who was without children (G. Wilson, 1953:38). According to Wilson, this was because children from other ethnic groups were genealogically "free," unidentified with any Tatoga patrilineage, and therefore able to be incorporated into any lineage. This would not be true of children born to other Tatoga. If a child was born out of wedlock among the Tatoga, that is, if it had no "clan" by virtue of its illegitimate birth, there was no mechanism of adoption for this child within Tatoga society (G. Wilson, 1953:38). Again, such a child would be killed, or perhaps more frequently, traded to the Iraqw for foodstuffs. The ideology of kinship among the Tatoga, and the ideology of the ritual purity of the *aya* among the Iraqw, therefore, produced a complementary pattern of population exchange among these two peoples.

Before the effective consolidation of an Iraqw identity, and of ritual control over the land by Iraqw ritual experts, the direction of this flow appears to have been from the Barabaig and other Tatoga subtribes toward the Iraqw in Irqwar Da'aw. Tatoga peoples who moved into the upland regions turned to agriculture under the ritual control of the *qwaslare* and *kahamuse* and contributed a large part of the population of Irqwar Da'aw.

Then the balance seems to have shifted. Irqwar Da'aw probably became crowded. Although it was reasonably fertile and well-watered, there was eventually no more land to distribute among new immigrants. The population began to grow rapidly. Today, this area has one of the highest population growth rates in Tanzania (Winter and Molyneaux, 1963; Thomas, 1977) and they have consequently turned the tide, expanding into the lands that were formerly Tatoga. It seems likely that economic pressures forced many young people into the frontier regions, but the development of ritual during the same period provided the means and the justification for forcing many other young people to move out of Irqwar Da'aw and into the lower, drier pasturelands. This process was disruptive of family and kin unity. The spatial mode of organization that had already been applied in response to this same contingency permitted, even required, such dissolution of kin bonds in the case of exile and movement to the frontier.

The fate of the exile, the orphan child (*panay*), or others who stray or are sent into the bush is a favorite theme of Iraqw stories (Wada, 1976). One story known to all Iraqw can be seen as a reasonably accurate representation of this important social crisis in Iraqw society. The story of Simboya has been collected by a number of people in almost identical form (Wada, 1976; Whiteley, 1958).

In brief, the story is about a boy named Simboya who takes pity on an elephant caught in his father's trap and releases it. By releasing the elephant, Simboya has directly wronged his father. He has committed *irange* (what we have defined as 'sin') and he is punished. His father learns what has happened and on the pretense of sending Simboya up a tree to gather honey, abandons him there by removing the ladder. Eventually the elephant comes along, and Simboya enlists his aid in getting out of the tree. To repay his debt to Simboya, the elephant carries Simboya to a vast pastureland where he helps him to overcome a Tatoga herdsman. Simboya takes the cattle of the Tatoga and marries a Tatoga wife. Seeing himself wealthy at last, Simboya finally sends for his family. At first they will not accept that Simboya is alive, but when proof is brought to them, they all follow Simboya to the plains where he has found new wealth in cattle.

This story reflects fairly closely what has in fact occurred. Young men who have been driven from the *aya* go into the surrounding lands that are better suited to cattle-rearing than to agriculture. Many acquired herds and land and later they were followed by members of their families or by others from their neighborhoods. In the story, Simboya is at first driven into the frontier because of his sin against his father (and against the economic well-being of the whole domestic group). Later, after he has lived in the frontier, he is forgiven, he makes up for his transgressions by bestowing wealth on those whom he had earlier wronged. He is reincorporated into the group.

Interestingly, this story is a metaphorical representation of two passages. In climbing the tree, Simboya passes out of the *aya* and out of his *boyhood*. Here the tree, symbol of the bush and the "outside," mediates his passage into the frontier, and into the status of elder. When he is reincorporated into the group, it is as an economically independent individual in a new land. In practice, the differentiation between age and spatial categories are linked, as the structural evidence of this story suggests. The elders are necessarily those who have lived in a place for the longest length of time. They are also responsible for the ritual condition of the land in which they live. Youth, on the other hand, have much less stake in the land. They are subject to the elders and they are the ones who may be exiled or forced to leave. Thus, growing up may entail, and for the majority of Iraqw usually did entail, leaving not only their youth but the place of their birth behind them. Those who remained were usually the youngest members of the family and they usually inherited the land of the fathers (Winter, 1955). The elders were those who managed to remain in the *aya* of their birth untainted by sin or pollution. The youth were forced into the frontier.

Exile is no longer practiced on the same scale as it must once have been, but even today there are enough cases of it to cause the movement of significant numbers of people out of the area. There were two clear cases of it during my period of research in the approximately 4 square miles that I had been in intensive contact with. If this were to be generalized over the larger area, it would involve perhaps as many as 30 or more persons a year. But what is significant is not that one person was forced to leave the area, but that his family followed. This is a clearly marked pattern even now. A son will frequently "pioneer" a location and he will then be followed by other brothers or father's brothers. The same may equally be the case for a woman who is exiled and marries a Tatoga or a

"Swahili" and who is then followed by her brothers to the new place. Thus, exile is, in itself, an organization of territorial expansion. The sin that caused the initial expulsion is either erased by time, or by the act of living outside, and that person then becomes the "foot in the door" followed by greater and greater claims on the land by his or her relations who follow.

Initially, the area settled by the exiles is considered to be cursed (*lu'us*). The frontiers so occupied are called *sehha*, which we may translate simply as 'frontier', but with the additional specification that this frontier is an "outer region," a place of exile (Figure 9.1). In time, as the population of the *sehha* increases, and as social intercourse becomes more frequent and important among those of the *sehha* and those of the home territory, inhabitants of the frontier may be absolved of the curse. The pioneers and inhabitants of the *sehha*, which until such time are neither within or entirely without the fold, are readmitted to the community. The

FIGURE 9.1. *A tembe-type house on the Irqwr Da'aw periphery. These solid, low, earth-walled, and roofed houses are partly excavated and some are dug deep into the hillside. They afford protection from both the sun and cattle thieves for remotely situated families on the frontiers of the Iraqw settlement.*

TEXT 30
Slufay: **The Cursing of Harar**

Ang Harar aga lu'usaan	Long ago we cursed Harar
Daxta kawa laqwali	And now they have multiplied
Masombar Harar ne toren	The youth of Harar and our youth
Ti tlu'er ar tu	Jostle one another
Ar tlakw ang a Harar	The evil of long ago (That evil)
Daxta sehha ngi ker	For which they were sent to the frontier
Asma lo'o da aga amohhoomaan	That curse is now forgiven

---

case of Harar, to the southwest of Irqwar Da'aw and at the extreme limit of Iraqw movement in that direction, is an example, as an excerpt from a *slufay* illustrates (see Text 30).

This combination of exile and cursing, followed by forgiveness and reincorporation, constitutes an organization of territorial expansion. But the motive here is not, it would seem, territorial expansion per se. Instead it is the result of the means by which the society maintains order within itself.

Among the Iraqw of Irqwar Da'aw there is no sort of hierarchically constituted authority with power to punish or coerce. Social sanctions are of the indirect sort: It is the disapprobation of the community in response to *irange* that forces the offender out of his home area. In consequence of this, the domain of the society has expanded, but with respect to the social institutions that I have so far discussed, it was not the conscious intention of those involved to expand the Iraqw land.

Along with this process there was, as well, a direct and intentional expansion movement led by a class of ritual experts, the *kahamuse*. The expansion under the *kahamuse*—and the expansion that resulted from the practice of exile—affected different categories of Iraqw society. Those who were exiled, as a consequence of *irange* or *metimani*, were the younger members of society who had not yet established themselves in society, or who had less stake in the economic structure of their society. In the case of women, in general it was the unwed girls who had the misfortune of becoming pregnant before the protracted engagement and marriage ceremonies had reached the stage where pregnancy was legitimate. Beneath the seemingly extreme disapprobation attached to premarital pregnancy, there seems to have been, sub-rosa, a relatively high degree of sexual license. There is a high level of sexual activity among the young, and a lot of drinking also. Drinking, of course, caused fights. Since no Iraqw man ever goes abroad without his stick, these fights would frequently lead to bloodshed, and as I have said, the shedding of blood upon the earth angered the *netlangw*. Both of these offenses put the offender in the state of *metimani*, and exile was the usual result. *Irange*, or sin against the elders, could only, by definition, be committed by the younger members of society.

On the other hand, the movement led by the *kahamuse* involved those with a greater stake in the establishment. Only these people could afford the fees for the medicines that were designed to protect them from disease and the raids of the Masai in the areas that they pioneered. Thus, all parts of society could, theoretically, be involved in the movement, albeit in different ways.

The *kahamuse* who led settlers directly into the frontier were able to use their role in the process of expansion to their own advantage, developing outright political powers in the newly settled areas that they did not have in the established *aya*. Within the established *aya*, the *kahamusmo* was a mere ritual executor and chairman of meetings. The "frontier" attracted certain charismatic individuals who attempted to lead groups of people into new areas under their authority. In the new areas these *kahamuse* became, in many instances, outright political authorities in their own right. In some cases, their position was recognized and legitimated by the colonial government.

Ralph Austen (1968:142) discusses a similar process among the Nyamwezi.

> The notion that administrative power could be exercised in terms of controlling a particular piece of territory represented a revolution in Western Bantu political thinking. Up to the period of the Arab trade, the occupation of land had been considered a secondary function of the organization of labor, always on a village scale and periodically at different locations. With the advent of the Arabs, however, caravans were requested to cross over and even rest and supply themselves on more or less fixed and relatively large scale tracts. These areas were larger than those normally within the sphere of village organizations while for the *ntemi* (ritual specialist) to assert practical territorial control contradicted the basic conditions of his ritual leadership. Thus, the early period of Arab penetration of Nyamwesi land was characterized by breaking up of a number of chieftainships into smaller units ruled by men who were not legitimately *batemi*, but *Banangwa*, that is parish subchiefs.

The change of territorial organization among the Nyamwezi was similar to the change which I have described for the Iraqw, in that the increase in authority of the *kahamuse* is like that of the *banangwa*, parish subchiefs, of whom Austen speaks.

The case of Bura Ma'ala is illustrative. In the late 1920s Bura Ma'ala gathered a group of people together and attempted to lead them northward out of Mbulu toward the Karatu area. Bura Ma'ala invented a ritual form that he used to "call" people; that is, to enlist them in his movement. He went into the bush and found the wood of a certain tree called *baqaramo* (I was unable to identify it). He then used a branch of this tree to "call" people. Standing on a small hill near groups of houses in the established *aya* around Mbulu town and in Irqwar Da'aw, Bura Ma'ala would swing this branch around his head. This action, according to his son, had the effect of drawing to him people who wanted to move to new lands.

Bura Ma'ala's first attempt to move north was thwarted by the colonial government. He and a small group of followers were intercepted by government patrols and returned to Mbulu. They were told then that the land was a game preserve and was not to be inhabited by people. Bura Ma'ala then attempted to lead a settlement party down the escarpment towards Babati. This was apparently successful, but Bura Ma'ala did not remain with this group of people. In 1926 the zealous reformer, Michael Ahho, was appointed chief of the district by the colonial government, and he began to pressure the government to open the northern part of the district to Iraqw settlement. This was a concerted effort by other elements of the Iraqw ritual and political leadership, since at around the same time, the paramount ritual specialist Nade Be'a called Bura Ma'ala to return from the Hanang region where he had gone after his attempt had failed. Nade Be'a gave Bura Ma'ala special medicines and ritual authority to lead a group to the north again. This time they were not intercepted by the government, and they reached Karatu. Here Bura Ma'ala an assistant by the name of Ganako, and six followers set up the first Iraqw settlement in the northern part of the district in 1929.

When they reached Karatu, there had already been some settlement by British planters. A few German planters remained as well. They made their first settlement in the abandoned cattle enclosure of one of the white settlers, a man by the name of Oban (O'Brian), and from this place Bura Ma'ala began to oversee the distribution of land to his followers and to others who continued to come. From his base near the settler Oban, Bura Ma'ala continued to press his claim to more and more land. The testimony of Stefano Ne'ema, the ex-subchief of Karatu, shows how Bura Ma'ala relied on a combination of British force and medicine from the *qwaslarmo* (Text 31).

The success of Bura Ma'ala depended as much on his political astuteness as on the magical powers with which he was attributed. He used his "control" over the rain, that is, the power that was supposed by the Iraqw

---

TEXT 31
Early Iraqw Settlement in Karatu

These people lived near the white settler Bwana Oban. They stayed in the *boma* that he had abandoned when he moved to another place a little ways away. Some of them went [east] to Mbulumbulu with their cattle. The Masai stole their cattle. They returned to the first place near Oban and complained to the Serikali [the British administration]. The Serikali then followed the Masai and caught them. They continued to steal cattle. Masai came from Ngorongoro to steal 900 cattle. Then the D.C., the police, and others followed them and later returned some of the cattle to the Iraqw.

Then Bura Ma'ala and Ganako carried medicine from Nade Be'a to prevent the Masai from stealing their cattle. They gave him many cattle in return for his medicine. Now the Masai are quiet.

---

settlers to be his, in a directly political way. In 1932 the British administration built the first local court or *baraza* in Karatu. They appointed a subchief over the area whose name was Hhaytsianay. Bura Ma'ala immediately quarreled with the appointed subchief over matters of jurisdiction, since, until that time, he, as *kahamusmo,* was effectively the authority in charge. It is said that he went to Nade Be'a to obtain medicine to prevent the rain, but in any case, there was a drought and famine following upon the appointment of Hhaytsianay. The people brought pressure to bear on the administration, eventually forcing them to remove Hhaytsianay. A close relative of Bura Ma'ala, Hhawu Muhale, was then appointed. People say that the rain fell immediately after Hhaytsianay was removed. Whether or not Nade Be'a and Bura Ma'ala actually controlled the rain, they used the belief to good effect in achieving their political ends. Bura Ma'ala continued to wield a certain amount of power until his death, and his son, Qambesh Bura, became a government-appointed headman in Mbulumbulu, a position he held until independence.

Qambesh Bura, the son of the original *kahamusmo,* was able to parlay his traditional authorities into a considerable amount of political power and wealth. During World War II, the British colonial government began to use the newly settled lands in northern Mbulu district for a "wheat scheme." The region very rapidly became highly productive. Because of his traditional authority over land distribution, Qambesh Bura was able to become intimately involved in the colonial apportionment of land to the Iraqw settlers. He ended up with large tracts for his own use. The development of the Iraqw Farmers Cooperative and the rapid inflow of capital meant that people like Qambesh were able to invest heavily in tractors, combine harvesters, trucks, and buses. Qambesh became a government subchief of Mbulumbulu in 1952. A year later he became, as well, the *kahamusmo* after the death of his father, Bura Ma'ala. After independence, however, the old colonial office of subchief was abolished. For a decade after that, Qambesh remained one of the principal capitalists in the area, but in the late 1960s a series of new government policies and redistribution of lands finally deprived him of much of his former wealth.

The case of Bura Ma'ala and his son Qambesh illustrates the way in which the organized movement of settlers out of Irqwar Da'aw and into the frontier areas significantly changed political relationships and statuses. The innovative ritual and the determination of Bura Ma'ala enabled him, and later his son, to achieve qualitatively different forms of authority and power. Although this was certainly dependent on the colonial government, the Iraqw see themselves as having acted quite independently, manipulating the English just as they manipulated Masai and fellow Iraqw, through the ritual and magic of the ritual specialists and the *kahamuse*.

Bura Ma'ala and those who followed him to Karatu were among the first settlers who moved out of Irqwar Da'aw under an organized campaign led by a ritual specialist. The old man who originally directed me to Irqwar Da'aw, Tua Masay, was among a group of other *kahamuse* who led similar expeditions to other points on the plateau. I cannot detail the history of these others here, but merely indicate that there is much interesting research yet to be done on the settlement movements led by these people. Tua Masay, for example, went west to Maghan; others went to Haidom, Harar, and elsewhere to the south and north of Irqwar Da'aw. Each of these separate movements of a *kahamusmo* and his clients was, as I believe I have shown, the most recent development in a history of ritual innovation. Beginning with the leader of the first Iraqw-speaking group to enter Irqwar Da'aw, Haymu Tipe, through subsequent ritual experts, such as Ido and Naman, each ritual expert garnered a following through effective and meaningful integration of old ritual practices and beliefs with the creation of new ones.

Ritual institutions, as well as ritual experts, rose and fell during the formation and consolidation of Iraqw culture. The case of *marmo*, a women's rite that involved seclusion and instruction in a secret lore, and which led to initiation into a system of ranked ritual statuses, provides an example of innovation and change. What we have called the "spatial mode of organization" is another similar example. The ideology and practice of this form of organization derives from and depends on a ritual of encirclement, enclosure, and purification, which is applied to either the house or the *aya*. We have seen that the elements of this ritual belief and practice exist in many forms in the cultures of other Tanzanian peoples. Their integration into a distinctively Iraqw culture, and the particular form that they took in the Iraqw instance, is the result of their application by ritual experts and a community of clients who used these rituals to protect themselves, to insure fertility, and to provide a basis of organization among immigrants who could not trace other links (such as links of kinship or common descent) among themselves.

Chapter 10

Conclusions

In my description of society, culture, and history of the Iraqw people, I have focused rather strictly—some, perhaps, would say, narrowly—on relations of space. Moreover, I have concerned myself primarily with a limited range of spatial relations. This subset of all possible notions and constructions of space I have called "topology," and I have sought to give an ethnological, rather than a mathematical, content to this set of ideas. Topological relations include the relations of neighborhood or proximity, continuity, boundary or partition, and open–closed or included–excluded. I have tried to show that these ideas are present in the ethnographic material itself—that is, they have not been "applied" as a "model" of social action or cultural structures—and that these ideas provide a useful and appropriate way of talking about the cultural material that does no violence to the form in which it was presented to me in the field as oral texts, layouts of houses and territories, or in conduct of daily affairs. In choosing to focus on this aspect of cultural and social life I have, I admit, given less attention to other aspects that are also important; for example, kinship and marriage, other rites and rituals, such as those attendant upon death or birth, economics and trade, the impact of the Colonial period and the relationship of the Iraqw political structure to encompassing national governments (colonial and independent), among many other topics that might have been considered and were not. Nevertheless, I hope that I have made some contribution to the understanding of a difficult, perhaps insoluble problem: What is the nature of space?

This study of the Iraqw, although a study of space, is only partially a study of territory as Morgan (1977) and Maine (1961) used the term and defined for posterity. "Territory" is only one aspect of all spatial

249

phenomena. It is a composite concept including many distinguishable primary spatial notions together with political and economic relations and practices. In the Iraqw case, spatial ideas of boundary, enacted in ritual and other forms of behavior, is applicable to illness as well as to land. The development of a political idea of territory in the organization of expansion from Irqwar Da'aw out into the whole Mbulu Plateau can be traced from a ritual and cognitive image of protection, *pa'asamo,* and enclosure. The spatial image precedes the creation of territory. For this reason, I have avoided talking in terms of "social space"—the space of behavior—for this limits the study to the observable and neglects the cognitive aspects. A behavioral focus in this matter leads to theoretical errors.

The notion that territory is that which is defended, for instance, puts the cart well before the horse. Territory is space that is shared. The idea of defense of territory is secondary. It is the sharing of common space, when seen as sharing and positively valued, that gives territory its meaning, its raison d'etre, just as it is the idea of shared substance (blood, spirit, family estate) that gives kinship its meaning and raison d'etre. It is because territory is shared that it is defended and extended, not the other way round. It would be absurd to say that an area was defended first, and then shared, for who would defend it if it were not shared? Equally, it is absurd to say that an area was extended and then shared, for on behalf of whom would it be extended? The primacy of defense as a definitional attribute clearly results from a behaviorist bias, since defense can be observed while sharing is clearly an idea that imparts meaning to action. Action associated with space may include defense of that space; but it need not, as the retreat and assimilation of the Tatoga in the Mbulu Plateau has shown.

The concept of a political space, space at the macro level which is mostly politicized space—used, shared, public, and the object of competition—has not advanced very far beyond the formulation of a concept of territory that implies both boundaries and dominion or proprietorship. This is the concept formulated by Maine (1961), Morgan (1977), and Weber (1978), and which has become the stock-in-trade of sociology and geography since the publication of their works. This idea of territory is limited as a theory of political space because it allows no alternative, and the practice of politics is everywhere the exploration of the possible. The centered, transhumant polity of the Masai or Tatoga pastoralist, for example, does not define a territory in the sense just mentioned, but is concerned instead with a locus of use, variously conceived according to season, size of the herd, and multiple sociopolitical considerations such as possibility of competition or conflict with other groups. The Iraqw image of territory is very much different. The *aya* is invariant with respect to herd size, population, or politics.

Maine showed that the European concept of territory, the bounded and politicized limits of sovereignity, had specific historical roots in Roman law. The concept was not given for all time, but developed at a particular time under certain conditions. For Maine and for Morgan who seems to have followed him in this, the development they discovered in reading the Greek and Roman legal records was the only development of which they could conceive. They were limited by the knowledge and concerns of their time. From our perspective, however, we may just as well reason that if a social form arose at a particular time under certain conditions, it therefore represents a possibility for all human societies that may or may not be realized under given conditions at other times and in other places. This was Lowie's position, formulated in opposition to Morgan, when he argued that there was a "germ" of territoriality even among the Andamanese (Lowie, 1927:50,60). Politicized territory is a specific social realization of the cultural images of space that serve to order many sorts of phenomena. Macro space, at the scale of topographic or geographic reality, may be used politically, more or less, and in different ways. The historical interactions on the Mbulu Plateau lend support to this assertion.

The fundamental point to which most of the argument of this book has been directed, then, is that territory is a made thing, a sort of artifact that is fundamentally no different from other made things from pots to pastures, halters to houses. If there is a difference, it is one of scale relative to the human organism. This difference is not in the quality of the phenomena themselves, but in our means of perceiving them. It is the increasing levels of scale that are dealt with in Chapters 2 and 3. In these chapters, the spatial form and symbolic significance of the house, *do'*; the neighborhood, *papahhay;* the ridge community, *gayemo;* and the larger scale units of the section, *hhay;* the ritually defined *aya;* the wilderness, *slaa';* the frontier, *sehha;* and the lands inhabited by other groups, *tumbo,* are described in order to show how fundamental spatial images serve a multiplicity of functions at many levels in the daily life of the Iraqw.

I have tried to show that the house, *do',* defines a group of people by virtue of their living in one place (*do'* means, literally, *'the* place'). It may include, together with biologically related family, numbers of adopted children, or children acquired in exchange for maize during famine years (if the family is well off). Each household group is an independent unit of production, consumption, and trade. The physical structure of the house represents or "stands for" the group of people that occupy it. In the event of social sanctions being applied to members of the house, it is the house itself (the physical structure) that is marked by symbolic means. Force is never applied in social interactions.

The physical structure of the house is in some ways a microcosm of the territorial unit called the *aya*. It is set off from its surroundings by its threshold (*duxutamo*), which is the conceptual analogue of the border (*digmu*) of the *aya*. Inside there is a space for public discussion (*matla'angw*) just as there are places (*tlahhay*) for public discussion in the *aya*. (The morpheme /*tla'*/, appearing in these, means 'focus' or 'center'.)

The courtyard and surrounding pasture are dominated by the household group, and anyone passing across this space must greet the inhabitants of the house. To cross without greeting them, whatever the time of day, signifies ill intent. The back of the house is called *papay*. It is negatively valued. *Papahhay*, derived from this word, means roughly, 'neighbors'. Neighbors, while valued for their cooperation, are also a source of competition for limited resources and so are valued somewhat ambiguously. Political rhetoric constantly exhorts the residents of the *aya* to get along with their neighbors.

The house, like the *aya*, is oriented with respect to the cardinal directions. Most houses face west, which is positively valued. The east is negatively valued. The same distinctions apply to topographic features: The west slope of a hill is the "good" side of the hill (*geto hho*; literally, 'good side') while the east side, *intsi*, is frequently spoken of as the side of witches and evil persons. With respect to hills, we observe that a natural distinction of micro-climates and topographic features is appropriated into a culturally valued system of social discrimination.

There are rituals for the demarcation and protection of the household that exactly parallel the rituals used to define the territory of the *aya*. The solidarity that exists among household members is exploited in political rhetoric at the level of the *aya* to create a sense of solidarity in the members of the ritually defined territory. Only the residential group, however, recognizes any relationship to its past; that is, to its own forebears. Occasionally sacrifice is made by the household group to the *gii*, spirits of ancestors (usually recently deceased parents or grandparents, never to ancestors more distantly removed). This occasional recognition of ancestors is *only* done at the household level: There are no lineages or larger kin groups that motivate or serve as the focus for ritual or other social action.

On the next level, the ridge community is defined as a neighborhood of people living on or near a common ridge of land. It is an informal economic organization of cooperation and friendship. Its boundaries, however, are not defined, and there are no formal activities or rituals that mark its existence.

On the third level, the section, *hhay,* represents a group formally organized for the maintenance of cattle pastures, walkways, field boundaries, and so on. The section is named and has definite borders. The section is "governed" by the consensus of a group of elders, *barise.* The elders are led by a speaker (*kahamusmo*) who acts as *primus inter pares* in meetings for the adjudication of disputes, assigning responsibility for certain tasks, or "affixing blame" (*kwasleemuut,* "accuse"; literally, 'to strike by the meeting').

While the section is the smallest bounded territorial unit, the *aya* is the largest. The *aya* is a historical alliance of sections. It exists by ritual for the Iraqw who create or make it (*tlehh-*) out of the bush (*slaa'*). The *aya* is the focus of a ritual practice that is meant to create consensus (there is no centrally constituted authority) by which social order is maintained. Consensus is believed to be the condition under which the spirits of the sky and earth will bless the land. The man who can create consensus, therefore, has power. Consequently, it is the ritual specialists— those who are skillful in the manipulation of symbols and the use of rhetoric—who occupy positions of political power. Everyone else is a client to these specialists.

The *aya* is corporate with respect to this ritual: It is conducted for the residents of the *aya* by their representatives—the elders and speakers. The symbolism of solidarity that is used to create the *aya,* derives from the house and the residential group. Thus, the *aya* is tied (*tsegiin*) with the same lianas that are used to tie the house beams. The solidarity of the *aya* is symbolized in commensal feasts during rituals that mark its borders. It is governed by consensus of the meeting which, if legitimate, is conducted in one of a few designated places near the center of the *aya* located on a main pathway.

Surrounding the *aya* is the contiguous outside, the area beyond the ritually demarcated boundary, *digmu.* There are three categories of outside: the bush or wilderness (*slaa'*), the frontier (*sehha*) where exiles traditionally went, and the lands inhabited by other ethnic groups (*tumbo*).

In Chapter 4, I discussed the *masay* ritual, a central cultural observance of the Iraqw in which the territorial borders are marked and the land purified. It constitutes a cultural creation and appropriation of space that becomes an economic expropriation of territory in an expansion movement in this century.

This ritual is preeminently political since it defines the conditions under which force may operate, and it legitimates the use of force. First of all, since it is the elders and speakers of the *aya* community who "create the *aya*," the ritual legitimates their use of power. Since the ritual draws up boundaries for the inhabitants of the *aya*, thereby laying claim to a piece of land, the ritual has an important bearing on the political structure of the region. Where the Iraqw have expanded into the lands of other peoples, they have used this ritual to legitimate their claim to the land. The cultural separation of one piece of land from an expanse of what is seen to be undifferentiated bush creates an important political tension. The Iraqw ethnic identity entails, among other things, submission to the authority of the *kahamuse* and elders of the *aya*, in whom responsibility for the land is vested. Their power rests on the submission to authority by those who live in the *aya*. In most cases their authority does not derive from use of violence or force. Wrongdoing and political transgressions are sanctioned first by resort to symbolic acts directed against the house of the offender. Ultimately wrongdoing is punished by suspension of all social contact and eventually by exile into the bush; that is, by the forceful assertion of boundary. Political force and violence are attributed to the outside while peaceful consensus is attributed to the inside. The two sides of the political coin, force and submission to force, are thus separated by the *masay* ceremony which creates, primarily, a spatial division. This ritual is the key feature in the political structure of the region.

The ceremony is held once a year, more or less, and involves the sacrifice of an animal on the border of the *aya*. The skin and chyme (inside and outside of the animal) are distributed around the border of the *aya* to seal it. On the second day, another sacrifice is made in the center of the *aya*. This time the animal has been identified with the earth by feeding the animal some ritually prepared white earth (white equals purity, health). The animal is killed, and young men carrying strips of skin and packets of chyme run from the center of the *aya* to the borders driving the evil spirits before them and flinging them over the edge of the *aya*.

The Iraqw present this ritual as a way of creating a political and social space, without which, they claim, they would not exist. An important aspect of the conduct of this ritual is the kinesthetic modeling of the *aya* by means of the body of the sacrificial animal. The identification of the animal's body first with the border, and then with the land, and the subsequent modifications of the body produce, in icons of reality, statements about definition and enclosure of the political territory.

This ritual is a creation of space on two levels: for the *aya*, and for the household, for which a nearly equivalent ritual is performed to protect and define it. The symbolic equivalences that are drawn in Iraqw ideology and in practice of ritual serve to conceal and obfuscate the objective economic solidarity that derives from their relationship to productive resources. By drawing a parallel between the territorial group and the domestic group, the solidarity of the smaller unit is projected onto the higher level of organization where it becomes the principal metaphor of organization for a grouping that is not based on direct and simple productive relations.

The *masay* ritual is the objectification of certain Iraqw ideas about the space in which they live. In the competition for land, ritual forms that were at first used for controlling natural forces eventually came to be used, beginning around the turn of this century, as a means of claiming land. A ritual that functioned originally as an instrument in an agricultural "magic" became a key instrument in a social movement of expansion.

Chapter 5 describes the way in which fundamental spatial ideas serve to define social groups and to provide a basis for evaluation of them. The composition of the domestic group, the neighborhood, and so on, is detailed. The household consists of from one to eleven persons, and usually includes a married couple (but not always) and children, together with adopted children and sometimes other residents and visitors. Only a few houses contained more than two generations. Residence patterns are strongly neolocal after marriage. The value of economic independence of the household is stressed. The ridge community frequently consists of a set of siblings and their household, together with houses of unrelated or immigrant families. In the case of the household and the ridge group, it is the space they live in and share that defines their identity as a group.

In contrast to this, there is a genealogical group, the *tlahhay*, that appears to be a bilateral kindred. It is spatially dispersed and is never the focus of ritual activity, is rarely mentioned in oral texts of any sort, and never serves to mobilize either wealth or labor for any purpose. It does provide a means of reckoning degree of relatedness between potential marriage partners. One cannot marry into the *tlahhay* of grandparents.

Within the *aya*, categories of age and sex do mobilize social resources and provide a structure of statuses. Men's and women's ritual hierarchies are quite separate and distinct, and both appear to be derived from institutions in other societies in Tanzania. Among men, age is the basis for a simple polarity of elders and juniors. Juniors are expected to honor the elders, but in the event they do not, they are exiled into the frontier by a meeting of the elders. The polarity of age—elders and youths—is referred to the spatial dichotomy of inside and outside in the political practice. Elders are those of the pure inside, while most youths end up being people of the impure outside. The age dichotomy is in practical terms a dichotomy of space.

The structure of space also provides the framework into which other ethnic groups are fit in order to classify and evaluate them. Bantu agriculturalists are all grouped together as either "Bantu-of-the-east" (*manda'aw*), or "Bantu-of-the-west" (*manda uwa*). Since the west is "good" and the east "bad," this classification strongly influences patterns of trade and interaction in the region. Trade is conducted primarily with people to the west. In oral traditions, the Masai are always associated with the north, and the Tatoga peoples are usually associated with the south. In these same traditions they say they shall "push to the north," "take the lands to the north," and so on. By the same token, they usually represent events that have taken place in the past as having happened in the south. These classifications reflect the "truth" of these matters very partially, and must be seen therefore as the product of an ideology that influences both economic activity and their symbolic representation of the environment.

Chapter 6 shows how the ideology of space which has been described in previous chapters provides a means and an ideology of authority and social control. Here the three sets of fundamental political and cultural oppositions between youth and elders, between inside and outside, and between good and bad, are discussed in more detail. The cultural definition of the outside as "bad" or "dangerous" is used as an effective threat by the elders in their exercise of power. By attributing political force to the outside, the idea of internal consensus, crucial for the functioning of an egalitarian society, may be maintained. In this connection the ideas of witchcraft, sin, and personal pollution are defined, and the means for dealing with each is described. The willfully sinful person is sent, by consensus of the meeting and by withdrawal of social contact, to the outside, beyond the boundary. The polluted person is secluded in his or her house for a period of up to a year in some cases. Pollution results from a wide range of events, such as bloodshed in certain instance, death of a fetus, being cut by iron, being clawed by a leopard, being struck by lightning, and others, all of which involve in one way or another the crossing or weakening of certain significant boundaries. We note, however, that both sin and pollution are dealt with by asserting boundaries in either exile or seclusion.

In all instances, the means of exerting social control are verbal, either by the curse or by accusation of the meeting. The legitimacy of a political proceeding is marked by the performance of another type of speech called *slufay,* a poetic sermon-cum-prayer. All of these verbal forms are only appropriate to certain undertakings and certain places. For example, the *slufay* performed at a wedding is performed as an *example* of the *slufay* performed at the meeting and so legitimates the wedding. Performed in the house, however, it could only be a joke! The spatial criteria of performance control the conditions under which certain powerfully effective verbal forms may be used. In the case of the *slufay* or the accusation of the meeting, these formulas are reserved to the public activity of the elders who represent the *aya* and who are responsible for maintaining its ritual condition (which in turn depends on the degree of consensus they have been able to muster). The *slufay,* in particular, provide a means of talking about other rituals, even of being critical, although always in the context of formalized consent since, in practice, each cadenced line is always given assent by the assembly.

Chapter 7 is about the internal structure of oral narrative. In this chapter some of the salient characteristics of Iraqw oral narrative are detailed in order to understand more fully the function of narrative in Iraqw society. The Iraqw narrative tradition lacks a central chronology by which events may be placed in relation to one another. The narratives talk about conduct of ritual, ritual states, and social types, and so on. They are, in short, nothing like a "historical" tradition since they deal not with events themselves, but with the meaning of events. They are not, therefore, "charter myths" that legitimate a status quo by reference to a positively valued past. I try to show that they are taken by the Iraqw as instances of the effective performance of ritual. They are models of ritual process rather than charters of social status. The lack of a chronology means that there must be another way to relate events one to another. This is done by relating events to one another in terms of spatial proximity rather than in temporal sequence. Narration of events that "happened in the south" follows the narration of stories about other events that "happened in the south." For the Iraqw things go on in places, primarily; only secondarily do they happen in time. This characteristic of Iraqw narrative I have called a "topology of time." It is consistent with other aspects of their culture.

Finally, Chapters 8 and 9 present a historical sketch of social and cultural development in Irqwar Da'aw, so far as this can be determined. The Iraqw atemporal world view notwithstanding, a skeleton chronology is constructed from ethnological and linguistic materials in order to present some aspects of Iraqw culture in a time dimension. The cultural ideology of spatial order, and the ritual creation of space, are shown to be the historical product of large-scale migration and resettlement in small groups that deprived "kinship" of its practical value at levels of organization above the immediate household group and permitted the substitution for it of a preexisting ritual organization of spatial categories, revalued under specific historical conditions. The Iraqw mode of organization simply places a high value on a feature of social organization that exists in most Tanzanian societies. Spatial order has been discussed by Monica Wilson in *Good Company,* Philip Gulliver in *Neighbors and Networks,* Peter Rigby in *Cattle and Kinship* (and in other texts). All of these discussions concern Tanzanian peoples who have been subjected to intense disintegrating forces by Ngoni raids, Arab slave trade, frequent and widespread intertribal raiding, and by the colonial administration. All of this has served to make neighbors more reliable than kinsmen. In the Iraqw case, ritual experts and elders, using the immediately available ideas of spatial order, provided an ideology, a rhetoric, and ritual practices that effectively organized small family units into larger territorial units that preserved and regulated their access to resources.

References

Adam, V.
    1962   *Social composition of Isanzu villages.* Conference papers, East African Institute of Social Research. Kampala: East African Institute of Social Research.
    1963   Migrant labour in Isanzu. *Proceedings of the East African Institute of Social Research.* Kampala: East African Institute of Social Research.

Austen, Ralph A.
    1968   Ntemiship, trade and state building: Political development among the western Bantu of Tanzania. In *Eastern African history,* edited by Daniel F. McCall, N. R. Bennett and J. Butler, Boston University Papers in African Studies, Vol. 3. New York: Praeger.

Bagshawe, F. J.
    1925   Peoples of the Happy Valley, East Africa. *Journal of the Royal African Society* 24:25–33, 117–129, 219–247.
    1926   Peoples of the Happy Valley (Part IV), *Journal of the Royal African Society* 25:59–74.

Bailey, F. G.
    1960   *Tribe, caste and nation: A study of political activity and political change in highland Orissa.* Manchester: Manchester Univ. Press.

Balandier, George
    1972   *Political anthropology.* London: Penguin Editions.

Barth, Fredrik
    1969   *Ethnic groups and boundaries.* Boston: Little, Brown.

Baumann, Oscar
    1895   *Durch Massailand zur Nilquelle: Reisen und forschungen der Massai-expedition.* London: Johnson Reprint (1968).

Beidelman, Thomas O.
    1967   *The matrilineal peoples of Tanzania.* London: International African Institute.
    1971   *The Kaguru, a matrilineal people of East Africa.* New York: Holt.

259

Bernardi, I. M. C.
  1959   *The Mugwe, a failing prophet.* London: International African Institute.
Black, Max
  1962   *Models and metaphors: Studies in language and philosophy.* Ithaca, N.Y.:
          Cornell University Press.
Boas, Franz
  1897   Secret societies of the Kwakiutl. *Race, language and culture.* New York:
          Macmillan.
  1962   *Anthropology and modern life* (1928). New York: Norton.
Bourbaki, Nicholas, (pseud.)
  1966   *General topology.* Reading, Massachusetts: Addison-Wesley.
Bourdieu, Pierre
  1977   *Outline of a theory of practice.* London: Cambridge Univ. Press.
Brain, James L.
  1976   Less than second class: Women in rural settlement schemes in Tanzania.
          In *Women in Africa,* edited by N. J. Hafkin and E. G. Bay. Stanford:
          Stanford Univ. Press.
Calame-Griaule, G.
  1970   *Le theme e l'arbre dans les contes Africaines.* Paris: Klinksieck.
Cohen, Abner
  1976   *Two dimensional man: An essay on the anthropology of power and sym-
          bolism in complex society.* Berkeley: Univ. of California Press.
Colson, Elizabeth
  1968   Political anthropology: The field. *Encyclopedia of Social Science.* New
          York: Macmillan and the Free Press.
Copland, B. D.
  1933   A note on the origin of the Mbugu with a text. *Zeitschrift für Eigebor-
          enen-Sprachen,* 24:241–245.
Cory, Hans
  1951   *The Ntemi: The traditional rites in connection with burial, election,
          enthronement and magic powers of a Sukuma chief.* London: Macmillan.
  1954   *The indigenous political system of the Sukuma and proposals for politi-
          cal reform.* East African Studies, (2), East African Institute of Social
          Research. Kampala: Eagle Press.
Cunnison, Ian
  1951   *History on the Luapula.* Rhodes-Livingston Paper, (21). Lusaka: Rhodes-
          Livingston Institute.
Douglas, Mary
  1966   *Purity and danger: An analysis of concepts of pollution and taboo.* Lon-
          don: Routledge and Kegan Paul.
  1970   *Natural symbols.* New York: Pantheon Books.
Dumont, Louis
  1970   *Homo hierarchicus.* Mark Sainsbury, trans. Chicago: University of Chi-
          cago Press.
Durkheim, Emile
  1915   *The elementary forms of the religious life.* London: Allen and Unwin.
Dyen, Isadore
  1962   The Lexico statistical classification of the Malayo-Polynesian languages.
          Language 38:38–46.

Dyson-Hudson, Rada, and E. A. Smith
    1978   Human territoriality: An ecological reassessment. *American anthropologist* 80:21–42.
Ehret, Christopher
    1970   *Southern Nilotic history.* Evanston, Illinois: Northwestern Univ. Press.
    1974   *Ethiopians and East Africans: The problem of contacts.* Nairobi: East African Publishing House.
Eisenstadt, S. N.
    1965   African age groups, a comparative study. In *Essay on comparative institutions,* edited by S. N. Eisenstadt. London: Wiley.
Evans-Pritchard, E. E.
    1936   *Witchcraft, oracles and magic among the Azande.* Oxford: Clarendon Press.
    1940   *The Nuer.* Oxford: Oxford University Press.
Feierman, Stephen
    1974   *The Shamba kingdom: A history.* Madison: Wisconsin University Press.
Fleming, H. C.
    1969   Asa and Aramanik: Cushitic hunters in Masai land. *Ethnology* 8(1).
Fortes, Meyer
    1969   *Kinship and the social order.* London: Routledge and Kegan Paul.
Fosbrooke, H. A.
    1954   The defensive measures of certain tribes in north-eastern Tanzania: Pt. 2. Iraqw housing as affected by inter-tribal raiding. *Tanganyika Notes and Records* 36, 50–57.
    1958   Blessing the year: A Wasi/Rangi ceremony. *Tanganyika Notes and Records* 50, 21–29.
Geertz, C.
    1963   *Agricultural involution.* Berkeley: Univ. of California Press.
Gluckman, Max
    1955   *The judicial process among the Barotse of northern Rhodesia.* Manchester, England: Manchester Univ. Press.
    1962   *Essays on the rituals of social relations: Introduction.* Manchester, England: Manchester University Press.
Godelier, Maurice
    1977   *Perspectives in Marxist anthropology.* Cambridge Studies in Social Anthropology, (18). Cambridge: Cambridge Univ. Press.
Goodman, M.
    1971   The strange case of Mbugu. In *Pidginization and creolization of languages,* edited by Dell Hymes. Cambridge: Cambridge Univ. Press.
Government of Tanganyika
    n.d.   *Agricultural district book,* Mbulu District. Unpublished manuscript compilation in Mbulu District administrative offices, Mbulu, Tanzania.
    n.d.   *District book,* Arusha Region, Tanganyika Territory. Microfilm in Cooperative Africana Materials Project (CAMP).
Gray, Robert F.
    1955   The Mbugwe tribe, origin and development. *Tanganyika Notes and Records* 38, 39–50.
    1963a   Some structural aspects of Mbugwe witchcraft. In *Witchcraft and sorcery in East Africa,* edited by J. Middleton and E. Winter. New York: Praeger.

1963b The Sonjo of Tanganyika: An anthropological study of an irrigation-based society. Oxford: Oxford University Press.
1974   Personal communication, letter dated 5 November 1974.
Greenberg, Joseph H.
1966   The languages of Africa. Bloomington: Indiana Univ. Press.
Gulliver, Philip H.
1971   Neighbours and networks: The idiom of kinship in social action among the Ndendeuli of Tanzania. Berkeley: California University Press.
Gwassa, G. C. K.
1969   The German intervention and African resistance in Tanzania. In A history of Tanzania, edited by I. N. Kimambo and A. J. Temu. Evanston, Illinois: Northwestern Univ. Press.
Hallowell, I. A.
1955   Culture and experience. Philadelphia: Univ. of Pennsylvania Press.
Hallpike, C. R.
1972   The Konso of Ethiopia. Oxford: Clarendon Press.
Hartnoll, A. V.
1942   Praying for rain in Ugogo. Tanganyika Notes and Records 13:59–60.
Jackson, C. H. N.
1942   Mangati. Tanganyika Notes and Records 10(8).
Jaeger, Fritz
1911   Das hochland der reisenkrater und der unliegenden hochlander in Deutsch Ostafrika. Berlin: Mittler.
Johnston, H. H.
1925   Introduction. In Peoples of the Happy Valley, Journal of the Royal African Society 24:25–26.
Kidamala, D., and E. R. Danielson
1961   A brief history of the Waniramba people up to the time of the German occupation. Tanzania Notes and Records 56, 67–79.
Kimambo, I. S.
1969   The political history of the Pare kingdom. Nairobi: East African Publishing House.
1970   The interior before 1800. In History of Tanzania, edited by J. A. Temu and I. S. Kimambo. Nairobi: East African Publishing House.
Klima, George
1970   The Barabaig, East African cattle herders. New York: Holt.
Levine, Donald N., Ed.
1971   Georg Simmel: on individuality and social forms. Chicago: University of Chicago Press.
Lewin, Kurt
1936   Principles of topological psychology, F. Heiden, trans. New York: McGraw-Hill.
Lienhardt, Peter
1966   A controversy over Islamic custom in Kilwa Kivinje, Tanzania. In Islam in Tropical Africa, edited by I. M. Lewis. Oxford: Oxford University Press for International African Institute.
Lowie, Robert
1921   Primitive society. London: Routledge and Kegan Paul.
1927   The origin of the state. New York: Harcourt.

Maine, Sir Henry Sumner
  1861 *Ancient law.* London: J. Murray.
  1875 *Lectures on the early history of institutions.* New York: Holt.
Marriott, McKim
  1968 Caste ranking and food transactions, a matrix analysis. In *Structure and Change in Indian Society,* edited by Milton Singer and Bernard S. Cohn. Chicago, Aldine Press.
Moore, Sally F.
  1976 The secret of the men: A fiction of Chagga initiation and its relation to the logic of Chagga symbolism. *Africa* 46 (357).
Morgan, Lewis Henry
  1871 *Systems of consanguinity and affinity of the human family.* Washington, D.C.: Smithsonian Institution.
  1877 *Ancient society.* New York: World Publishing. (Reprinted with Introduction by L. A. White, 1964, Cambridge, Mass.: Belknap Press.)
Murdock, George P.
  1959 *Africa, its peoples and their culture history.* New York: McGraw-Hill.
Needham, Rodney
  1960 The left hand of the Mugwe. *Africa* 30:20–33.
Nicholas, Ralph
  1968 Rules, resources and political activity. In *Local level politics,* edited by M. Swartz. Chicago: Aldine.
Oliver, Roland
  1963 Discernible developments in the interior, 1500–1800. In *History of East Africa, Vol. I,* edited by R. Oliver and G. Matthew. Oxford: Clarendon Press.
Oliver, R., and G. Matthew
  1963 *History of East Africa.* Oxford: Clarendon Press.
Pender-Cudlipp, Patrick
  1975 Personal communication.
Piaget, Jean
  1970 *Structuralism.* New York: Harper Torchbooks, Harper & Row.
  1973 *Main trends in interdisciplinary research.* New York: Harper Torchbooks, Harper & Row.
Plumb, John Harold
  1970 *The death of the past.* Boston: Houghton Mifflin.
Prins, A. H. J.
  1953 *East African age class systems.* Groningen, Netherlands: J. B. Wolters.
Radcliffe-Brown, A. R.
  1965 The study of kinship systems. *Structure and function in primitive society,* New York: Free Press.
Ramadhani, Mzee Hemedi
  n.d. *Mapokeo ya historia ya Wa-Iraqw Mbulu.* Dar es Salaam: East African Literary Bureau.
Rigby, Peter
  1967 The structural context of girls puberty rites. *Man* 2 (3):434–444.
  1968 Some Gogo rituals of purification. In *Dialectics in practical religion,* edited by Edmund Leach. Cambridge Paper in Social Anthropology, (5). Cambridge: Cambridge Univ. Press.
  1969 *Cattle and kinship among the Gogo.* Ithaca, N.Y.: Cornell Univ. Press.

Roberts, Andrew
  1969   Political change in the nineteenth century. In *A History of Tanzania,* edited by I. N. Kimambo and A. J. Temu. Evanston, Illinois: Northwestern University Press.
Sahlins, M.
  1963   The segmentary lineage: An organization of predatory expansion. *American Anthropology* 63. 323–345.
  1972   On the sociology of primitive exchange. In *Stone age economics,* edited by M. Sahlins, Chicago: Aldine-Atherton.
  1976   *Culture and practical reason.* Chicago: University of Chicago Press.
Sanches, M., and Ben Blount, eds.
  1975   *Sociocultural dimensions of language use.* Chicago: Academic Press.
Schneider, H. K.
  1970   *The Wahi Wanyaturu.* Chicago: Aldine.
Sutton, J. E. G.
  1966   The Archeology and early pre-history of the highlands of Kenya and northern Tanzania. *Azania* 1 (37).
  1969   The peopling of Tanzania. In *History of Tanzania,* edited by I. N. Kimambo and A. J. Temu. Nairobi: East African Publishing House.
Stocking, George
  1974   *The shaping of American anthropology, 1883–1911: A Franz Boas reader.* New York: Basic Books.
Stoeltje, Beverly
  1978   Cultural frames and reflections: Ritual, drama, and spectacle. *Current Anthropology* 19(2):450.
Swartz, Marc
  1968   Introduction. In *Local level politics,* edited by Marc Swartz. Chicago: Aldine.
Swartz, M. J., V. W. Turner, and A. Tuden
  1966   Introduction. In *Political Anthropology,* edited by M. J. Swartz, V. W. Turner and A. Tuden. Chicago: Aldine.
Ten Raa, E.
  1970   The couth and the uncouth: Ethnological, sociological, and linguistic divisions among the Sandawe. *Anthropos* 65 (1). 127–153.
Terray, Emmanuel
  1972   *Marxism and primitive societies.* London: Monthly Review Press.
Thomas, G.
  1977   AID baseline inf. and situational overview requisite to the design of rural development project in Mbulu district Tanzania. Mimeograph. Ithaca: New York: Ithaca College.
Thompson, Joseph
  1885   *Through Masai land.* London: Sampson, Low and Marstone & Co.
Thornton, R. J.
  1974   *The Kibuga of Buganda: spatial symbolism in an Africa state.* Unpublished M.A. thesis, University of Chicago.
Trognon, Alain, J. L. Beauvois, and G. Lopez
  1972   Topologies et theorie de la metaphore. *Homme* 12 (3), 10–83.
Tomikawa, M.
  1970   *The distribution and the migration of Datoga tribe.* Kyoto Univ. African Studies, 5 Kyoto, Japan: Kyoto Daigaku.

1979   The migrations and inter-tribal relations of the pastoral Datoga. *Senri Ethnological Studies,* No. 3. Osaka, Japan: National Museum of Ethnology.

Tucker, A. N.
1967   Fringe Cushitic: An experiment in typological comparison. *Bulletin of the School of African and Oriental Studies* 30:655–680. London: University of London.

Tucker, A. N., and Mary Bryan
1956   *Handbook of the non-Bantu languages of northern East Africa.* London: Oxford Univ. Press for International African Institute.
1966   *Linguistic analyses.* London: Oxford Univ. Press for I.A.I.

Turner, Victor
1967   Color classification. In *Forest of symbols,* edited by V. Turner. Ithaca, New York: Cornell Univ. Press.
1969   Forms of symbolic action. *Proceedings of the American Ethnological Society,* pp. 3–25. Seattle, Washington: University of Washington Press.
1974   *Dramas, fields, and metaphors.* Ithaca, New York: Cornell Univ. Press.

Van Gennep, A.
1960   *The rites of passage.* Chicago: Univ. of Chicago Press.

Vansina, J.
1961   *Oral tradition: A study of historical methodology.* Chicago: Aldine.

Wada, S.
1971   *Marriage ceremonies and customs among the Iraqw of Tanzania.* Kyoto Univ. African Studies, 6. Kyoto, Japan: Kyoto Daigaku.
1975   *Political history of Mbulu district.* Kyoto Univ. African Studies, 9. Kyoto, Japan: Kyoto Daigaku.
1976   Hadithi za mapokeo ya Wa-Iraqw (Iraqw folktales in Tanzania). In *African Language and Ethnography,* edited by V. Tomikawa. Tokyo: Institute for the Study of Language and Culture of Asia and Africa.

Weber, Max
1978   *Economy and society.* Berkeley: University of California Press.

Werther, C. Waldeman
1898   *Zum Victoria Nyanza: Eine Antisklaverei Expedition und Forschungsreise.* Berlin: Gergonne.

Wheatley, Paul
1969   *The city as symbol.* London: University College.

Whiteley, W. H.
1954   *An introduction to the study of Iraqw.* Kampala: East African Institute of Social Research.
1958   *A short description of item categories in Iraqw.* London: School of Oriental and African Studies.
1960   *The verbal radical in Iraqw.* African Language Studies. London: School of Oriental and African Studies.

Wilson, G. McL.
1952   The Tatoga of Tanganyika, Pt. I. *Tanganyika Notes and Records* 33, 35–47.
1953   The Tatoga of Tanganyika, Pt. II. *Tanganyika Notes and Records* 35, 35–36.

Wilson, Monica
1951   *Good company.* Oxford Univ. Press for the International African Institute.

Winter, Edward
   1966   Territorial groupings and religion among the Iraqw. In *Anthropological Approaches to the Study of Religion,* edited by M. Banton. London: Tavistock.
   1955   *Some aspects of political organization and land tenure among the Iraqw.* Kampala: East African Institute of Social Research.
Winter, E., and L. Molyneaux
   1963   Population patterns and problems among the Iraqw. *Ethnology* 2 (4), 490.
Yoneyama, T.
   1970 *Some basic notions among the Iraqw of north Tanzania.* Kyoto Univ. African Studies, 5. Kyoto, Japan: Kyoto Daigaku.
Zuidema, R. T.
   1964   The Ceque system of Cuzco: Social organization of the capital of Inca. *International archives of ethnology (Supplement to Volume 50).* Leiden: E. J. Brill.

Index

STUDIES IN ANTHROPOLOGY

Under the Consulting Editorship of E. A. Hammel,
UNIVERSITY OF CALIFORNIA, BERKELEY

Andrei Simić, THE PEASANT URBANITES: A Study of Rural-Urban Mobility in Serbia

John U. Ogbu, THE NEXT GENERATION: An Ethnography of Education in an Urban Neighborhood

Bennett Dyke and Jean Walters MacCluer (Eds.), COMPUTER SIMULATION IN HUMAN POPULATION STUDIES

Robbins Burling, THE PASSAGE OF POWER: Studies in Political Succession

Piotr Sztompka, SYSTEM AND FUNCTION: Toward a Theory of Society

William G. Lockwood, EUROPEAN MOSLEMS: Economy and Ethnicity in Western Bosnia

Günter Golde, CATHOLICS AND PROTESTANTS: Agricultural Modernization in Two German Villages

Peggy Reeves Sanday (Ed.), ANTHROPOLOGY AND THE PUBLIC INTEREST: Fieldwork and Theory

Carol A. Smith (Ed.), REGIONAL ANALYSIS, Volume I: Economic Systems, and Volume II: Social Systems

Raymond D. Fogelson and Richard N. Adams (Eds.), THE ANTHROPOLOGY OF POWER: Ethnographic Studies from Asia, Oceania, and the New World

Frank Henderson Stewart, FUNDAMENTALS OF AGE-GROUP SYSTEMS

Larissa Adler Lomnitz, NETWORKS AND MARGINALITY: Life in a Mexican Shantytown

Benjamin S. Orlove, ALPACAS, SHEEP, AND MEN: The Wool Export Economy and Regional Society in Southern Peru

Harriet Ngubane, BODY AND MIND IN ZULU MEDICINE: An Ethnography of Health and Disease in Nyuswa-Zulu Thought and Practice

George M. Foster, Thayer Scudder, Elizabeth Colson, and Robert Van Kemper (Eds.), LONG-TERM FIELD RESEARCH IN SOCIAL ANTHROPOLOGY

R. H. Hook (Ed.), FANTASY AND SYMBOL: Studies in Anthropological Interpretation

Richard Tapper, PASTURE AND POLITICS: Economics, Conflict and Ritual Among Shahsevan Nomads of Northwestern Iran

George Bond, Walton Johnson, and Sheila S. Walker (Eds.), AFRICAN CHRISTIANITY: Patterns of Religious Continuity

John Comaroff (Ed.), THE MEETING OF MARRIAGE PAYMENTS

Michael H. Agar, THE PROFESSIONAL STRANGER: An Informal Introduction to Ethnography

Robert J. Thornton, SPACE, TIME, AND CULTURE AMONG THE IRAQW OF TANZANIA

Linda S. Cordell and Stephen Beckerman (Eds.), THE VERSATILITY OF KINSHIP

Peggy F. Barlett (Ed.), AGRICULTURAL DECISION MAKING: Anthropological Contributions to Rural Development

in preparation

Eric B. Ross (Ed.), BEYOND THE MYTHS OF CULTURE: A Reader in Cultural Materialism

Thayer Scudder and Elizabeth Colson, SECONDARY EDUCATION AND THE FORMATION OF AN ELITE: The Impact of Education on Gwembe District, Zambia